OHIO
GAZETTEER

OHIO
GAZETTEER

American Historical Publications, Inc.
725 Market Street
Wilmington. Delaware 19801

FOREWORD

A gazetteer is a dictionary of places. This is a (historical) gazetteer. Its primary function is to give detailed information on events that have occurred in this State and the people who have participated in them.

It is also intended to serve as a contemporary directory of certain basic reference data of frequent interest. Most prior geographical references were prefaced with lengthy explanations interpreting codes, abbreviations, keys and other space-saving, but confusing symbols. This gazetteer needs no such explanations. The abbreviations used have obvious interpretations.

Larger cities are, of course, covered extensively in general encyclopedias and numerous monographs. An important service offered in this gazetteer is in arranging material systematically and in providing information on the vast majority of places that are not well covered elsewhere.

The Biography Index should be of particular value for researchers in making readily accessible information on famous persons related to their places of origin or activity.

New editions are planned basis for updating material currently listed and for adding new information to expand the usefulness of the publication.

Acknowledgment is made to the many Chambers of Commerce in that have provided information, the many libraries and especially the Library of Congress for the use of its facilities. Credit is also due the U.S. Geological Surveys for reference to their most recently published material. Also to the U.S. Census Bureau for expediting the availability of the latest population data for our use. Considerable use has been made of the Federal Writer's Project State and City Guides and a special tribute is offered to the hundreds of celebrated writers who contributed to that unprecedented collection of Americana.

INTRODUCTION

Ohio is truly a land of variety, a small microcosm of the rest of American landscape, culture and economy. About 2500 lakes dot this small (thirty-fifth in size) state, including the one that forms its northern border, Lake Erie. In fact, the towns along Erie can be considered ocean ports because of their access to the Atlantic Ocean via the St. Lawrence. Ohio also is a land of rivers, namely the Muskingum, Scioto, Maumee and Miami as well as the great Ohio and its many tributaries.

Geographical features make for cultural differences and in Ohio there are three distinct ways of life determined by the natural surroundings. In the cities such as Toledo and Cleveland along the banks of ocean-going Lake Erie, life is cosmopolitan and carries much of New England's heritage. The southern part of the state is centered around the great river and the city built upon it, Cincinnati. Here, trade with the west and southern states is important. The heartland of rivers, valleys, and hills is taken up mainly by farmlands that spread outward from the capital.

Even before it was named the seventeenth state in the union on March 1, 1803, Ohio grew because it served as a passageway to the Northwest Territories. Small settlements of New Englanders have since grown into several major cities as canals, railroads, and highways traveling in and out of the state were built. With the need for steel came Ohio's importance as the holder of fine lake and river transportation between the iron ore deposits in Minnesota and Michigan and the coal mines of the East. In 1870, about 2,600,000 lived in Ohio, which is the approximate size of Cleveland today. The 1970 census showed 10,657,423 persons residing here, with two-thirds of those in 9 urban areas. That made Ohio the sixth largest state in population, with a reputation as a nationwide provider of manufactured items such as steel and rubber products as well as farm goods. As of April 1, 1980, the population of the state was 10,772,342, according to a preliminary count of the returns of the 1980 census. This figure represents an increase of 114,919 or 1.1 percent, from the 10,657,423 inhabitants enumerated in the 1970 census.

THE NAME

The state of Ohio was named after the river that flows along its southern border. The French took the name from Wyandot Indians' word, *O, he, zuh*, meaning "great, grand, fair to look upon", and pronounced it Ohio. The Iroquois also had a word, *Oheo*, that meant "beautiful", and some historians suggest that the Wyandots may have used it in naming the river. Other Iroquoian words, such as *O-y-o*, meaning "a stream very white with froth", and *Ohion-hiio*, or "beautiful river", are also possible roots for the current state name.

One historian suggests that there may be a connection between the Delaware Indian name Kittanning, or "at the Great River", and an Iroquoian word, *Ohio*, meaning the same thing. The secondary meaning of *io*, he says, was "grand" and "beautiful", and only was applied to the Ohio River after the French arrived.

In any case, the French first brought the word into common usage to describe the section of the country now known as Ohio.

NICKNAMES

Ohio's nicknames are as follows: the Buckeye State, the Modern Mother of Presidents, and the Yankee State.

"Buckeye" is derived from a legendary incident before Ohio became a state. The first court conducted by the settlers in Ohio was located at Marietta in a large wooden fortress known as the Campus Martius. On September 2, 1788, while the judges marched in a body to the fort, a large, robust man named *Colonel Sproat* so impressed the onlooking Indians that they excitedly shouted "Hetuck! Hetuck!" which meant "Big Buckeye". From that incident onwards, in addition to the fact that there were many buckeye trees (Aesculus glabra) in the area, Ohio was known as the "Buckeye state". However, the nickname was not made official until 1840, when it was approved by the legislature after a bitter fight.

Ohio's reputation as being the "Modern Mother of Presidents" stems from the fact that eight presidents hail from the state. They are as follows: *James A. Garfield, Ulysses S. Grant, Warren G. Harding, Benjamin Harrison, William H. Harrison, Rutherford B. Hayes, William McKinley*, and *William H. Taft*.

Before 1820, the more staid settlers in Virginia and Kentucky called Ohio the "Yankee State" because of its more freewheeling institutions.

THE STATE FLAG

Although the state was nearly a century old already, Ohio's flag was not designed until 1901, to be shown at the Pan-American Exposition in Buffalo, New York. On May 9, 1902, the state legislature approved the flag, which is eight-thirteenths as wide as it is long. Designed by *John Eisenmann*, the flag has three red and two white horizontal stripes (symbolizing the roads and waterways), a blue triangular field in which there are 17 white, five-pointed stars, (symbolizing Ohio as the seventeenth state), all grouped around a red disc superimposed over a white "O" for Ohio.

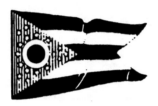

STATE FLAG

THE STATE MOTTO

Between the years 1865 and 1868, the state had as a motto, "Imperium In Imperio", Latin for "An empire within an empire". However, this motto offended many settlers in the state because it sounded too much like a passage from *The Life and Times of Thomas Becket* which read: "The Church, an imperium in imperio, however corrupt in practise, was encroaching on the state with organized system..." (Froude, *Sir James Anthony*, New York 1878).

Effective October 1, 1959, a new state motto was enacted, "With God All Things are Possible". This saying was taken from Matthew 19:26 in the Bible, and was suggested by a 12 year old boy from Cincinnati, *James Mastronardo*.

Between 1868 and 1959, the state had no motto.

THE STATE SEAL

In 1803, the legislature of the new state of Ohio approved a state seal designed by *Secretary of State William Creighton*. The seal was inspired by a view of the rising sun between the hills of Mount Logan as seen from the home of *U.S. Senator Thomas Worthington*. In the foreground were a sheaf of wheat and a bundle of 17 arrows, and in the background was the sun spreading its rays over a mountain, signifying both that Ohio was the seventeenth state and the first state west of the Alleghenies.

The first law authorizing this seal was repealed in 1805, and various other seals were introduced until 1868 when an act reinstated the original seal, with a minor change: the single mountain was replaced with a range of hills. Surrounding the circular sign are the words, "The Great Seal of the State of Ohio".

STATE SEAL

THE STATE FLOWER

The legislature of the state in 1904 voted for the scarlet carnation (Dianthus) as the state flower, in memory of native-born *President William McKinley* who had worn the bloom in his buttonhole. McKinley had been assassinated three years before, but the legislators had not forgotten the president's use of the carnation as a good luck piece in all of his campaigns. "It is fitting and proper that a state should honor and perpetuate the memory of its illustrious sons," the 1904 law read.

THE STATE BIRD

The songbird *cardinalis cardinalis*, or red cardinal, was adopted as Ohio's favorite bird in 1933 by an act of the legislature. The bird is bright red in color, and the male of the species has a high-crested tuft of feathers on his head.

STATE FLOWER   **STATE BIRD**

THE STATE SONG

Although for many years one of at least seven tunes could be used as substitutes for a state song, "Beautiful Ohio" was officially named the state song in 1969. Written in 1918 by *Ballard McDonald* and *Mary Earl*, the song is mainly concerned with the Ohio River:

BEAUTIFUL OHIO
Long, long ago,
Someone I know
Had a little red canoe
In it room for only two
Love found its start,
Then in my heart
And like a flower it grew.

Chorus:
Drifting with the current
down a moonlit stream
While above the Heavens
in their glory gleam
And the stars on high—
Twinkle in the sky—
Seeming in a Paradise
of love divine
Dreaming of a pair of eyes
that looked in mine
Beautiful Ohio,
in dreams again I see
Visions of what used to be.

Beautiful Ohio

Drift - ing with the cur - rent down a moon - lit stream

THE CAPITOL BUILDING

The Ohio capitol building at Columbus, begun in 1838 and completed in 1861, cost $1,644,677. The architects who designed it were *Henry Walter* of Cincinnati, *Martin E. Thompson* of New York City, and *Thomas Cole* of Catskill, New York. From 1848 to 1861 the supervising architects were *William Russell West* and *J.O.Sawyer*. West resigned in 1854 and *N.B.Kelly* was appointed to take his place. This statehouse is "built of limestone taken from the state owned quarry, five miles northwest of the city. The labor was done by convicts from the state penitentiary." The style of architecture is Doric Greek, of which it is a splendid specimen. This state capitol is 304 feet long, 184 feet wide, and 158 feet high. An annex or judicial building was constructed on the east front of this structure, begun in 1898 and dedicated in 1901. This addition, 220 feet long, and 99 feet wide, constructed of the same material as the building proper, cost $400,000.

11

OHIO GAZETTEER

•**ABERDEEN**, Village; Brown County; Pop. 1,566; Area Code 513; Zip Code 45101; Elev. 500'; SW Ohio; is the Ohio River terminus of Zane's Trace.

For more than a century people and goods were ferried over to Limestone, later Maysville, Kentucky, the gateway into the Bluegrass country.

•**ADA**, Village; Hardin County; Pop. 5,669; Area Code 419; Zip Code 45810; 16 m. E of Lima in NW Ohio; Est. in 1853 as Johnstown. To avoid confusion with another Ohio town changed to Ada in 1855 for postal reasons.

> *Agriculture* - Cattle, corn and varied farming
> *Industry/Mfg.* - Lumber, animal feed, dairy products
> *Higher Education* - Ohio Northern University
> *Mayor* - Larry E. Hubbell 634-8876
> *Chamber of Commerce* - Box 225

•**ADAMS COUNTY**, S Ohio; Area 587 sq. miles; Pop. 24,328; County seat - West Union; Est. July 10, 1797; Named for *John Quincy Adams*, sixth President of the United States (1797-1801); Bordered to S by Ohio River; Hilly region.

•**ADAMSVILLE**, Village; Muskingum County; Pop. 229; Area Code 614; Zip Code 43802; SE Ohio; Rural.

•**ADDYSTON**, Village; Hamilton County; Pop. 1,195; Area Code 513; Zip Code 45001; Elev. 510'; SW Ohio; Had a few settlers as early as 1789, but did not become a town until 1871 when *Matthew Addy* of Cincinnati established a large pipe foundry here.

•**ADELPHI**, Village; Ross County; Pop. 472; Area Code 614; Zip Code 43101; S Ohio; On Salt Creek; Site of several Indian burial grounds.

13

•ADENA, Village; Harrison and Jefferson Counties; Pop. 1,062; Area Code 614; Zip Code 43901; 16 m. S of Stubenville in E Ohio; Named by *John McLaughlin* a member of Ohio General Assembly after a country place of the same name owned by a friend.

•AKRON, City; Seat of Summit County; Pop. 237,177; Area Code 216; Zip Code 443 + zone; Elev. 950'; on the little Cuyahoga River, 36 m. SE of Cleveland in NE Ohio; spreads saddle-wise over the watershed dividing the drainage of northern Ohio into the St. Lawrence and the Mississippi River systems. Appropriately named by a scholarly young man long ago, Akron is derived from the Greek akros, meaning "high".

Before the settlement of Akron, the Indian on his way from Lake Erie to the Ohio River crossed its site because it was on the eight-mile Portage Path over the watershed from the Cuyahoga River to the Tuscarawas. Worn smooth by moccasins, the path was so well known that the writers of the Greenville Treaty used it to designate to the Indians what they meant by the western border of the United States. The route crossed what is now the western section of the city, over the street known as Portage Path, and thence south over Exchange Street.

Settlement of this locality began in 1709 at Hudson, 12 miles northeast, with the arrival of *Deacon Hudson* and a party from Goshen, Connecticut; but the territory embraced in the present city limits of Akron was neglected, except by hunters and trappers, until 1807. Then *Captain Joseph Hart* deserted the sea and selected a spot two miles east on the Little Cuyahoga River for a settlement known as Middlebury, now East Akron. In 1811, *Major Miner Spicer* came from the East and began a farm in the section in which the University of Akron now stands. Around his cabin soon grew a settlement generally known as Spicertown.

From 1820 to 1825 there was much talk about how the proposed Ohio and Erie Canal would run when it came through Summit County. People in Middlebury wanted the canal so badly that *Laureen Dewey* easily raised funds ($204) for a paper to becalled the *Ohio Canal Advocate*. When he returned from Cleveland, where he had bought an old Ramage press and other primitive equipment, he found the village boiling with indignation. The Ohio legislature had authorized the building of the canal, but had routed it two miles west of Middlebury. Dewey's paper appeared

14

simply as the *Portage Journal*, and Middlebury became the sixth ward of modern Akron.

Akron proper owes its existence to the canal. *General Simon Perkins* of Warren, commissioner of the Ohio Canal Fund, foresaw the trade possibilities of the projected canal and the great future for a town on the summit of the canal course. In partnership with *Paul Williams*, who had been associated with *Major Spicer*, he laid out Akron in 1825. The village area was part of the 1,000 acres acquired by *General Perkins* for $4.01, the bill for its back taxes. The plat of 150 acres was divided into 300 lots and a public square. After the canal was opened to traffic in 1827, the town grew quickly.

For some time prior to the opening, carpenters in the crude boat yard at Lock No.1, just south of Akron, had been hurrying to get the "State of Ohio" ready for service. On July 3, 1827, this first packet on the Ohio and Erie Canal was ready to be launched. Akron's entire population of 250, and a few disappointed folk from Middlebury, came to the ceremonies. There were speeches and toasts and cheers; the trim black horses of *Job Harrington* strained at the ropes, and the *State of Ohio*, queen of the canal, moved away on its journey to Cleveland.

The canal brought a new people—virile, rowdy (scandalous, said the churchgoers)—and stimulated further development. *Dr. Eliakim Crosby*, an ironmonger in Middlebury, constructed a millrace and a two-story gristmill about a mile north of Akron. A settlement known as Cascade gathered around the mill and soon grew to be larger than Akron. The settlement lost its identity and name, however, when an act of the Ohio legislature in 1836 annexed it to Akron. By this time several blast furnaces were smelting native ore; potteries were making kitchen utensils and crockery from rich beds of fine clay; saws in the lumber mills buzzed continuously; and the primitive gristmills were taking on the dignity of "flouring" industries. When the panic of 1837 broke and wrecked struggling cities, Akron rode out the storm on the business of the canal.

In 1836 exports had reached a record high of $400,000, giving impetus to the successful movement for the Ohio-Pennsylvania. The first boat arrived from Beaver on April 4, 1840.

When Summit County was created in 1840, three villages began contending furiously for the trade advantages of the county seat. The result was a comedy of vacillation. When Akron was chosen, the people of nearby Cuyahoga Falls protested so strongly that a special commission was appointed to reconsider the question. Both factions were outraged when a third town, Summit City, was selected. But before the breaking of ground for the courthouse was completed, the commissioners reconsidered in favor of Cuyahoga Falls. Then, a year later, they returned to their original decision and gave the seat back to Akron. There it remained.

During the 1840's, when religion and religious controversies were burning issues throughout Ohio, the Millerites, a doomsday religious cult, almost disrupted the Congregational Church in Akron by their fervid preachings, which threw the villagers into hysteria. The fanatical wave passed, and the church survived. Later, in 1859, the town reached a new high pitch of excitement with the execution of *John Brown*, a former Akron citizen, for his raid at Harper's Ferry.

The railroad entered the city in 1852, foretelling eventual abandonment of the picturesque and leisurely trading life on the canal. With the Civil War came new demands, new industries, new developments. In 1863, the Empire Barley Mill, first of Akron's great cereal mills, was started by the German merchant *Ferdinand Schumacher* ; in 1865, Akron became a city of the second class; and in 1870 the Universalists founded Buchtel College, now the University of Akron.

Rubber came into Akron without much fanfare, and few people foresaw its future importance. In 1870 *Dr. Benjamin Franklin Goodrich*, lured by a local booster pamphlet, arrived here from Melrose, New York. Nineteen venturesome Akronites subscribed $1,000 each to start the new plant for manufacturing fire hose and similar articles. When, in 1879, the none-too-stable plant underwent one of its chronic reorganizations, the original backers were given their choice of cash or stock, and took the former. They were soon to regret it bitterly.

As the "gay nineties" began, a "horseless carriage" appeared on the streets of Detroit, rolling in on its wheels a vast new market for rubber. Of more immediate importance, however, was the racing trotter Nancy Hanks, who in 1892 lowered the record of the famous Maud S by four seconds. The sulky she drew had new-fangled pneumatic tires, and soon bicycle and buggy owners were clamoring for them.

16

The town began to bristle with names that were to become household words in rubber: *Goodrich, Miller, Seiberling, Firestone, Goodyear, Diamond, Swinehart, Star.* The story of Goodyear, organized in 1898 by *F.A.Seiberling* is typical. For weeks Seiberling made the rounds of acquaintances trying to raise money for his new plant and succeeding only after exhausting his eloquence. In 25 years $10,000 worth of the stock soared to a value of $1,000,000–after having paid a third of a million in dividends.   Through this period and continuing into the first few years of the next century, Akron's five large plants made the city famous as a national center for the manufacture of farm machinery. The clay and cereal industries also showed marked progress. In 1891 the Schumacher interests, which had suffered a $1,000,000 fire in 1886 but had recovered by means of a merger, incorporated as the American Cereal Company, absorbed other units, including the Quaker Oats Mills in Ravenna, and adopted "Quaker Oats" as a trade mark.

During the early 1900's the rubber industry grew steadily, experimenting with new techniques and trying desperately to adapt itself to constant changes in the automotive industry, wherein its future was now definitely seen to be bound up. Then, in a sudden rush, the madness of prosperity descended on the town.

By 1915 it was a boom town, and with a vengeance. The word spread over the country, "There's work in Akron," and men swarmed in by the thousands. Thirty thousand workers came to the city in 1916; in one decade, 1910-20, the population jumped from 69,000 to 209,000.

POINTS OF INTEREST

B.F.GOODRICH RUBBER CO. PLANT- Akron's

oldest and one of the world's largest; occupies 275 acres; a virtually autonomous community.
SUMMIT COUNTY HISTORICAL MUSEUM- Akron's first

educational structure; erected 1847; contains historical manuscripts.

Industry/Mfg. - Varied manufacturing, trade and services
Higher Education - University of Akron
Mayor - John S. Ballard 375-2121
Daily Newspaper - The Beacon-Journal, 44 East Exchange
      St.
Chamber of Commerce - 8th Floor, One Cascade Plaza
Community Event(s) : English Faire; Annual, February,
      Wonderful World of Ohio Mart; Annual, September

•ALBANY, Village; Athens County; Pop. 905; Area Code 614; Zip Code 45701; Elev. 774'; SE central Ohio; was laid out in 1831 and named for Albany, New York.

   Two colleges once functioned here: Atwood Institute, from 1851 to 1890, and Enterprise Institute for Negro students which was established in 1864.

•ALEXANDRIA, Village; Licking County; Pop. 489; Area Code 614; Zip Code 43001; central Ohio; approx. 31 m. NE of Columbus.

•ALGER, Village; Hardin County; Pop. 992; Area Code 419; Zip Code 45812; NW Ohio. Originally called Jagger after *Elias* and *Marie Jagger* who established the town in 1882. Changed to Alger in honor of *Russell A. Alger,* Michigan Governor who was born in Ohio.

•ALLEN COUNTY, NW Ohio; Area 410 sq. miles; Pop. 112,136; County seat - Lima; Est., February 12, 1820; Named for *Ethan Allen,* leader of the "Green Mountain boys" of Vermont during the Revolutionary War; Agricultural area; oil deposits discovered here in 1880's.

•ALLIANCE, City; Mahoning and Stark Counties; Pop. 24,315; Area Code 216; Zip Code 44601; 14 m. NE of Canton in NE central Ohio; In 1805, six Quakers from Virginia established homes on the banks of the Mahoning River north of what is now the city proper. Within the next 30 years three rival towns sprang up nearby and prospered--Greedom, Williamsport, and Mount Union. In 1854 the four communities were united under the name Alliance, and the town was incorporated in 1889.

         Agriculture - Corn, Wheat and varied farming
         Industry/Mfg. - Heavy equipment, dairy products, coal,
            oil, electronics
         Higher Education - Mount Union College
         Mayor - James P. Puckett 821-3110
         Daily Newspaper - The Review, 40 S. Linden Ave.
         Chamber of Commerce - 210 E. Main St.

•ALVORDTON, Village; Williams County; Pop. 362; Area Code 419; Zip Code 43501; NW Ohio; Near Michigan state line.

•AMANDA, Village; Fairfield County; Pop. 720; Area Code 614; Zip Code 43102; 30 m. SE of Columbus in central Ohio; the village was named by *William Hamilton*, surveyor.

•AMBERLEY, Village; Hamilton County; Pop. 3,422; Area Code 513; 10 m. NE of Cincinnati in SW Ohio; is mainly a suburban community.

•AMELIA, Village, Clermont County; Pop. 1,108; Area Code 513; Zip Code 45102; SW Ohio; 21 m. SE of Cincinnati.

•AMESVILLE, Village; Athens County; Pop. 247; Area Code 614; Zip Code 45711; SE Ohio; in a recreational region near several rivers.

•AMHERST, City; Lorain County; Pop. 10,638; Area Code 216; Zip Code 44001; 25 m. SW of Cleveland in N Ohio.

> *Agriculture* - Fruit, dairy products and varied farming
> *Mayor* - Anthony J. Depaola 988-4380
> *Chamber of Commerce* - PO Box 3

•AMSTERDAM, Village; Jefferson County; Pop. 783; Area Code 614; Zip Code 43903; approximately 21 m. NW of Steubenville in E Ohio.

•ANDOVER, Village; Ashtabula County; Pop. 1,205; Area Code 216; Zip Code 44004; Elev. 1,095; NE Ohio; rural trading village centering around its public square; Through the summer Andover bustles as visitors arrive for sport at the nearby reservoir.

> *Agriculture* - Varied farming
> *Industry/Mfg.* - Lumber, dairy products. Resort area

•ANNA, Village; Shelby County; Pop. 1,038; Area Code 513; Zip Code 45302; W Ohio; 9 m. N of Sidney.

•ANSONIA, Village, Darke County; Pop. 1,267; Area Code 5113; Zip Code 45303; W Ohio.

•ANTIOCH, Village; Monroe County; Pop. 113; Area Code 614; Zip Code 43710; SE Ohio; Near the Ohio River.

•ANTWERP, Village; Paulding County; Pop. 1,765; Area Code 419; Zip Code 45813; Elev. 719'; NW Ohio; named by Hollanders and Germans who settled the area. Antwerp came to life when the Wabash, Erie and Miami canals were built, prospered while they prospered, and declined when their usefulness ceased.

Agriculture - Wheat, corn and varied farming
Industry/Mfg. - Machine shops

•APPLE CREEK, Village; Wayne County; Pop. 741; Area Code 216; Zip Code 44606; SE of Wooster in NE Ohio.

•AQUILLO, Village; Geauga County; Pop. 355; Area Code 216; NE Ohio.

•ARCADIA, Village; Hancock County; Pop. 580; Area Code 419; Zip Code 44804; 9 m. NE of Findlay in a rural region in NW Ohio.

•ARCANUM, Village; Darke County; Pop. 2,022; Area Code 513; Zip Code 45304; W Ohio; 14 m. SE of Greenville along Twin Creek.

Agriculture - Corn, tobacco and varied farming
Industry/Mfg. - Sports equipment, grain processing, lumber

•ARCHBOLD, Village; Fulton County; Pop. 3,318; Area Code 419; Zip Code 43502; NW Ohio; 12 m. SW of Wauseon in an agricultural region.

Agriculture - Sugar beets, livestock, soybean and varied
    farming
Industry/Mfg. - Meat packing, lumber furniture
Mayor - William Lovejoy 455–1729
Chamber of Commerce - Rural Rt. 2, Box 218-F

•ARLINGTON, Village; Fulton County; Pop. 1,187; Area Code 419; Zip Code 45814; NW Ohio.

•ARLINGTON HEIGHTS, Village; Hamilton County; Pop. 1,082; Area Code 513; SW Ohio; residential suburb of Cincinnati.

•ASHLAND, City; Seat of Ashland County; Pop. 20,326; Area Code 216; Zip Code 44805; Elev. 1,077'; N central Ohio, NE of

20

Mansfield; has the quiet charm of mellowed age and gradual growth.

William Montgomery platted the town in 1815 and called it Uniontown, the stage line made it easily accessible to prospective settlers, many of whom came from New England. In 1822 the growing town was renamed Ashland, after *Henry Clay's* estate at Lexington, Kentucky.

Agriculture - Varied farming
Industry/Mfg. - Rubber products, clothing, grain milling, animal feed
Higher Education - Ashland College
Mayor - Don M. Richey 289-8622
Daily Newspaper - The Times-Gazette, 40 E. 2nd St., Box 128
Chamber of Commerce - 43 W. Main St.

•ASHLAND COUNTY, N Central Ohio; Area 424 sq. miles; Pop. 46,178; County seat - Ashland; Est., February 24, 1846; Named for "Ashland" *Henry Clay's* estate near Lexington, Kentucky; Agricultural region once frequented by *Johnny Appleseed.*

•ASHLEY, Village; Delaware County; Pop. 1,057; Area Code 614; Zip Code 43003; 40 m. N of Columbus on the E shore of the Delaware Reservoir in central Ohio.

•ASHTABULA, City; Ashtabula County; Pop. 23,449; Area Code 216; Zip Code 44004; Elev. 688'; 50 m. NE of Cleveland in NE Ohio; lies on the shore of Lake Erie. It is at the mouth of the Ashtabula River.

It was briefly named Mary Esther by *Moses Cleveland* when he visited in 1796. The name is thought to mean "River of Many Fish" in it's native Indian. Strong abolitionist sentiment made it a key terminus on the Underground Railroad. It is on the St. Lawrence Seaway route and freighters carry large quantities of iron and coal ore throughout the Great Lakes region.

Agriculture - Varied farming
Industry/Mfg. - Farm implements, shipbuilding, chemicals
Higher Education - Kent State University
Mayor - Clifford D. McClure 997-5791
Daily Newspaper - The Star-Beacon, 4626 Park Ave. 44004
Chamber of Commerce - PO Box 96

•ASHTABULA COUNTY, NE corner Ohio; Area 700 sq. miles; Pop. 104,215; County seat - Ashtabula; Est., February 10, 1807; Name is derived from Indian for "fish river"; Bordered to N by Lake Erie, to E by Pennsylvania state line; Level lake plain, covered with small fruit orchards, vineyards, and port towns.

•ASHVILLE, Village; Pickaway County; Pop. 2,046; Area Code 614; Zip Code 43103; S central Ohio; 30 m. S of Columbus.

Chamber of Commerce - 277 E. Main St.

•ATHALIA, Village; Lawrence County; Pop. 367; Area Code 614; on the Ohio River in S Ohio on Hwy. 7, 3 m. S of Wayne National Forest.

•ATHENS, City; Seat of Athens County; Pop. 19,743; Area Code 614; Zip Code 45701; Elev. 720; 30 m. W of Marietta; spreads across a series of hills above the Hocking River. Some of the bluffs rise 70 feet above the river, and unexpected views are afforded by the network of streets running up and down the town at odd angles. Athens is a magical place of saffron lights and gleaming rooftops. Athen's streets are enlivened the year round by hundreds of college students.

Athens owes its founding to the decision to establish a school here. When the Ohio Company of Associates purchased the Muskingum Valley lands in 1787, the contract set aside two townships for "the use of a university." The townships selected covered this area. In 1800 *General Rufus Putnam* and several other persons from Marietta came here to determine the site for the school and to survey a town. In the same year the territorial legislature approved the Putnam survey and named the village -comprising six cabins - Athens. Not until 1804 was the university chartered, but meanwhile a steady dribble of settlers arrived, and in 1805 Athens became the county seat.

Apart from the growth and development of Ohio Universtiy, Athens' progress was slow and unspectacular. In 1841 the first boat left Athens over the newly opened Hocking Canal. The Baltimore and Ohio Railroad sent the first passenger car through the town in 1856, but it was 1912 before Athens was incorporated as a city. Unconcerned with the nearby Hocking coal fields, Athens looks to its university and to its favored position as a county seat and commercial center for its prosperity.

Industry/Mfg. - Printing equipment, food packing
Higher Education - Ohio University
Mayor - Donald L. Barrett 593-7322
Daily Newspaper - The Messenger, Rt. 33 North & Johnson Rd.
Chamber of Commerce - Security Bldg.

•**ATHENS COUNTY**, SE Ohio; Area 504 sq. miles; Pop. 53,399; County Seat - Athens; Est., February 20, 1805; Named for the capitol of Greece; Livestock and dairying region, the site of part of the Wayne National Forest; Hocking River flows through county, bordered by small villages along its steep bluffs.

•**ATTICA**, Village; Seneca County; Pop. 865; Area Code 419; Zip Code 44807; on a branch of the Sandusky River in N Ohio; was named for the town in New York.

Agriculture - Cattle, dairy and varied farming
Industry/Mfg. - Rubber products, grain milling

•**AUGLAIZE COUNTY**, W Ohio; Area 400 sq. miles; Pop. 42,554; County seat - Wapakoneta; Est., February 14, 1848; Name is Indian, meaning "fallen timbers"; Former lumbering area; Birthplace of astronaut *Neil Armstsrong*.

•**AUGLAIZE RIVER**, River; W Ohio; Flows approx. 100 m. from a point near Wapakoneta in Auglaize County W and N to confluence with Maumee River at city of Defiance; irrigates flat corn farmlands. The name Auglaize comes from the French meaning "at the lick".

•**AURORA**, City; Portage County; Pop. 8,177; Area Code 216; Zip Code 44202; 21 m. SE of Cleveland and 21 m. NE of Akron in NE Ohio.

Mayor - Nignon Donaldson 562-6131
Chamber of Commerce - PO Box 48

•**AVON**, City; Lorain County; Pop. 7,241; Area Code 216; Zip

23

Code 44011; S of Lake Erie shoreline in N Ohio, 20 m. W of Cleveland.

•AVON LAKE, City; Lorain County; Pop. 13,222; Area Code 216; Zip Code 44012; Elev. 628'; 19 m. W of Cleveland in NE Ohio; extending for 5 m. along Lake Erie with many beaches for water sports. Local officials are chosen by a community caucus similar to the New England town meeting.

•BAILEY LAKES, Village; Ashland County; Pop. 397; Area Code 419; Zip Code Rural; N Central Ohio; Near city of Ashland in a recreational area.

•BAINBRIDGE, Village; Ross County; Pop. 1,042; Area Code 614; Zip Code 45612; Elev. 716'; S central Ohio; is a rural trading center.
 Nathaniel Massie, prominent landowner and surveyor started a town on the site in 1805, after a previous attempt at settlement on swampy ground near by had failed. The village was named for *Commander William Bainbridge*, War of 1812 fame.

•BAIRDSTOWN, Village; Wood County; Pop. 151; Area Code 419; NW Ohio; rural community.

•BALLAST ISLAND, Island; Ottawa County; SW Lake Erie; small tree-covered island with an abandoned clubhouse and a government light. Just before his naval encounter with the British in 1813, *Commodore Perry* secured stones here to ballast his ships.

•BALTIC, Village; Tuscarawas County; Pop. 563; Area Code 614; Zip Code 43804; E Ohio; the Village was first named Rowville after founder *Lewis Row*. The second name was Buena Vista and later changed to Baltic. In a hilly river and stream region, once heavily mined for coal.

24

•**BALTIMORE**, Village; Fairfield County; Pop. 2,689; Area Code 614; Zip Code 43105; S central Ohio; 30 m. SE of Columbus.

•**BARBERTON**, City; Summit County; Pop. 29,751; Area Code 216; Zip Code 44203; Elev. 965'; 7 m. SW of Akron NE Ohio; In the center of the city lies beautiful Lake Anna, serene in the midst of squat industrial plants and smoking stacks.

Barberton was laid out in 1891 by *Ohio Columbus Barber*, whose extravagance of name is surpassed only by his fabulous accomplishment and folly. Having organized the Diamond Match Company in 1880, Barber platted his extensive land options, promoted the town successfully, and attracted industries by generous offers of land. The demand of these early factories for cheap labor brought large numbers of foreigners.

Until his death in 1920, Barber was the most important and interesting figure in the city. Retiring from the presidency of the Diamond Match Company in 1913, he poured his boundless energies and $3 million into the Anna Dean Farm in the southeastern section of the town.

> *Industry/Mfg.* - Auto tires and steam boilers
> *Mayor* - Lawrence A. Maurer 753-6611
> *Chamber of Commerce* - 524 Wooster Road W.
> *Community Event(s)* : Cherry Blossom Festival Annual, May

•**BARNESVILLE**, Village; Belmont County; Pop. 4,633; Area Code 614; Zip Code 43713; 40 m. SW of Steubenville in SE Ohio; in a hilly region. The town was named after *James Barnes* who was the founder in 1808.

> *Mayor* - Allen Phillips 425-1880
> *Chamber of Commerce* - Box 376

•**BARNHILL**, Village; Tuscarawas County; Pop. 327; Area Code 216; E central Ohio; Near several streams; Rural.

•**BASS ISLANDS**, Islands; Ottawa County; Elev. 689'; N Ohio, north of Catawba Island Village by ferry, includes Middle, North and South Bass Islands in Lake Erie. All derived their names from the prevalence of bass in the surrounding waters.

Middle Bass is 1 m. wide with wooded bluffs which encircle

750 acres, largely given over to vineyards. As part of the Western Reserve, the islands became the property of *Pierpont Edwards* ; his heirs sent laborers in 1811 to clear land and plant wheat, but they were driven away by British soldiers in the following year. In 1854 the three Bass and several adjacent islands came into the possession of *Jose de Rivera*. He planned to introduce sheep raising, but hearing of the successful grape culture on North Bass Island, he persuaded some immigrants from wine-making centers in Germany to settle here.

•NORTH BASS ISLAND, Elev. 595'; is the most northerly of the Bass group and lies one and one-half miles south of the international boundary. The island contains 740 acres. To the Post Office Department it is known as Isle of St. George. In the early 1820's its first settler was a lonely squatter called George; not until the 1840's and 1850's did other settlers arrive.

The *Fox brothers* came from Pelee Island in 1853, bought 500 acres, found wild grapes of exceptional quality growing here, and introduced the culture of Concords, Catawbas and Delawares.

•SOUTH BASS ISLAND, Elev. 642'; is the largest and most southerly of the Bass Islands. Shaped like a pudding bag (which gave rise to one theory for its common name, Put-in-Bay), it is five miles long and lies a mile south of Middle Bass Island behind a broad, semicircular harbor.

•BATAVIA, Village; Seat of Clermont County; Pop. 1,896; Area Code 513; Zip Code 45103; on the E fork of the Miami River, 20 m. E of Cincinnati in SW Ohio.

> *Agriculture* - Tobacco, grain, and varied farming
> *Industry/Mfg.* - Dairy products, soft drinks machinery
> *Higher Education* - University of Cincinnati

•BATESVILLE, Village; Noble County; Pop. 129; Area Code 614; Zip Code 43715; SE Ohio; is named for *Rev. Timothy Bates*, Methodist preacher.

•BAYVIEW, Village; Erie County; Pop. 804; Area Code 216; Elev. 598'; 10 m. W of Sandusky in N Ohio; is a resort community with bathing, boating, camping and summer cottage facilities.

•**BAY VILLAGE**, City; Cuyahoga County; Pop. 17,846; Area Code 216; Zip Code 44140; Elev. 630'; NE Ohio; is a suburb of Cleveland overlooking Lake Erie.

Mayor - James H. Cowles

•**BEACHWOOD**, City; Cuyahoga County; Pop. 9,963 Area Code 216; Zip Code 44122; NE Ohio; Near Cleveland on Lake Erie; Suburban.

•**BEALLSVILLE**, Village; Monroe County; Pop. 601; Area Code 614; Zip Code 43716; SW Ohio; in a hilly region once mined for coal.

•**BEAVER**, Village; Pike County; Pop. 330; Area Code 614; Zip Code 45613; S Ohio; In a hilly region near the Scioto River.

•**BEAVERCREEK**, Village; Greene County; Pop. 31,589; Area Code 513.

•**BEDFORD**, City; Cuyahoga County; Pop. 15,056; Area Code 216; Zip Code 44146; Elev. 946'; 10 m. SE of Cleveland in NE Ohio; was the site of a temporary settlement by Moravian missionaries in 1786; the settlement was called Pilgerruh, meaning "pilgrim's rest".

The name was chosen as the same town in Connecticut. *Daniel Benedict* was the founder of Bedford when he settled here in 1821.

In 1810 the town site was surveyed by the Connecticut Land Company, and three years later the first permanent settler arrived. *Benjamin Fitch*, credited with starting the manufacture of chairs in Bedford, came in the same year. The town grew slowly and it was not until the 1920's when its population nearly tripled within the decade, that it achieved a city status.

Archibald M. Willard (1836-1918), painter of "The Spirit of '76", was born here.

Industry/Mfg. - Furniture, auto pars, rubber products
Mayor - Andrew V. Romito

•**BEDFORD HEIGHTS**, City; Cuyahoga County; Pop. 13,214; Area Code 216.

Mayor - Lucille J. Reed 439-1600

•**BELLAIRE**, City; Belmont County; Pop. 8,241; Area Code 614; Zip Code 43906; Elev. 655'; 35 m. S of Steubenville on the Ohio River in E Ohio; Bellaire's real growth took place after the entrance of three railroad lines in the 1850's.

Industry/Mfg. - Coal, clay, limestone, glass
Mayor - John Fialkowski 676-6539
Chamber of Commerce - First Natl Bank Bldg. Room 204

•**BELLBROOK**, City; Greene County; Pop. 5,174; Area Code 513; Zip Code 45305; 14 m. SE of Dayton in SW Ohio; suburban; is named after *Stephen Bell* in 1816.

Industry/Mfg. - Lighting products
Mayor - G. David Bucalo 848-4666

•**BELLE CENTER**, Village; Logan County; Pop. 930; Area Code 419; Zip Code 43310; W central Ohio near Indian Lake; Rural.

Agriculture - Grain and varied farming
Industry/Mfg. - Animal feed, quarrying

•**BELLEFONTAINE**, City; Seat of Logan County; Pop. 11,888; Area Code 419; Zip Code 43311; Elev. 1,200'; is 30 m. N of Springfield in W Ohio; was named for the springs of limestone according to an early writer. Prior to 1800 was the location of a Shawnee Indian village. The place was settled in 1806, but did not get under way until 1820 when it became the county seat.

With the coming of the railroads and the establishment of several industries in the latter half of the nineteenth century, Bellefontaine assumed its present character: a railroad town which also serves as the trading center for a rich agricultural region.

Mayor - William S. Meyer 599-3015
Daily Newspaper - The Examiner, 127 E. Chillicothe
Ave. (43311)

28

•**BELLE VALLEY**, Village; Noble County; Pop. 329; Area Code 614; Zip Code 43717; SE central Ohio; On Duck Creek in a hilly region.

•**BELLEVUE**, City; Huron and Sandusky Counties; Pop. 8,187; Area Code 216; Zip Code 44811; Elev. 753'; 15 m. SW of Sandusky in N Ohio; first settled in 1815; Named in 1839 by *James Bell*, who was then building the Mad River and Lake Erie Railroad from Sandusky.

> *Agriculture* - Fruit, grain and varied farming
> *Industry/Mfg.* - Auto parts, electrical products
> *Mayor* - Phillis A. Robertson 483-7720
> *Daily Newspaper* - The Gazette, PO Box 269, 107 N.
>   Sandusky St.
> *Chamber of Commerce* - 202 W. Main St.
> *Community Event(s)* : Cherry Festival; Annual, June

•**BELLVILLE**, Village; Richland County; Pop. 1,714; Area Code 419; Zip Code 44813; Elev. 1,144'; N central Ohio; farm community surrounded by apple and peach orchards.

Bellville was the center of a mild furor when gold was discovered here in 1853 by *Dr. James C. Lee*, a former California miner. Since the amount found equaled only $30 in value, Bellville's dreams of becoming another Eldorado vanished.

•**BELMONT**, Village; Belmont County; Pop. 714; Area Code 614; Zip Code 43718; E Ohio; In 1808, *Joseph D. Wright* planned out this community and named it Wrightsville. The name was changed to that of the county in hope that it would become the county seat because of its central location.

•**BELMONT COUNTY**, E Ohio; Area 534 sq. miles; Pop. 82,569; County seat - St. Clairsville; Est., September 7, 1801; Named by French trappers for the "beautiful mountains", or rather, hills in this county; Bordered to S and E by Ohio River; Coal mining, farming.

•**BELMORE**, Village; Putnam County; Pop. 205; Area Code 419; Zip Code 45815; NW Ohio; 20 m. NE of Ottawa.

•**BELOIT**, Village; Mahoning County; Pop. 1,093; Area Code 216; Zip Code 44609; E Ohio; Steel manufacturing; Residential area; 30 m. SW of Youngstown.

•**BELPRE**, City; Washington County; Pop. 7,193; Area Code 614; Zip Code 45714; Elev. 622'; S Ohio; It's name means beautiful meadows in French; 10 m. SW of Marietta. Belpre lies by the Ohio River on a fertile bottom devoted to large-scale fruit growing and truck gardening.

Belpre began in 1789 when *Captain Jonathan Stone* and a party of about 40 persons, principally Revolutionary War veterans, came here from Marietta to examine their pruchase of land from the government. The Belpre Farmer's Library, established in 1796 by *Colonel Israel Putnam*, was one of the first subscription libraries in the Northwest Territory. The Blennerhassett Island is close-by.

Mayor - Ivan C. Smith 423-7592
Chamber of Commerce - 713 Park Dr.

•**BENTLEYVILLE**, Village; Cuyahoga County, Pop. 381; Area Code 216.

•**BEREA**, City; Cuyahoga County; Pop. 19,567; Area Code 216; Zip Code 44017; Elev. 788'; 10 m. SW of Cleveland in N Ohio; frequently called the grindstone city because of its quarries. Its oldfashioned, serene appearance is emphasized by its proximity to the clamorous, industrial city of Cleveland. Winding narrow streets converge at the center of town, which is called "the square" though triangular in shape. Abandoned quarries dot the town.

This area was purchased from the Connecticut Land Company by *Gideon Granger*, Postmaster-General under *President Thomas Jefferson*, and the toss of a coin determined its name. In 1827 *John Baldwin* came to the settlement. He built the first frame house, the first Sunday school, opened the first quarry, laid out the first building lots, turned the first grindstone, and had a guiding hand in establishing Baldwin-Wallace College. While digging a cellar for his house, Baldwin struck a thick vein of perfect abrasive sandstone. With its commercial possibilities in mind, he acquired title to most of the valuable land of the vicinity. Today quarrying, the manufacture of building blocks, and the raising of onion crops are the town's major industries.

In 1845 *John Baldwin* offered to the North Ohio Conference of the Methodist Episcopal Church a building and lands in Berea for founding an institution of learning. Accepting the gift, the conference appointed a board of commissioners who, with Baldwin, organized Baldwin Institute, later chartered as Baldwin University. In 1856 German-Wallace College was founded by the university trustees as a department to provide for the educational needs of the German Methodist Church. The two schools operated separately until 1913 when they were combined to form Baldwin-Wallace College, a liberal-arts school under the control of the Methodist Episcopal Church.

Industry/Mfg. - Metal products, small appliances, plastics
Higher Education - Baldwin-Wallace College
Mayor - Jack Kafer 234-5436
Chamber of Commerce - 106 Front St.
Community Event(s) : Bach Festival; Annual, May

•BERGHOLZ, Village; Jefferson County; Pop. 914; Area Code 614; Zip Code 43908; E Ohio; In a hilly region 25 m. NW of Steubenville.

•BERKEY, Village; Lucas County; Pop. 306; Area Code 419; Zip Code 43504; NW Ohio; On Michigan state line; 10 m. W of Toledo city border; Suburban-rural.

•BERLIN HEIGHTS, Village; Erie County; Pop. 756; Area Code 216; Zip Code 44814; Elev. 604'; N Ohio; in the heart of an important apple and peach district. Fruit growing got its start in this part of Ohio in 1812 when *John Hoak* and *John Fleming* brought from Canada a number of young fruit trees. The favorable climate and the skill of the farmers eventually made fruit growing profitable.
        During the 1850's and 1860's men and women from the East settled in Berlin Heights and vicinity, and soon proved themselves able orchardists and businessmen. Their neighbors called them Free Lovers. Never very numerous, they were, nevertheless, a perpetual goad to the solid citizenry. *Artemus Ward* visited Berlin Heights and wrote a bit of foolery about the Free Lovers in "Artemus Ward: His Book". In time many of them moved to other places; those who remained became respectable.

•BERSTON, Village; Harrison County; Pop. 487; Area Code 614; Zip Code 44695; E Ohio; In a hilly region.

•**BETHEL**, Village; Clermont County; Pop. 2,231; Area Code 513; Zip Code 45106; SW Ohio; 30 m. SE of Cincinnati.

Agriculture - Fruit, cattle and varied farming
Industry/Mfg. - Cement, auto parts, dairy products

•**BETHESDA**, Village; Belmont County; Pop. 1,429; Area Code 614; Zip Code 43719; E Ohio; Hilly region.

•**BETTSVILLE**, Village; Seneca County; Pop. 752; Area Code 419; Zip Code 44815; N Ohio; 25 m. NE of Findlay in a stock raising region.

•**BEVERLY**, Village; Washington County; Pop. 1,471; Area Code 614; Zip Code 45715; Elev. 631'; SE Ohio; was settled in 1789 by 19 adventurers from the Marietta settlement. After the Big Bottom Massacre, Fort Frye, a triangular stockade, was constructed here near the river bank. It was abandoned in 1794 and a new community was established on the Muskingum at the mouth of Olive Green Creek. Beverly has a large nursery, which may account for the beautiful landscaping of the residential district overlooking the river. The town lies in one of the most profitable truck garden areas in the state, and is the home of many retired farmers who maintain its air of trim prosperity.

From 1842 to 1875 the Beverly Academy served as the educational center for the district, attracting students from many miles around. After the shcool closed, the academy building was converted into a print shop. At present it is used as a Roman Catholic church. Sandstone quarries just south of Beverly yielded abundantly in former years.

•**BEXLEY**, City; Franklin County; Pop. 13,405; Area Code 614; Zip Code 43209; Elev. 775'; E side of Columbus in central Ohio; is mainly a residential community of Columbus. Many affluent families have their estates here.

Mayor - David H. Madison 235-8694

•**BLAKESLEE**, Village; Williams County; Pop. 136; Area Code 419; Zip Code 43505; NW Ohio; Near the St. Joseph River; Rural.

•**BLANCHESTER**, Village; Clinton County; Pop. 3,302; Area Code 513; Zip Code 45107; approx. 30 m. NE of Cincinnati in SW Ohio; The town was first settled in 1832. Today is chiefly an industrial village.

Mayor - Stephen Valentine 783-2431
Chamber of Commerce - 111 W. Main St.

•**BLOOMDALE**, Village; Wood County; Pop. 744; Area Code 419; Zip Code 44817; NW Ohio; 13 m. NE of Findley.

•**BLOOMINGBURG**, Village, Fayette County; Pop. 869; Area Code 614; Zip Code 43106; SW Central Ohio; Rural.

•**BLOOMINGDALE**, Village; Jefferson County; Pop. 254; Area Code 614; Zip Code 43810; 10 m. E of Steubenville in E Ohio; Farm center.

•**BLOOMVILLE**, Village, Seneca County; Pop. 1,019; area Code 419; Zip Code 44818; N Central Ohio.

Agriculture - Varied farming
Industry/Mfg. - Quarrying

•**BLUE ASH**, City; Hamilton County; Pop. 9,506; Area Code 513; NE of Cincinnati; Residential.

Mayor - Paul D. McKinney 791-0330

•**BLUFFTON**, Village; Allen County; Pop. 3,310; Area Code 419; Zip Code 45817; Elev. 823'; 14 m. NE of Lima in NW Ohio; founded in 1833, took its present name from a Mennonite community in Indiana. Many of its residents are Mennonites of Swiss descent. At present the distribution of crushed stone and lime produced from the limestone outcroppings of the vicinity is an important local activity.

Agriculture - Grain, truck and varied farming
Industry/Mfg. - Electrical products, clothing
Higher Education - Bluffton College
Mayor - James P. King 358-2981
Chamber of Commerce - Box 142

33

•**BOLIVAR**, Village; Tuscarawas County; Pop. 989; Area Code 614; Zip Code 44612; E Ohio; resembles a New England village and was originally named Kelleysville after the father of the Ohio Canal, *Alfred Kelley* who declined the offer.

It was an important grain market for a half dozen counties during the boom days of the Ohio and Erie and the Sandy and Beaver canals in the last century. A mile and a half southwest of Bolivar a marker indicates the site of the first cabin built in Ohio by a white man, *Christian Frederick Post*, a Moravian missionary who came in 1761.

●**BOSTON HEIGHTS**, Village; Summit County; Pop. 781; Area Code 216; Zip Code (with Akron); NE Ohio; Near Cuyahoga River, 15 m. N of Akron city center.

●**BOTKINS**, Village; Shelby County; Pop. 1,372; Area Code 513; Zip Code 45306; W Ohio; Rural.

●**BOWERSTON**, Village; Harrison County; Pop. 487; Area Code 614; Zip Code 44695.

●**BOWERSVILLE**, Village; Greene County; Pop. 329; Area Code 513; Zip Code 45307; SW Central Ohio.

●**BOWLING GREEN**, City; Seat of Wood County; Pop. 25,728; Area Code 513; Zip Code 43402; Elev. 700'; 20 m. SW of Toledo in NW central Ohio; Laid out in 1835 and named by *Joseph Gordon* for his home town in Kentucky.

In 1886 the Fulton well spouted oil, followed by the Royce gusher and other wells, and the town became a maelstrom of activity. Derricks popped up in the meadows and industries, especially glass factories, were attracted to this region. An industrial boom followed, but petered out with factories. The H.J. Heinz Company established a large tomato-products plant here, and a state normal school opened its doors. Today Bowling Green is an inviting educational center with nothing to remind a stranger of its oil spree except the elaborately trimmed and turreted houses that were built on the crest of expansion.

Agriculture - Grain, cattle and varied farming
Industry/Mfg. - Farm equipment, auto parts, campers, dairy products
Higher Education - Bowling Green State University
Mayor - Alvin L. Perkins 352-3541
Daily Newspaper - The Sentinel-Tribune 300 East Poe Rd., PO Box 88
Chamber of Commerce - 121 E. Wooster St.

●BRADFORD, Village; Miami County; Pop. 2,166; Area Code 513; Zip Code 45308; 15 m. W of Greenville and 30 m. NW of Dayton in W Ohio.

●BRADNER, Village; Wood County; Pop. 1,175; Area Code 419; Zip Code 43406; NW Ohio.

●BRADY LAKE, Village; Portage County; Pop. 470; Area Code 216; Zip Code 44211; NE Ohio; Adjacent to Kent in a region of small lakes; Residential.

●BRATENAHL, Village; Cuyahoga County; Pop. 1,485; Area Code 216; Zip Code (with Cleveland); NE Ohio; On Lake Erie, 10 m. NE of Cleveland city center.

●BRECKSVILLE, City; Cuyahoga County; Pop. 10,132; Area Code 216; Zip Code 44141; Elev. 955'; 10 m. S of Cleveland in NE Ohio; was settled about 1811 and named for *John* and *Robert Breck*, early land owners in the region. Its old inn, church and various civic buildings are grouped around the customary soldier's monument on the village green; Annual displays of fruits, flowers, and vegetables, accompanied by much dancing and merry-making, are important events.

●BREMEN, Village; Fairfield County; Pop. 1,432; Area Code 614; Zip Code 43107; 10 m. E of Lancaster in N central Ohio; is named for the German City. The town was first settled by *George Berry* in 1834. In 1907 oil was discovered and the town rapidly expanded.

●BREWSTER, Village; Stark County; Pop. 2,321; Area Code 216; Zip Code 44613; NE Ohio; 18 m. SW of Canton; Along the Sugar Creek.

● **BRIARWOOD BEACH,** Village; Medina County; Pop. 628; Area Code 216.

● **BRICE,** Village; Franklin County; Pop.93; Area Code 614; Zip Code 43109; SW of Columbus in central Ohio; within the city's metropolitan area; Residential subdivision.

● **BRIDGEPORT,** Village; Belmont County; Pop. 2,642; Area Code 614; Zip Code 43912; Elev. 660'; on the Ohio River in E Ohio; across the river is Wheeling, West Virginia; was called Canton when platted by *Ebenezer Zane* in 1806, but has been called by its present name since 1836.

Boatbuilding was an important industry during the first half of the nineteenth century, and glass-making during the latter half. Today many of Bridgeport's residents work in Wheeling, West Virginia.

Mayor - Samuel C. Loften 635-2424

● **BRILLIANT,** Village; Jefferson County; Pop. 1,751; Area Code 614; Zip Code 43913; E Ohio; On the Ohio River, 7 m. S of Steubenville.

● **BROADVIEW HEIGHTS,** City; Cuyahoga County; Pop. 10,920; Area Code 216; Zip Code (with Cleveland); NE Ohio; Suburban development, 20 m. S of Cleveland.

Mayor - Edna M. Deffler 526-4357
Chamber of Commerce - 8938 Broadview Rd.

● **BROOKLYN,** City; Cuyahoga County; Pop. 12,342; Area Code 216; Zip Code 44144; NE Ohio; S suburb of Cleveland; Residential.

● **BROOKLYN HEIGHTS,** City; Cuyahoga County; Pop. 1,653; Area Code 216; Zip Code 44142; NE Ohio; Residential subdivision adjacent to city of Brooklyn.

● **BROOK PARK,** City; Cuyahoga Coutny; Pop. 26,195; Area

Code 216; Zip Code 44142; NE Ohio; SW suburb of Cleveland, site of the Cleveland International Airport.

Mayor - Angelo Wedo 433-1300
Chamber of Commerce - 15734 Harrison Dr.

● BROOKSIDE, Village; Belmont County; Pop. 887; Area Code 614; Zip Code (not listed); E Ohio; Near Ohio River and Wheeling, West Virginia.

● BROOKVILLE, Village; Montgomery County; Pop. 4,322; Area Code 513; Zip Code 45309; SW central Ohio; 20 m. NW of Dayton.

Mayor - Robert N. Apgar 833-2135

● BROUGHTON, Village; Paulding County; Pop. 171; Area Code 419.

● BRUNSWICK, City; Medina County; Pop. 27,689; Area Code 216; Zip Code 44212; 25 m. SW of Cleveland in N Ohio; is named for Brunswick township.

Mayor - Helen L. West 225-9144
Chamber of Commerce - PO Box 82

● BRYAN, City; Seat of Williams County; Pop. 7,879; Area Code 419; Zip Code 43506; Elev. 764'; 50 m. W of Toledo in NW Ohio; is named for *Hon. John A. Bryon* who held offices in the state and also developed this part of the state. Early growth was due to the discovery of artesian wells.

Agriculture - Grain and varied farming
Mayor - William C. Runkle 636-4232
Daily Newspaper - The Times, 127 S. Walnut St.
Chamber of Commerce - PO Box 586

● BUCHTEL, Village; Athens County; Pop. 585; Area Code 614; Zip Code 45716; SE Ohio; In the Wayne National Forest, 18 m. N of Athens.

● BUCKLAND, Village; Auglaize County; Pop. 271; Area Code 419; Zip Code 45819; W Ohio.

37

●BUCYRUS, City; Seat of Crawford County; Pop. 13,433; Area Code 419; Zip Code 44820; Elev. 1,006'; 20 m. NE of Marion in N central Ohio, along the Sandusky River; settled 1818, became county seat 1830.

When *Samuel Norton* and 17 other persons came from Pennsylvania in the fall of 1819 to build the first homes on the site, the forests abounded in wild turkey, deer and other game. *Col. James Kilbourne* bought the land, and then surveyed the village in 1822. Because *Cyrus*, a leader of the ancient Persians, was one of Kilbourne's favorite heroes, and because the country was attractive, he is said to have named the community by prefixing Cyrus with "bu", signifying "beautiful".

Visitors may see coper kettle production at a factory started here in 1879. The Pickwick Farms nearby produce standardbred horses.

> *Agriculture* - Varied farming
> *Industry/Mfg.* - Clothing, utensils, hydraulic equipment, road machinery, glass works
> *Daily Newspaper* - The Telegraph Forum, 119 W. Rensselaer St., PO Box 471
> *Chamber of Commerce* - 334 S. Sandusky Ave.
> *Community Event(s)* : Bratwurst Festival; Annual, August

●BURBANK, Village; Wayne County; Pop. 365; Area Code 216; Zip code 44214; NE central Ohio; 27 m. SW of Akron.

●BURGOON, Village; Sandusky County; Pop. 244; Area Code 419; Zip Code 43407; N central Ohio; Rural.

●BURKETTSVILLE, Village; Mercer County; Pop. 295; Area Code 513; Zip Code 45310; W Ohio; Rich agricultural region.

●BURTON, Village; Geauga County; Pop. 1,401; Area Code 216; Zip Code 44021; Elev. 1,310'; NE Ohio; near the Cuyahoga River; Agricultural community; is named for the son of the founder of Titus St.

Outside of town is a restored Western Reserve village with nineteenth century antiques and documents. A genealogical library is open to the public.

●BUTLER, Village; Richland County; Pop. 955; Area code 419;

Zip Code 44822; N central Ohio; On the clear Fork of the Mohican River, 16 m. SE of Mansfield; hilly region, with a ski area nearby.

●BUTLER COUNTY, SW Ohio; Area 471 sq. miles; Pop. 258,787; County seat - Hamilton; Est., March 24, 1803; Named for *Richard Butler*, Indian fighter, who died while working with *Arthur St. Clair's* expedition against northwest Indian tribes in this region; Miami River flows through this region, with heavy industry centered to S.

●BUTLERVILLE, Village; Warren County; Pop. 223; Area Code 513; SW Ohio; Rural.

●BYESVILLE, Village; Guernsey County; Pop. 2,572; Area Code 419; Zip Code 45820; Elev. 804'; E Ohio; named for *Jonathan Bye*, who built the first flour mill in the vicinity early in the nineteenth century. The place was first called Bye's Mill and in 1856 the name was changed to Byesville.

●CADIZ, Village; Seat of Harrison County; Pop. 4,058; Area Code 614; Zip Code 43907; Elev. 1,210'; 20 m. SW of Steubenville in E Ohio; Designated "the proudest small town in America" in 1938 when a Hollywood publicity group sought the American town with a population under 5,000 having the most illustrious roster of famous sons. Cadiz won easily. The 10 names submitted by Cadiz included *John A. Bingham*, statesman of Civil War days; *Bishop Matthew Simpson*, prominent abolitionist; *Edwin M. Stanton*, Lincoln's Secretary of War; and *Clark Gable*, actor.

> *Agriculture* - Grain, cattle and varied farming
> *Industry/Mfg.* - Coal mining, machine shops
> *Mayor* - Christopher Wood 942-2310
> *Chamber of Commerce* - Box 224
> *Community Event(s)* : International Mining and
> Manufacturing Festival; Annual, September

●CAIRO, Village; Allen County; Pop. 596; Area Code 419; Zip Code 45820; NW central Ohio; Small community named for city in Egypt.

●CALDWELL, Village; Seat of Noble County; Pop. 1,935; Area

Code 614; Zip Code 43724; Elev. 748'; 27 m. N of Marietta in a rich coal mining region in SE Ohio.

Lying along the west fork of Duck Creek, this village has been important in large scale Freeport coal production since 1880. Founded in 1857, it is named for the owners of the town site. When the railroad came through in the 1870's the town began to grow and continued to expand with the coal mining business.

Agriculture - Corn, tobacco, and varied
    farming
Industry/Mfg. - Campers, lumber, coal, oil,
    dairy products
Chamber of Commerce - PO Box 41

•CALEDONIA, Village; Marion County; Pop. 759; Area Code 614; Zip Code 43314; N central Ohio; 8 m. NE of Marion; Rural; was named by early Scotch-Irish settlers.

•CAMBRIDGE, City; Seat of Guernsey County; Pop. 13,573; Area Code 614; Zip Code 43725; Elev. 799'; 20 m. NE of Zanesville in E Ohio.

In 1806 *Jacob Gomber* and *Zacheus Beatty* laid out the town and named it for Cambridge, Maryland, from which came many of the first settlers. Decades of commercial activity and social excitement followed the arrival in 1826 of the National Road and Cambridge grew and took on life with the road. After the road's commercial importance had declined, agricultural, milling and salt-making pursuits kept the community busy.

Manufacturing got started in the 1880's when oil and gas were discovered in the vicinity and coal mining became a large-scale industry in eastern Ohio. The large glass factory was founded in 1901. Near-by deposits of clay led to the establishment of several potteries and fire-clay concerns. A large steel mill helped cement Cambridge's steady industrialization by employing in peak years nearly 900 workers. The mill closed in the early 1930's, but other industries, a plastics plant among them, started, and these have absorbed most of the mill hands.

Agriculture - Corn, grain and varied farming
Industry/Mfg. - Coal Mining, machine shop,
    dairy products, lumber, furniture
Mayor - Jack D. Hendricks 439-1050
Daily Newspaper - The Jeffersonian, 821
    Wheeling Ave

•CAMDEN, Village; Preble County; Pop. 1,971; Area Code 513; Zip Code 45311; SW Ohio; On Sevenmile Creek, 19 m. N of Hamilton.

Agriculture - Varied farming
Industry/Mfg. - Pre-fab homes, cement, steel

•CAMPBELL, City; Mahoning County; Pop. 11,619; Area Code 216; Zip Code 44405; on the Mahoning River, 5 m. SE of Youngstown in NE Ohio; Suburb.

Industry/Mfg. - Steel and iron works
Mayor - Rocco F. Mico 755-1451

•CAMPBELL HILL, Large hill; Logan County; Elev. 1,550'; W central Ohio; near the city of Bellefontaine; Shawnee Indians used to live near this highest point in Ohio, now surrounded by farmlands.

•CANAL FULTON, Village; Stark County; Pop. 3,481; Area Code 216; Zip Code 44614; Elev. 947'; NE Ohio; Formerly Milan, lying on the Tuscarawas River (so-called because an Indian tribe of this name lived along its banks); A busy distributing point on the Ohio and Erie Canal during the 1840's and 1850's.

When the canal was being built, Milan changed its name to Canal Fulton in honor of *Robert Fulton*, inventor of the steamboat.

Agriculture - Grain and varied farming
Industry/Mfg. - Cement, dairy products,
electronics, lumber
Mayor - E.M. Fellmeth 845-2225
Community Event(s) : Canal Days; Annual,
July

•CANAL WINCHESTER, Village; Fairfield and Franklin Counties; Pop. 2,749; Area Code 614; Zip Code 43110; 15 m. SE of Columbus in central Ohio; located on the branch of the Ohio Canal;

41

was named for settlers from Winchester, VA and then Canal was added because of the location.

Agriculture - Fruit, grain and varied farming
Industry/Mfg. -Meat packing, food processing,
glassware
Mayor - K.L. Miller 837-7493

•CANFIELD, City; Mahoning County; Pop. 5,535; Area Code 216; Zip Code 44406; Elev. 1,157'; 10 m. SW of Youngstown in NE Ohio; fans out from oval-shaped village green; was named for *Johnathan Canfield* an early landowner.

Surveyed in 1798, the town grew and prospered and saw an oil boom come and go.

Agriculture - Fruit and varied farming
Industry/Mfg. - Publishing, animal feed,
steel and aluminum
Mayor - Francis McLaughlin 533-4927

•CANTON, City; Seat of Stark County; Pop. 94,730; Area Code 216; Zip Code 444 + zone; Elev. 1,050'; 20 m. SE of Akron in NE Ohio.

The city lies on the flood plain where the three branches of the Nimishillen Creek comes together 12 miles south of the Tuscarawas watershed. It fits snugly into its peninsula at the forks, being roughly in the shape of an equilateral triangle, with its principal apex inclining to the southwest.

Canton's history goes back almost to the time when Indians used to camp here before going over the Old Portage Trail, and to the time when, in 1784, *Delaware Chief Turtle Heart* deeded this land to unremembered white traders.

After the French and the early Colonial traders, there came in 1793 five Government land scouts, who reported the fertility and suitableness of the land. But permanent settlement did not begin until 1805, when a half dozen pioneers from New England set their homes on the flood plain at the forks of the creek. The next year *Bezaleel Wells*, the "Father of Canton" (and also Steubenville), together with his friend *James Leonard*, platted the town. Despite criticism of his "willful waste of good land," Wells insisted that the streets be made amply wide - an unusual bit of foresight for the Ohio country.

When the settlement became the county seat of the newly

organized Stark County in 1809, it had a gristmill, sawmill, resident physician, post office, tavern, tannery, pay school, and two stores. On March 30, 1815, *John Saxton*, grandfather of *Mrs. William McKinley*, brought out the first edition of the Ohio Repository, which is still being published as the Canton Repository. Canton was incorporated as a town in 1822.

Two events of the late 1820's are especially important. In 1827, *Joshua Gibbs* of Canton, who had been experimenting with the shape of plow moldboards, brought out a greatly improved metal plow, and soon became one of the most important plow manufacturers west of the Alleghenies. The other event affected Canton quite differently. The great Ohio and Erie Canal connecting Cleveland with the Ohio River passed Canton by and went through Massillon, eight miles west. Canton languished for a time, but the presence of the canal in the county raised wheat to almost a dollar a bushel and other products proportionately. The rich land and highly improved machinery attracted many dollars to Canton.

The plow was helping not only the farmer but also the mechanic. People became more interested in working steel and designing new machinery. In 1851 the C. Aultman Company was established in Canton to manufacture reapers; soon its business had so increased that it erected branch plants in Akron and Mansfield. With the help of these new machines and better agricultural technique, farming became easier and more profitable. At one time as many as six kinds of reapers were manufactured in Stark County.

Canton sent companies to the Mexican War, organized its common school system in 1849, welcomed the railroads in 1853, and became a city in 1854 with a population of 2,600.

In 1867 young *Major William McKinley*, who had returned from the Civil War and prepared for the bar, moved in from Poland, Ohio, and opened a law office. In the same year the first portentous shipload of Minnesota iron ore arrived in Cleveland harbor. This high quality ore, together with the ready resources of coal, limestone, and water necessary for making steel, gave northeastern Ohio a tremendous steel business. Canton's population figure rose from 4,041 in 1860 to 26,189 in 1890.

In 1888, by offering bonuses of land and money, Canton acquired the Hampden Watch Manufacturing Company of Springfield, Massachusetts, and the Dueber Watch Company of

Newport, Kentucky. These concerns were merged and became the Dueber-Hampden Company, employing 2,300 workmen. This plant attracted to Canton a large number of skilled German and Swiss artisans, to whom is due much of the neighborliness and order of the present steel city.

In 1898 *Henry H. Timken,* a carriage manufacturer of St. Louis, Missouri, secured a patent on the tapered roller bearing and, because of Canton's rising fame in steel, selected the city as a place for his factory. Designed originally for buggies, carriages, and farm implements, the bearing later became a necessary part of the automobile. Timken's plant expanded phenomenally until it became Canton's biggest factory and the world's largest manufacturer of roller bearings.

William McKinley's fame had also been growing. He had served in Congress for 14 years (1876-90) and was Governor of Ohio from 1892 to 1896, in which year he conducted from his home in Canton the original "Front Porch Campaign" for the presidency. After his assassination in Buffalo in September 1901, his remains were brought back to Canton for interment. A memorial tomb, realized through contributions from more than a million Americans, was started in 1904 and dedicated in 1907. Because McKinley loved the red carnation, it was made the State flower.

POINTS OF INTEREST

CANTON PUBLIC LIBRARY- Erected in 1905 with funds given by *Andrew Carnegie* ; contains important McKinley manuscripts.

MCKINLEY MONUMENT- Bears minor resemblance to Tajmahal of India and Tomb of Hardrian; designed by *Harold Van Buren Magonigle* of New York.

Industry/Mfg. - Mining, quarrying, office equipment, engines, steel

Higher Education - Malone College

Mayor - Stanley A. Cmich 489-3000

Daily Newspaper - The Repository, 500 Market Ave., S.

Chamber of Commerce - 229 Wells Ave.

Community Event(s) : Pro Football Hall of Fame Festival; Annual, August

•CARDINGTON, Village; Morrow County; Pop. 1,665;

Area Code 614; Zip Cdoe 43315; N central Ohio; 14 m.
SE of Marion.

Agriculture - Grain, cattle and varied farming
Industry/Mfg. - Medical supplies, machine shop, truck
  bodies
High Education - Cedarville College

•CAREY, Village; Wyandot County; Pop. 3,674; Area Code 419;
Zip Code 43316; Elev. 823'; 15 m. SE of Findlay in a large farming
region, NW central Ohio; the place was named for *Judge John
Carey.*

Carey is the site of the National Shrine of Our Lady of Con-
solation, founded by Franciscans. The image of the *Virgin Mary,*
brought to Carey in 1875, is carried in processions each Sunday
from May to October.

Mayor - Dallas K. Risner 396-7681
Chamber of Commerce - 101 E. Findlay

•CARLISLE, Village; Warren and Montgomery Counties; Pop.
4,276; Area Code 513; Zip Code 45005; 15 m. SW of Dayton in SW
Ohio; Between the Twin and Miami Rivers; Near Middletown.

Mayor - Kelly C. Borad 732-4158

•CARROLL, Village; Fairfield County; Pop. 641 Area Code 614;
Zip Code 43112; S central Ohio; 10 m. NW of Lancaster.

•CARROLL COUNTY, E Ohio; Area 390 sq. miles; Pop. 25,598;
County seat - Carrollton; Est., December 25, 1832; Named for
Charles Carroll, signer of the Declaration of Independence and
Maryland senator; Rural region, cut through by the Sandy River.

•CARROLLTON, Village; Seat of Carroll County; Pop. 3,065;
Area Code 614; Zip Code 44615; 20 m. SE of Canton in E Ohio; was
named for *Charles Carroll* who signed the Declaration of
Independence.

Carrollton is the site of the McCook House, the renovated
home of the "Fighting McCooks" of the Civil War. Historical
museum houses local artifacts and documents.

Agriculture - Grain and varied farming
Industry/Mfg. - Steel and rubber products, coal and
   clay products
Mayor - Lynn R. Fox 627-2411
Chamber of Commerce - Second St. SW

•CASSTOWN, Village; Miami County; Pop. 331; Area Code 513;
Zip Code 45312; W Ohio; Rural trading center near Troy.

•CASTALIA, Village; Erie County; Pop. 973; Area Code 216; Zip
Code 44824; Approx. 6 m. S of Sandusky Bay, Lake Erie in N
Ohio; Site of Blue Hole, an artesian spring of fresh water at a constant 48 degrees F. The town was named for the Grecian Font at
the Foot of Mt. Parnasus. The village was settled in 1836 by *Mar-
shall Burton*. The village was formerly known as Margaretta.

•CASTINE, Village; Darke County; Pop. 147; Area Code 513; Zip
Code 45313; 15 m. S of Greenville in W Ohio.

•CATAWBA, Village; Clark County; Pop 314; Area Code 513; Zip
Code 43010; Elev. 587'; W Ohio; on the island of the same name. It
lies at the northeast end of the peninsula overlooking the lake and
the Bass Islands. The local ferry, Erie Isle, makes three round
trips daily to Middle and South Bass Islands from mid-April to
mid-June, and five round trips daily from mid-June to mid-
September. The village derived its name from an Indian tribe
formerly living along the Eastern seaboard.

•CECIL, Village; Paulding County; Pop. 267; Area Code 419; Zip
Code 45821; NW Ohio; Near the Maumee River; Rich
agricultural land.

•CEDAR POINT, Elev. 580'; at the tip of the peninsula at the entrance of Sandusky Bay on Lake Erie in Erie County, N Ohio. In
1760, *George Croghan*, an English trader landed here and found
Ottawas and Wyandot Indians camping.
   The site was formerly a wild, heavily timbered tract of
1,200 acres with a large sandy beach. Officially a resort in 1882,
the point soon attracted such crowds that boats were hard put to
accommodate them. Railroad and steamer excursions from all
parts of Ohio and nearby states have maintained Cedar Point's
popularity as a summer playground; it is a noted convention
center, and a large hotel accommodates the summer residents.

46

Today the large Cedar Point Amusement Park attracts hundreds of thousands of vacationers from all over the midwest and east. The park is accessible by pleasure craft.

•CEDARVILLE, Village; Greene County; Pop. 2,799; Area Code 513; Zip Code 45314; Elev. 1,055'; NE of Xenia in SW central Ohio; was named for cedar trees in the area. The place was formerly known as Milford but was changed for postal reasons.

The place was first settled in 1816 by *Jesse* and *William Newport*. A sedate college town, Cedarville was once characterized by the editor of a leading British newspaper as "a Puritan oasis in America". The entire congregation of a Covenanter church from Chester, South Carolina, established their new homes here.

Cedarville College, west side of State 72 near the north village limits, chartered in 1887 and opened in 1894 under the auspices of the Reformed Presbyterian Church, offers arts, sciences, and normal courses to approximately 175 students. In 1913 the theological seminary of the Reformed Presbyterian Church was combined with the institution. Cedarville College "was founded and is maintained to give a sound Christian training to both sexes".

•CELINA, City; Seat of Mercer County; Pop. 9,137; Area Code 419; Zip Code 45822; Elev. 768'; on the W end of Lake St. Marys in W Ohio; was named for a New York town Salina. Settled in 1834.

Mills were set up which attracted woodworkers and cabinet makers, and the manufacture of furniture became the leading industry. It retains that importance today. Celina is an attractive, clean town, well known as a summer resort and as a shopping center for sportsmen from Ohio and neighboring states who come to fish and hunt at Lake St. Marys.

Agriculture - Grain, cattle, poultry and varied farming
Industry/Mfg. - Dairy products, soft drinks, furniture,
     cement. Resort area
Mayor - Don H. Grimes 586-7051
Daily Newspaper - The Standard, 123 E. Market St.
Chamber of Commerce - 108 S. Walnut St.
Community Event(s) : Celina Lake Festival; Annual,
     July

•CENTERBURG, Village; Knox County; Pop. 1,275; Area Code 614; Zip Code 43011; Elev. 1,197'; 30 m. NE of Columbus in central Ohio; is named for the location in the state.

> *Agriculture* - Cattle, grain, poultry and
> varied farming

•CENTERVILLE, City; Montgomery County; Pop. 18,886; Area Code 513; Zip Code 454–; 10 m. S of Dayton in SW central Ohio.

> *Mayor* - Victor A. Green 433-7151
> *Chamber of Commerce* - Po Box 123

•CENTERVILLE, Village; Gallia County; Pop. 148; Area Code 614; S Ohio; Rural area near Raccoon Creek.

•CHAGRIN FALLS, City; Cuyahoga County; Pop. 4,335; Area Code 216; Zip Code 44022; Elev. 985'; NE Ohio; Lies in a wide loop of the Chagrin River, which is said to have been named by *Moses Cleaveland* and his party of surveyors. There are two other name origin explanations. The Indian word meaning clear water. The other is that it sounds like Shagreen, a description of the surrounding sycamore trees.

   Noah Graves, a native of Massachusetts, built a gristmill here in 1833. Abundant water power and extensive water led to the establishment of several small factories along the river; but the village was isolated from canal, railroad, and transportation and became a residential community.

> *Agriculture* - Fruit, grain and varied farming
> *Industry/Mfg.* - Food processing, paper, hatchery
> *Mayor* - James H. Solether 247-5050
> *Chamber of Commerce* - 13-1/2 N. Franklin St., PO Box 255

•CHAMPAIGN COUNTY, W central Ohio; Area 432 sq. miles; Pop. 33,649; County seat - Urbana; Est., February 20, 1805; Name is derived from French word meaning "a plain"; Cut through by Mad River; Rolling landscape, with sheep, corn and wheat raising, as well as dairy farming.

•CHARDON, Village; Seat of Geauga County; Pop. 4,434; Area Code 216; Zip Code 44024; Elev. 1,230'; 25 m. NE of Cleveland in NE Ohio; the maple syrup and sugar center of Ohio.

The town is named for *Peter Chardon Brooks*, first owner of the site. Annually during the latter part of March or the first week in April, Chardon stages the Geauga County Maple Festival. Thousands of visitors come to watch the modern and old-fashioned methods of rendering sap, and to taste syrup and sugar fresh from the vats.

Agriculture - Cattle and varied farming, grain
Industry/Mfg. - Dairy products, rubber goods
Mayor - Robert F. Weber 285-3585
Daily Newspaper - The Geauga Times Leader, 111 Water St.
Chamber of Commerce - 107 N. Hambden St.
Community Event(s) : Maple Festival; Annual, April

•CHATFIELD, Village; Crawford County; Pop. 228; Area Code 419; Zip Code 44825; N central Ohio; 12 m. N of Bucyrus.

•CHAUNCEY, Village; Athens County; Pop. 1,050; Area Code 614; Zip Code 45719; Elev. 680'; SE Ohio; had a mere sprinkling of houses left from its salt-mining days when the first coal shaft was sunk in 1896. Since then Chauncey has had the ups and downs of a coal town.

•CHERRY FORK, Village; Adams County; Pop. 210; Area Code 513; Zip Code 45618; S Ohio; In a farming region producing vegetables and fruits.

•CHESAPEAKE, Village; Lawrence County; Pop. 1,370; Area Code 614; Zip Code 45619; S Ohio; On the Ohio River across from Huntington, West Virginia; Small port.

•CHESHIRE, Village; Gallia County; Pop. 297; Area Code 614; Zip Code 45620; S Ohio; On the Ohio River; Small port.

•CHESTERHILL, Villge; Morgan County; Pop. 395; Area Code 614; Zip Code 43728; SE central Ohio.

•CHESTERVILLE, Village; Morrow County; Pop. 242; Area Code 419; Zip Code 43317; N central Ohio; On the Kokosing River.

•**CHEVIOT**, City; Hamilton County; Pop. 9,888; Area Code 513; 10 m. NW of Cincinnati in SW Ohio corner; in a hilly area; Residential.

Mayor - Louis E. Von Holle 661-2700
Chamber oF Commerce - 3814 Harrison Ave.

•**CHICKASAW**, Village; Mercer County; Pop. 381; Area Code 513; Zip Code 45826; W Ohio; Near Grand Lake St. Marys in a corn farming region.

•**CHILLICOTHE**, City; Seat of Ross County; Pop. 23,420; Area Code 614; Zip Code 45601; Elev. 643'; lies in a bent elbow of hills on the west side of the wide Scioto River Valley, 45 m. S of the State capital in S Ohio. Above the valley rises Mount Logan, familiar to all Ohioans because it is stamped on the Great Seal of the State. A Shawnee Indian word meaning a place where people dwell.

Four years after *Nathaniel Massie* established a settlement here in 1796, Chillicothe became the capital of the Northwest Territory. In 1798, *Edward Tiffin* arrived from Virginia. Others from his home state soon followed. By the turn of the centruy, the town's rough pioneer image was replaced by the splendor of a capital town. Among the beautiful houses was Adena, *Thomas Worthington's* home, built by the famed British architect, *Benjamin Latrobe*. In 1803, Ohio became a state, with Chillicothe its capital and Tiffin its first governor. The city's political importance was shortlived, however, as the capital was moved to Zanesville from 1810 to 1812, and then permanently to Columbus in 1816. Although its political importance was diminished, its economic growth had just begun. By the early 1820's, Chillicothe became a center of trade with New Orleans. As overland routes were completed connecting it with Aberdeen and Cincinnati, and with the completion of the Ohio and Erie Canal, Chillicothe boomed as a port town. Over the years, everything from automobiles to razor blades have been produced here. Today, it continues to be a major industrial city, although its importance in the state is no longer what it once was. Outside of town lies Camp Sherman. There is also a Hopewell Mound group nearby.

Agriculture - Grain, truck and varied farming
Industry/Mfg. - Footwear, paper, housewares, floor tile
Higher Education - Ohio University
Daily Newspaper - The Gazette, 50 West Main St.
Chamber of Commerce - 85 W. Main St.

•**CHILO**, Village; Clermont County; Pop. 173; Area Code 45112; Elev. 507'; SW Ohio; on the Ohio River.

This village was once a boatbuilding center and river port for the back country; as many as 14 steamboats lay at the landing at one time, and 10 river boats made this a terminus for their regular trips.

•**CHIPPEWA-ON-THE-LAKE**, Village; Medina County; Pop. 245; Area Code 216; Zip Code 44215; N central Ohio; On a small lake by the same name, the headwaters of the Chippewa River; Named for the Indian tribe.

•**CHRISTIANSBURG**, Village; Champaign County; Pop. 593; Area Code 513; Zip Code 45389; W Central Ohio; 35 m. N of Dayton in a corn farming region.

•**CINCINNATI**, City; Seat of Hamilton County; Pop. 385,457; Area Code 513; Zip Code 452 + zone; Elev. 540'; SW corner of Ohio on Ohio River; was first named Losantiville meaning town opposite the mouth of the Licking River. This name is a combination of different language/origin. The "L" is taken from the Licking River "os" is Latin for mouth, "ant" is from the Greek meaning opposite and finally "ville" is French for town. The name was changed to Cincinnati by *Gen. Arthur St. Clair* in 1709 in honor of the "Order of Cincinnati" - an association of American Revolution Veterans. It is the second-largest city in Ohio and spreads back from the Ohio River over a disarray of rugged hills.

Cincinnati has been known as the "Queen City" for over a century, although it is no longer the most important metropolis west of the Alleghenies.

Before the white man's first boats came down the Ohio, the site of Cincinnati was an important crossing on the river. Indians from as far as Detroit and beyond traveled through here into the Bluegrass and the Carolinas. Valleys gave easy ascent through the hills north of the Ohio; on the southern side, the Licking River penetrated through a deep channel into the Kentucky Bluegrass.

Although explorers visited the region from 1669 on, there was no settlement until *Benjamin Stites*, a Pennsylvania trader, interested *John Cleves Symmes*, Congressman and land speculator, in the profits to be made from this land. Symmes bought hundreds of thousands of acres from the Continental Congress, but the site of Cincinnati he sold to three other speculators.

They platted the basin in 1788 and brought in the first settlers that winter.

During the summer of 1789 the army had begun the construction of Fort Washington, base of operations against the Indians for the next five years. It was from there that *Governor St. Clair*, and later *General Harmar*, led militia armies against the Indians - and fled back defeated.

To the village in April 1792 came *General Anthony Wayne* with a third army. For more than a year, amidst the jeers of the loungers who wanted him to go out and fight, he drilled his raw militiamen beside a prehistoric mound at the village waterfront. Then he went north and broke the resistance of the Ohio Indians. Under the circumstances, the village saw little actual warfare, although an occasional Indian was killed in its vicinity, and livestock was stolen and crops were destroyed.

The census of 1795 showed 500 persons in the village, sheltered in 94 log cabins and 10 frame houses. Despite catastrophes - smallpox, a plague of squirrels that devoured the crops, caterpillars that killed the poplar trees, and floods that destroyed at least one river-front settlement -14,892 settlers came by flatboat and overland trail during the next five years. Only 250 of them settled in the village proper. The rest cleared farms in surrounding Hamilton County, but brought their business into the bustling little village.

Meanwhile, in the crowded East, oppressed men were hearing about an empire of the West. They went to take it, migrating in ever-increasing masses. The way there was the Ohio River; on flatboats, keelboats, rafts, they floated down. All of them stopped at the new village halfway down the river's length. Some settled there; others traded and went farther west.

In October 1811 the first river paddle-wheeler, the Orleans, came down river at unprecedented speed. There was an earthquake that year, and a few believed the clanking, smoking boat presaged the end of the world. Exploitation of the new contrivance was held back by the War of 1812, but after the war the river steamboat and the new town boomed together. West-bound migrants flocked to the cheap boats. Cincinnati not only got most of the river commerce and business, but also set up marine ways and built steamers. The town soon became a city, the largest in Ohio, and a gathering point for western immigration.

Meanwhile, the rich lands of the Ohio country were becoming thick with settlers. These inland farmers raised hogs and corn, but had no means of getting them to market. In 1825 work was begun on the Miami and Erie Canal; the first section was finished two years later and immediately large loads of corn, hogs, and wheat came down to Cincinnati. Plants were built in the city, and these raw products were processed into pork and flour and whisky and shipped down river.

The year 1828 brought *Mrs. Frances Trollope*, writer and mother of *Anthony Trollope*, Victorian novelist. Mrs. Trollope's Bazaar, with its collection of dry goods and trinkets, was housed in a grotesque building near the site of Fort Washington. Although her pen was usually dipped in acid in writing about the manners of Americans, she was kind to the growing community. Despite its recent origin and its bent for money-grubbing, she decided it had possibilities. *Charles Dickens*, who came here in 1842, was even more kindly. Few other cities visited during his trip through the Middle West were informed that they were "a place that commends itself ... favorably and pleasantly to a stranger."

The city's fame as a prosperous place where work could be found spread through Europe. Immigrants who could not speak English managed somehow to have themselves routed straight through to the new city on the Ohio River. In 1830, the Germans, fleeing religious and political persecution, began a mass migration there. In 1840, when a potato famine ravaged Ireland, thousands of people left the island for America. That year, Cincinnati's population soared to 46,338.

The impoverished newcomers settled in the slums. Although many of the Germans soon built their own homes, so crowded were they that only their Teutonic cleanliness saved the area from squalor. Riots, murder, assault, and stabbings were now frequent in the frontier river town. The descendants of the first settlers banded together into the Order of the Star Spangled Banner, and murdered and fought street battles with the immigrants. Cholera, which had first struck in 1830, returned in 1849 to kill 7,500 in two years.

Meanwhile, because of English demand for cotton, the South had boomed; the flat lands around the lower Mississippi had been turned into plantations. Cotton land was too valuable to be used to raise produce; it was cheaper for the Southern planters to buy salt pork, produce, flour, and whisky from Cincinnati, and ship it down river by steamboat. With the canals being extended, Cincinnati was able to supply this demand for the product of the farms of central Ohio, and the farmer in turn bought more Cincinnati goods. The foundations of the great Cincinnati fortunes were laid in this boom period. Before 1850 Cincinnati was the world's greatest center of pork-packing, surpassing even Dublin, Ireland.

Social and religious institutions also flourised. The first

53

school had been established by *John Reilly* in 1790. All schools were private until 1824, when *Thomas Hughes* bequeathed the income from 20 acres of land to the support of a school for paupers. After a long struggle, free public schools were provided by the city in 1830. The first public high school was built 17 years later.

The first church, Presbyterian, was established in 1790; others were organized by 1810. Catholics heard their first local mass in 1815, and built a church in 1821. The first Jewish services in the Northwest Territory were held in the city in 1819, but no synagogue was built until 1835.

At midcentury, Cincinnati business still centered about the public landing. Steamers came and went, whistles blew, the wharf was piled high with merchandise and crowded with people. When a packet was in dock it seemed as if the whole world were there. The men of the boats were of a fabled race - pilots in their "texas" high above the river, suave gamblers, and the roustabouts, singing chanteys while bearing the river's trade up and down the gangplanks.

By 1859 the city had a population of 160,000 and a river front six miles long. The city was getting the first chance at the commerce of a western empire; its manufactured products, worth $18,000,000 in 1841, had tripled in value by 1851, and soared to $112,000,000 in 1859. Imports and exports of that year were valued at $122,000,000. The 1859 city directory told of two high schools and 16 elementary schools, with more than 17,000 pupils. It listed 180 Christian societies, 6 synagogues, 53 periodicals, and 16 insurance companies.

In 1846 the city's first railroad was constructed to Springfield, and shortly there were other lines. But contented Cincinnati businessmen were too busy with the river trade and booming real-estate values to bother much with railroads. Their trade prospered until 1860, when a depression smashed the Nation's business. River trade and Cincinnati were hit especially hard, since transcontinental freight was being increasingly shipped by railroad through Chicago. Already Chicago had suplanted Cincinnati as the meat-packing center of the Nation. But the Civil War came in time to rescue Cincinnati business for a while.

The war tore the city apart. Located on the Mason and Dixon Line, and with the South the mainstay of its trade, it had known internal conflict for more than 30 years. Every year rioters had attacked the small Negro colony. When, in 1836, *James G. Birney* published one of the first abolitionist newspapers, "The Philanthropist," his presses were thrown in the river and he had to flee from arrest. Later, public pressure forced *Dr. Lyman Beecher*, head of the Lane Theological Seminary, to stop abolitionist work at the school. Yet *Levi Cof-*

fin, president of the Underground Railroad, made his head-quarters in a suburb, and *Salmon P. Chase* defended the liberty of a fugitive slave in a nationally famous case.

When the guns first began to roar, Cincinnati merchants howled about the loss of their Southern markets - until they began to get government contracts. In the main, they were loyal, but some were not above smuggling to the Confederacy. The *Cincinnati Enquirer,* Peace-Democratic newspaper, branded Lincoln "king" and charged him with suppressing the freedom of the press and the Constitution.

The city was the Copperhead center of the Northwest. Bombs made here were used to blow up federal gunboats on the river, and arms and munitions were shipped from here to Indiana Copperheads trying to foment rebellion farther west. But as a whole, the city did magnificently in supplying soldiers to the Union. Whole regiments were outfitted and the city served as the recruiting center for southern Ohio, part of Indiana, and Kentucky. In 1862 the city was threatened when *Kirby Smith* and his raiders came north through Kentucky. Martial law was declared; thousands of farmers streamed in to the city to help Cincinnatians defend it, but Smith turned back.

The war had saved river trade; old and new steamboats, lying idle on the banks, had been pressed into service transporting troops and supplies. After the war the river continued to boom; blockaded Southern products had to be moved, the Southwest was opening, and the still incomplete railroad lines were willing to share traffic with it. The public landing was gay with paddle-wheeler palaces and their orchestras and calliopes.

The prosperous period after the war was accompanied by a cultural urge, and Philanthropic leaders presented the city with Fountain Square, the Music Hall, the Zoo, the Art Museum, the Art Academy, the Conservatory of Music, and the Public Library. The well-known May Music Festivals were started, as well as a professional baseball team. The city itself spread. In the 1860's with 200,000 persons living in the Basin, it had been the most crowded city in America, but at the end of the decade it annexed more than a score of adjoining communities and began the move outward.

The city blazed with revelry. About the bright hotel district, where were held the spectacular balls of the new and old rich, were scores of casinos, gambling houses, and bagnios. Professional gamblers numbered more than 1,000. The all-surrounding slums were dangerous for strangers. Men were robbed and slain, and not infrequently their bodies were tossed in the river.

Prosperity, however, died abruptly in the 1870's when the river trade declined almost permanently before the rise of the railroads. From end to end the river was paralleled by tracks. The lines not only refused to transship freight with the steamers, but brought about a crisis by slashing rates. In its extremity the city turned again to the Southern markets, now ruined and disrupted. They had finally managed to make arrangements for a Southern railroad. Rushed to completion in 1880 at a cost of about $20 million, it revived the Southern trade and rescued business.

In the summer of 1883 there were nine murders in nine successive days. Justice was lax; of 50 men tried for murder, four had been sentenced to death, 23 were in the county jail; the rest were at liberty. The public was bitter, and newspapers and civic leaders denounced the courts in inflammatory words.

Public anger exploded the following March when a jury found two youths accused of murder guilty only of manslaughter. Leading citizens called a mass meeting in Music Hall, and afterwards the crowd forced the jailer to lynch the convicted men. Following this incident, the crowd remained orderly until the militia came and opened fire. Then began three days of fighting, in which the $500,000 courthouse was burned and more than 300 men were killed and wounded. Two militiamen were slain. But still the crime wave increased.

In the elction that fall the Republican party won a sweeping victory. One of its minor leaders was *George Barnsdale Cox*, a tavern keeper who had entered politics because of the police protection it would secure him. The Republican Governor, *Joseph B. Foraker*, a Cincinnati corporation lawyer, soon afterwards placed the city's Board of Public Affairs and its 2,000 jobs at Cox's disposal. Cox became head of his party, and at the next election turned out a plurality for Governor Foraker.

From then on Cox was absolute boss of both his party and the city. Although people talked about "conditions", only three times during the next 25 years were his candidates defeated by reformers. And each time Cox won back his power.

The city won notoriety with Cox and corruption. Scandal was buzzed about concerning the 1892 "gas franchise", which was defeated by two votes in council, and the later attempt, defeated in a general election, to sell the city's railroad, already earning more than $1,000,000 a year.

Cox handled city affairs cavalierly: tax assessments, street-paving contracts, public-service franchises, and not a few court decisions. He made for himself and his lieutenants fortunes of several millions of dollars and kept his Republican party in power.

The city's pace slackened; new industry hesitated to start here; two great automobile manufacturers were rebuffed in their offer to build their plants here. The river trade was nearly dead, but the already-established industries were solid and strong, and the great fortunes were safely set in rBasin real estate and high rents.

It was Cox's bluntness in an interview with *Lincoln Steffens* that perhaps more than anything else helped to defeat him.

Reformers gathered their forces, and in 1911 *Henry Hunt* was elected Mayer. Although Cox came back to beat him, it turned out to be a meaningless victory. Scandal broke in a bank Cox owned, in the matter of the disposal of interest on deposited city money, and in verdicts returned by judges who knew Cox too well.

Cox's power descended to *Rudolph Hynicka*, one of his lieutenants, who operated the city from the East where most of his business interests were centered. When the state legislature passed a home-rule act, the reform charter party not only defeated the old parties and the old voting system (birds on the ballot), but also brought city managership. Administration abuses and corruption were cleaned up quickly, but the other damage that had been done -wretched streets and street lighting, public franchises, poor facilities - took longer to repair. But the city soon acquired the title "best governed."

During and after World War II, another economic boom caused unrestricted growth in the downtown area or "Basin" of Cincinnati. Master Plan was adopted in 1948 to accomodate urban renewal but no progress was made on the Plan until the 1960's. By this time the decay and griminess of the Basin's oldest sections had become acute. Century-old tenements were torn down and replaced by steel and concrete apartment buildings and offices. In the 1960's a new Convention Hall, Provident Towers, a federal bank building and an underground garage were completed. Soon afterwards a $40 million sports stadium was constructed along the riverfront. A few old neighborhoods were preserved and restored, but most have been razed and rebuilt.

Fountain square, named for the large Tyler-Davidson fountain with figures cast in Munich Germany in 1871, is a social and cultural focal point in Cincinnati. The city library holds over three million volumes. Printing and publishing are strong traditions in the city, as evidenced by several major publications such as the *Enquirer* and the *Post.* Several parks grace the area, and a good skyline view of the city may be obtained by crossing the Suspension Bridge to the Covington-Kentucky banks of the river.

POINTS OF INTEREST

HAMILTON COUNTY MEMORIAL BUILDING

Dedicated 1908 as permanent memorial to pioneer and military
heroes; designed by *Samuel Hannaford and Sons.*

EDEN PARK - Most noted of city's parks:
Navigation Monument. a 30 foot granite obelisk, dedicated
1929:
The Cincinnati Art Museum contains the best
Duveneck collection in the country; the original
building built 1886 with wings added 1907 and
1937:
Art Academy established 1859

THE TAFT HOUSE MUSEUM - Example of Adams
Federal architecture (1820); formerly home of
style Early *Charles P. Taft* family.

FOUNTAIN SQUARE - Originally deeded to the city
as a market place, became public square (1870); The
Tyler Davidson Fountain (1817).

MOUNT AIRY FOREST - Begun in 1913. now con-
tains more than 1,304 acres; contains Arboretum, Warder
Nursery Plant. Lodge House.
UNIVERSITY OF CINCINNATI OBSERVATORY

On Mt. Lookout: established 1842; in 1844 its 11-inch
telescope was largest in the U.S.

Industry/Mfg. - Varied manufacturing, trade and
services
Higher Education - Xavier University, Hebrew Union
College. God Bible School, University of Cincinnati,
Edgecliff College
Mayor - Ms. Bobbie Sterne 352-3000
Daily Newspaper - The Enquirer. 617 Vine St.
Chamber of Commerce - 120 W. Fifth St.
Community Event(s) : Cincinnati May Festival;
Annual. May. College Conservatory Jazz
Festival; Annual, February. Ohio Valley
Kool Jazz Festival; Annual, July. Summer
Opera Festival; Annual, July.

•CIRCLEVILLE, City; Seat of Pickaway County; Pop. 11,700; Area Code 614; Zip Code 43114; Elev. 687'; on Scioto River 25 m. S of Columbus in S central Ohio.

Circleville was laid out inside the round enclosure from which it took its name. Two streets formed complete circles around the town; the center was a round public "square" in the middle of which was built an octagonal courthouse and from this center four streets ran like the spokes in a cartwheel to the original circular ditch.

Mayor - Frank E. Barnhill 647-8484
Daily Newspaper - The Herald, PO Box 498, 200 N. Court St.
Chamber of Commerce - 135 W. Main St., PO Box 462
Community Event(s) : Pumpkin Show; Annual, October

•CLARINGTON, Village; Monroe County; Pop. 558; Area Code 614; Zip Code 43915; SE Ohio; is a small river community whose Swiss settlers have been gradually displaced by Slavs and Italians. Clock-making was once carried on here.

•CLARK COUNTY, W central Ohio; Area 402 sq. miles; Pop. 150,236; County seat - Springfield; Est., December 26, 1817; Named for *George Rogers Clark*, pioneer and Revolutionary War soldier; Rolling wooded hills and industry centered around Springfield.

•CLARKSBURG, Village; Ross County; Pop. 483; Area Code 614; Zip Code 43115; S central Ohio; 45 m. SW of Columbus in a farming area.

•CLARKSVILLE, Village; Clinton County: Pop. 525; Area Code 513; Zip Code 45113; SW Ohio; On the Todd Fork of the Miami River.

•CLAY CENTER, Village; Ottawa County; Pop. 327; Area Code 419; Zip Code 43408; 15 m. SE of Toledo and approx. 10 m. W of the Lake Erie shoreline; Named for clay deposits in area or *Henry Clay*.

•CLAYTON, Village; Montgomery County; Pop. 752; Area Code 513; Zip Code 45315; 12 m. NW of Dayton in SW Ohio.

•**CLEAR FORK RESERVOIR**, Man-made lake; Richland County; central Ohio; Formed by a damming of the Clear Fork of the Mohican River; Approx. 5 m. long; Formerly a swampy area where a giant serpent was said to live.

•**CLERMONT COUNTY**, SW Ohio; Area 458 sq. miles; Pop. 128,483; County seat - Batavia; Est., December 6, 1800; Name is French for "clear mountain", although there are no mountains in this rolling countryside, bordered to S by Ohio River.

•**CLEVELAND**, City; Seat of Cuyahoga County; Pop. 573,822; Area Code 216; Zip Code 441 + zone; Elev. 665'; at mouth of Cuyahoga River on Lake Erie in N Ohio; Ohio's largest city and one of the world's biggest steel-producing and ore handling centers, has grown fan-wise from the Lake Erie shore, radiating from the twisting Cuyahoga River to the east, south and west. Along the river are The Flats - Cleveland's industrial area - where mills, factories, loading machinery, and warehouses of immense proportions sprawl.

In the beginning of Cleveland's history, there was the deep and limitless forest. Into this wilderness in 1796 came *General Moses Cleaveland* with his band of surveyors and axemen to plat a town site for the Connecticut Land Company, owners of 120 miles of Lake Erie's shores west of the Pennsylvania line. Already the pressure of population along the Atlantic seaboard had sent new swarms across the Allegheny passes into the Ohio Valley to plant thriving settlements at Marietta and Cincinnati. Northern Ohio was almost entirely unoccupied, having been only recently cleared of Indian opposition by General Anthony Wayne's Treaty of Greenville.

At the mouth of the Cuyahoga River, in the exact middle of the Western Reserve's shore line, Cleaveland founded the town that was to confound his prophecy. Here on the high ground above the river he laid out his streets around a common ground that was a New England landmark. But *Father Moses* and his band remained but a few months before they hurried back to the comforts of Wyndham. It had been a miserable experience for most of them. Living in three small huts, they had suffered from dysentery, ague, and the bites of innumerable insects. Only three families remained on the site of the new town, and they soon went on.

Through the Mohawk Valley and Erie Lake Trail gateway, settlers were making their way. In Cleaveland, however, only one of the early arrivals stayed. He was *Lorenzo Carter*, a giant among the pioneers. For 15 months in 1799 and 1800, while others had sought the lands along the ridges away from the swampy river mouth, Carter and his wife stayed in the town site. When other settlers came, it was Carter's rifle and resourcefulness that forestalled starvation. Around him, his physical prowess, his control of wayward Indians, his residing over the improvised "law", and other feats has grown a legend of magnificent proportions. Officially, he held only the office of "fence viewer", but he kept the settlement together. His home was the social center of primitive Cleaveland; here were held the first ball, the first wedding, the first school, and the first church service. Here also the first prisoner was jailed, and here were fed and sheltered, in the absence of an inn, new settlers and arrivals.

With the year 1800 the population of the settlement was a mere seven. Already there were 45,000 people in Ohio, mostly along the Ohio River. The immediate growth of the potential metropolis was slow. By 1830 little more than 1,000 people called themselves Cleavelanders. But Cleaveland was feeling its way. In 1804 *Lorenzo Carter* launched the first boat, the 30-ton Zephyr, an impressive craft for an inexperienced builder to launch but a small prophecy of the huge freighters and passenger steamers that one day would enter the Cleveland harbor. In 1818 there arrived in the harbor from Buffalo the first steamboat on Lake Erie, the Walk-in-the-Water. All who watched the tiny vessel plod to the narrow river mouth felt that a new era was stirring. Soon there came talk from new arrivals that they were beginning the "Big Ditch" in New York State.

Cleaveland, according to one of several legends, altered its name by a casual quirk. On July 1, 1832, the compositor of a freshly launched newspaper, The *Cleveland Gazette and Commercial Register*, had to drop one letter from his masthead to fit his space, and he chose the first "a" in Cleaveland, simplifying the spelling for posterity.

When the Erie Canal was finished, clothing began to move in from the East to replace the homespuns, and machined goods to displace the crude improvisations of the frontier. Inspired by the immediate success of the New York canal, not only as a cheap carrier of products but also as a developer of the uninhabited lands contiguous to it, agitation began for a similar waterway to join the Ohio River with Lake Erie and to tap the resources of the Ohio lands. Competition between lake towns for nomination as the northern terminal of the Ohio and Erie Canal was furious. It was *Alfred Kelley*, Cleveland's first practicing attorney, who secured the necessary legislation to bring that important advantage to his city. Work began on the lower stretches of the canal, along the Licking River, and in 1827 the first section was completed from Cleveland to Akron. Within five years, barge traffic was moving uninterruptedly between the lake and the river and Cleveland was on its way to commercial supremacy on Lake Erie.

The city expanded phenomenally after the canal came. From 1825 to 1830 the population doubled, and in the next ten years increased 464 percent, the greatest percentage increase in the city's history. The first Cleveland directory (1837) states that 117,277,580 pounds of goods, with a value of $2,444,708, arrived by way of Cleveland. During 1836, 911 sailing vessels and 990 steamboats entered the port of Cleveland, and soon Cleveland, like Cincinnati at the head of a canal, was an important commercial center. In that same year Cleveland incorporated as a city.

Land prices boomed along the canal route. Cities fortunate enough to be on the canal thrived. On the west bank of the Cuyahoga River, Ohio City, which was to have a ship canal cut through to it, had grown rapidly. Soon a bridge spanned the river to give Cleveland better access to Brooklyn, Elyria, and distant points. But this bridge and the road from it by-passed Ohio City. A public meeting voted the bridge a nuisance, and the two communities went to war over it. Trenches, powder, firearms, and cannon were brought into play. The draw in the bridge was cut away; casualties resulted and the sheriff took a hand. The bridge was repaired but the squabbling continued until 1854, when Ohio City was annexed to Cleveland.

The panic of 1837 retarded the city but little, although the sudden contraction of credit bankrupted many of the firms. But a hint was given of governmental procedure 100 years hence. Public funds put 100 men to work in the panic year to open the old river bed for unimpeded passage to the lake.

The canal brought an influx of foreigners. In one fortnight after the canal opened, 600 immigrants came into town, a human river whose flood continued unabated for many years. Much of the burly life that infests water routes and port towns became part of the city's melange. But with all the bustling newness and

62

the makeshift expansion, Cleveland in 1840, a little city of 6,000, pleased the early Ohio historian, *Henry Howe*. "It is one of the most beautiful towns in the Union," he wrote, "and much taste is displayed in the private dwellings and the disposition of the shrubbery." Two years later *Charles Dickens* concurred, but condemned the local residents roundly.

The first 50 years of Cleveland were ending and the Cuyahoga River port had consolidated its place as a commercial city. Bigger days were immediately ahead. *Alfred Kelley* worked indefatigably to bring the railroad to the city. In 1845, Cleveland voted the sum of $200,000 to aid and insure the construction of the first steam road. Within two years the Lake Erie Telegraph Company had set up poles on the city's streets. Soon Cleveland's *Jephtha H. Wade* was to build a line farther west and begin the work that culminated in the first transcontinental telegraph line and the formation of the Western Union system.

Cleveland's second 50 years were to see the town burst out with an amazing record of industrial growth. The first successful pier was extended into the lake; in 1850 planking improved the city's streets; the next year the first train puffed into town; and in 1856 a few barrels of iron ore were sent down to Cleveland from the Lake Superior ranges. Business on the new railroad was so brisk that the "numerous and excellent hotels are constantly filled to overflowing". The low cost of shipping the 80 percent Superior ore was assured by the digging of the "Soo" canal in 1855; $60,000 was subscribed to build a blast furnace the next year. In 1859 the horse car was moving about Cleveland, and in Titusville, Pennsylvania, the first Pennsylvania oil well was brought in.

During the turmoil that accompanied these marks of progress, two young men, *John D. Rockefeller* and *Marcus Alonzo Hanna*, arrived with their parents. While these two striplings were continuing their educations in Cleveland schools and casting about for their future vocations, *William A. Otis* and *John Ford* were manufacturing iron castings in a foundry on Whiskey Island. And while *John Brown's* soul was beginning its march, Otis was building a rolling mill. Cleveland was recognizing its new advantage of position. The first soft coal, which had come up on the canal to be rejected as too dirty by housewives, found favor with the iron-makers. Coal and iron were wedded in Cleveland, and from these derived the first locomotives built

63

west of the Allegheny Mountains, the same "iron horses" that brought the early trains into the city. The proud parent of these wood-burners was the Cuyahoga Steam Furnace Company, the city's first manufacturing corporation. Among the railroads that extended their lines to Cleveland in 1836, the first was a through east-west road (now the Lake Shore and Michigan Southern Division of the New York Central System).

On the brink of the Civil War the Forest City was changing from a purely commercial community to a manufacturing and transportation center. With a populatin of 43,000, it had passed Columbus, the State capital, to become the second city in Ohio.

The outbreak of the war found Cleveland enthusiastic in its support of the Union. It had been at a boiling point over the slavery question as far back as 1807, when the state legislature, dominated by settlers along the Ohio River who had come in large numbers from slavery states, had passed the "black laws" that were so intolerable to the Cleveland New Englanders. The canals and the Underground Railroad brought human cargo on the run, escaped slaves headed for Canada and freedom. A friendly and important post on the Underground Railroad, Cleveland became a gathering place for slave-snatchers and kidnapers, who haunted the docks to intercept runaways leaving on Cleveland steamers.

Cleveland made no effort to hide its contempt for the institution of slavery. When *John Brown* was on trial, it had sent one of its ablest lawyers to defend him. The news of his death had tolled the city's bells for half an hour to "honor him who had been sacrificed to the Moloch of slavery;" newspapers appeared with black borders. Cleveland was the scene of the trial in the famous Oberlin-Wellington Rescue Case. During the trial, business was suspended and a protest meeting of 10,000 was held in the Public Square. There was a salute of 100 guns to honor the 27 imprisoned men who were hailed as martyrs and public heroes. When *President Lincoln* called for volunteers, Melodeo Hall was filled and within two days the first Cleveland Grays were on the march. Those who stayed behind labored to supply the war demands.

The Civil War gave an even greater impetus to the iron industry. After the peace had been won, the years to the end of the centruy were startling in the expansion of commerce and industry, in labor strife, vaster foreign immigration, and the rise of tremendous fortunes in steel and shipping, in railroads, in communictions, in manufactures, in the electrical field, and, most spectacularly of all, in oil.

Euclid Avenue, once the Lake Trail of the aborigines, blossomed out as "Millionaires Row," a mansion-studded street whose fame soon was far flung. Unbroken by cross streets for more than a mile, the avenue of "show places" and elaborately landscaped gardens dominated the social life of the community. Carriages rolled up and down the Avenue; in the winter the street was roped off from other traffic, and cutters raced before the gaping public. Farther down Euclid Avenue, the Public Square, according to the Mayor, was "... in a miserable, dilapidated, shabby, ragged condition."

Nevertheless, this interest in public open spaces brought the era of Cleveland's parks. *J.H. Wade*, of the telegraph and real estate fortune, in 1882 gave the city its first park, that now encircles the Museum of Art. To the assiduity of *Charles Bulkley*, president of the first Park Board in 1893, Cleveland owes its city park system. A definite plan was adopted in 1896. Other Clevelanders donated park lands. *W. J. Gordon* and *John D. Rockefeller* giving the adjoining Gordon and Rockefeller Parks. With these, Garfield, Lakeview, Lincoln, Brookside, Edgewater, and Washington and other parks combined to form the extensive present-day system, which has been co-ordinated with the greater Metropolitan Parkway.

The giants and the lesser ones of the steel era were having glorious days. The first cargoes of ores to come through the "Soo" canal were routed to Cleveland. The earlier report of a Cleveland mineralogist led to the formation of the Cleveland Iron Company to exploit the Superior region on a large scale. *Samuel L. Mather's* interests developed through the Cleveland Cliffs Iron Compnay and affiliates. From the Marquette fields west the ranges felt the impetus given by Clevelanders. And, from the mining of the ore, a tremendous shipping business developed, carrying iron down the lakes and coal up the lakes. Through the enterprise of the Mathers, the Bradleys, and their associates, fortunes rolled into Cleveland's coffers. Ships slid off the ways, new steel mills dotted the landscape, and the Flats of the Cuyahoga River grew into a solid body of manufacturing plants.

Organization of the Standard Oil Company in 1870 made Cleveland the oil center of the Nation, and today, while the drilling operations have shifted to other points, the gulley known as

Kingsbury Run, which separated the east side from the south side, is a forest of refinery domes and squat oil tanks. Rockefeller, the young commission merchant, and other Clevelanders had grasped the opportunity opened by *Colonel Ddrake's* well at Titusville. In 1865, six years after the Drake well came in, Rockefeller had made a profit of more than $100,000 in oil refining. Kerosene was the profit maker, gasoline being only a waste product for many years. When the Rockefeller eye fell upon the genius of *Henry M. Flagler,* a new team ws formed that revolutionized industrial organization. They had observed the Western Union telegraph merger of *Jephtha H. Wade* and the railroad system of *Commodore Vanderbilt.* With additional capital from *Stephen V. Harkness,* Cleveland's wealthiest man, these men formed the world's leading "octopus", an organization that brought riches to its orgnizers and stockholdrs.

While industry boomed, the common worker was not unaware of the lavish display of "Millionaires Row". Labor established itself in Cleveland with the headquarters of the Brotherhood of Locomotive Engineers, one of the most successful of trade unions. After the financial crisis of 1873, labor turned to politics, and the first Farmer-Labor representatives met in Cleveland in 1876. Two years later the Miners National Association met here for their second convention. In 1882 the Federation of Organized Trades and Labor Unions of the United States and Canada met in Cleveland for national organization, in a convention that paved the way for the May Day strikes in behalf of the eight-hour day.

With practical-minded Clevelanders more concerned with an industrial frontier than a cultural one, it is significant that the first college should have been a technical one - Case School of Applied Science, the result of a fund left by *Leonard Case,* scion of a pioneer family. Immediately the Western Reserve College moved up from Hudson where it had maintained a precarious existence for 50 years, and in 1882 the first building for Adelbert College of the university group was dedicated as a memorial to the son of the donor, *Amasa Stone.* Within four years, St. Ignatius College, of Jesuit founding, came to the city. In 1923 the name was changed to John Carroll University. Later days saw the opening of Notre Dame College for women, and Fenn College, a YMCA offspring. And for those who could not drop their work in pursuit of higher education, Western Reserve University established Cleveland College for part-time courses, day and night. Public education started late. Not until 1836 was the first "free school" opened for the education of male and female pupils of every religious denomination. In 1856 the first public high school was opened for boys; girls were admitted the following year. The maturing years brought an elaborate system, now administered from the beautiful Board of Education Building in Cleveland's Mall.

An opera house had been erected in 1875, and in the year following an art club took shape, with a nucleus of 12 members. The year 1878 launched the *Penny Press,* ridiculed because of its tabloid size and small columns, but destined to be the forerunner of the *Liberal Press* and of the Scripps newspaper chain. Already the *Plain Dealer,* which could be traced back to the *Herald* of 1819, was well entrenched. The list of defunct newspapers in Cleveland contains many names, a common enough experience in all cities in the early days of highly individualistic papers. For many years the *Leader* fought with the *Plain Dealer* for supremacy, until it merged with its afternoon counterpart, the *News.* Today, only the *Plain Dealer, Press,* and *News* operate as metropolitan dailies.

In addition to steel, oil, and shipping, new industries were born in the minds of Clevelanders. While *Thomas A. Edison,* native of Milan, Ohio, was still struggling with his incandescent globe, *Charles F. Brush* lighted the Public Square with the dazzling white light of his carbon arc lamp, which he had invented in his Cleveland workshop. By 1881 a central power station had been built and the Brush Electric Light and Power Company began to erect arc lamps throughout the city. Brush, to stabilize his lighting system, developed the first practical storage battery, today one of Cleveland's major products, and perfected the most efficient generator of the day. He gave $500,000 for the organization of the Brush Foundation, an institute of eugenics.

Two Connecticut mechanics, *Worcester R. Warner* and *Ambrose Swasey,* came to Cleveland in 1880 to manufacture machine tools and precision instruments, which were soon important local products. Their inventions and applications revolutionized the use of gears in the mechanical and automotive industries, and their designing and perfecting of astronomical instruments opened new spaces for scientists to explore. Many of the world's greatest telescopes are the products of their skilled craftsmen.

For all the industrial advancement and civic improvement - new streets, electric street railways (1884), the telephone, and street lighting - the laboring men looked with mistrust on the industrial giants. Labor began to test its strength. A walk-out of 500 men paralyzed the Lake Shore Railroad and won better conditions than the 12-hour day, 7-day week. The Newburgh steel workers walked out again in 1885, three years after their first strike. A general strike of switchmen tied up all the transportation lines in and about the city, and several other troubles, which included the historic Brown Hoisting Company strke of several months duration, were among the growing pains of the industrial giant.

In the last 50 years Cleveland's history has included a dramatic story of political giants and a rapid realignment of the city's population. The steel industry in this period absorbed all the available labor supply, and mass immigration from the Slavic and non-Nordic nations swung into fullest stride. It was in this chaotic era that *Thomas Loftin Johnson*, a steel and transportation magnate whose political ideas had been transformed through the reading of *Henry George*, came to power. Opposing him in the political war he waged with *Mark Hanna*, wealthy and powerful from his coal, iron, traction, and shipping interests, was a divergent and well entrenched political philosophy. Johnson came to sway Cleveland for 10 years; Hanna already was swaying the State as a molder of legislation and the Nation as a builder of Presidents. Johnson, who had sold his interests in his steel company at Lorain, arrived in Cleveland and was shortly elected its mayor, serving for five consecutive terms. So uprightly did he conduct the city government that Cleveland won even the praise of *Lincoln Steffens*, the crusader. From his studies of American municipalities, Steffens decided that Johnson was the "best mayor" and Cleveland "the best governed city in the United States."

From 1893 to 1900 a series of consolidations of the original nine grants for street railways combined them into the "Little Consolidated" and the "Big Consolidated." Hanna controlled the former; Johnson the latter. Their views of public service being as divergent as their political ideals, they locked horns. Johnson initiated the one-pay fare with through transfer; Hanna fought the plan, insisting on a double fare. Later Johnson entered politics to fight for the "people against privilege". The two rail groups had been merged into the popularly named "Concon." From the day of the merger, the war was on in earnest. On a three-cent fare platform Johnson rode into the mayor's office, and after an intense struggle, he organized the municipally controlled lines in 1907.

Hanna, bitter at Johnson's election, brought actions in the courts and lobbied legislation through the state legislature. He secured ouster proceedings against the federal plan of city government, which had been adopted in 1891, and made the mayoralty the only elective office. In 1902 Hanna placed before the legislature a plan putting the city government in the hands of elective boards, and giving the governor right to remove any mayor for malfeasance. He also sought perpetual franchises for utilities. Johnson moved his fight to Columbus and although he lost on the charter he won the franchise fight. Finally the streetcar war was settled by the adoption of the "Taylor Grant", written by Federal Judge *R.W. Tayler*. This went into effect in 1910, providing for a city-policed, privately operated company. But Johnson suffered defeat when he ran for a sixth term as mayor. His own explanation was, "I had been mayor for so many years that many people lost sight of conditions as they existed before that time".

Under Johnson many of Cleveland's "bright young men" rose in influence - *Newton D. Baker*, later the city's mayor and the World War Secretary of War; *Peter Witt*, caustic liberal fighter whose Town Hall speech has become an annual Cleveland event; and other professional men who worked to bring enlightened government to the city. During Johnson's regime, the parks had their "Keep off the grass" signs removed; band concerts and other recreational features were inaugurated. He introduced a municipal electric light plant to hold in check the private utilities. In addition he cleaned up dishonest weights and measures, established meat and dairy inspection, and built parks, playgrounds, and hundreds of miles of streets.

The fight against Johnson by "trenched interest" was so bitter that one resident said, "If a man don't like the way Tom L. wears his hat, he gets an injunction restraining him from wearing it that way." But on the statue of *Tom Johnson* in the Public Square is the inscription: "HE FOUND US GROPING LEADERLESS AND BLIND, HE LEFT A CITY WITH A CIVIC MIND."

While the political fight waged, Cleveland had ousted Cincinnati as the state's largest city and had witnessed the birth of the gigantic twentieth-century industry, automobile manufacture. While most of this business has concentrated in Detroit, *Alexander Winton* in 1898 sold the first gasoline buggy made in Cleveland and one of the first in the country. White developed the "steamer" before he concentrated on commercial vehicles. The early "electrics" flourished here also.

During World Wars I and II, a shortage of factory workers caused a large influx of blacks in the city from the rural south that continued into the 1950's and 1960's. However, the available jobs required precise skills, and no employers would provide the newcomers an opportunity to learn them. Many blacks had to take temporary or cheap labor jobs or were forced to go on relief. People crowded into small shanties and apartments without hope for a future. These problems contributed to the eruption of riots in some sections of the city in 1966.

Other ethnic groups found it difficult to survive in twentieth century Cleveland as well. Language barriers and customs kept nationalities apart and left them all at a much lower economic level than the English-speaking Clevelanders.

Although for years city officials ignored these problems, the 1960's brought a sense of urgency to urban renewal and improved educational opportunities for unskilled laborers. The city housing authority built hundreds of publicly financed dwellings.

The city also began to deal with air and water pollution caused by industry. For a long time, Erie was considered a "dead" lake, since hardly anything could live in its murky, oxygen-depleted waters. Industries had been dumping their wastes into Lake Erie and the Cuyahoga River for almost a century, and the toll was paid by the air over the city as well. Although the problems are far from solved, Cleveland has spent millions to improve the quality of its air and water since 1970.

The almighty steel industry, which in part may be blamed for many of the city's ills, has been experiencing a large decline recently. The demand for steel has lessened, and hundreds of thousands have lost their jobs as formerly important factories closed in the city. Some areas are veritable ghost towns, once thriving under the shadow of some of these steel and auto parts manufacturing centers. Today, Cleveland's leaders are trying to bring about an urban renaissance not unlike the attempts in

Detroit and Pittsburgh. By attracting new, high-technology businesses into the city, officials hope to make a complete turnabout in its fortunes.

They are battling disparate odds. Since World War II, the population has declined within city limits as more and more businesses and shopping centers were built. Also, the problems of black residents of Cleveland have not been solved. Discrimination and economic decline have left them outside of the wealthy citizens' attempts at rejuvenating the city. Although Cleveland did have a black mayor, *Carl B. Stokes* (1967-71), the business boom envisioned by new mayor *George Voinovich* and others does not include the manual skills many of these people learned in working for the steel industry.

The mayor before Voinovich, *Dennis Kucinich,* tried to maintain the traditional businesses in Cleveland, supporting the underrepresented work force and courageously shunning big corporate giants. Citizens saw Kucinich as a "white knight" figure, being elected to the mayor's seat when he was only 31 and still idealistic. However, his ability to keep track of the city budget was far from adequate and soon Cleveland was in debt over $14 million. With nothing to back it up and no clear figures on its financial standing, the city was forced to declare bankruptcy, the first major city to do so since the Great Depression. Increased city taxes and private financing may help Cleveland rebuild in the 1980's.

Many Clevelanders still take pride in the city despite its problems. Cultural attractions are numerous and vaired, such as the world-renowned Cleveland Orchestra, three repertory theaters, a ballet company, and several museums. A climb to the top of Terminal Tower (Cleveland's tallest building at 708 feet), gives a commanding view of the metropolis. Several old homes have been restored, such as the Weddell House, built in 1847, and the few remaining ornate Victorian mansions along the old "Millionaire's Row."

POINTS OF INTEREST

SITE OF MOSES CLEAVELAND'S LANDING - Marked by a plaque at foot of St. Clair Ave. hill.

TERMINAL TOWER BUILDING - Opened Jan. 26, 1930; 52
  stories high, 708 feet.

MOSES CLEAVELAND STATUE - Bronze figure of the
  general with surveyor's instrument in hand; executed
  (1887) by *G.C.Hamilton* of Cleveland.

CLEVELAND PUBLIC LIBRARY - Designed by *Walker
  and Weeks* (1925), French Renaissance style;
  includes *John Griswold White* collection of
  folklore; articles from *King Tutankhamen* tomb;
  library on chess, checkers and other move games.

CLEVELAND STADIUM - Opened July 3, 1931 for heavyweight championship fight between *Schmeling
  and Stribling* ; designed by *Walter and Weeks*.

CLEVELAND HORTICULTURAL GARDEN - Covers 75 acres;
  contains Cleveland Fine Arts Garden, Fountain of
  Waters, and Cleveland Museum of Art; Architects
  Hubbell and Benes of Cleveland.

ROCKEFELLER PARK - Comprises 273 acres donated
  (1896) by *John D. Rockefeller Sr.* contains
  Cleveland Cultural Gardens, English Gardens, Hebrew
  Garden, German Garden, Italian Garden.

Industry/Mfg. - Varied manufacturing, trade and services
Higher Education - Dyke College, Notre Dame
    College, Cleveland State University, Ursuline
    College, John Carroll University
Mayor - George V. Voinovich 664-2000
Daily Newspaper - The Plain Dealer,1801 Superior
    Ave., N.E.
Chamber of Commerce - 690 Union Commerce Bldg.
Community Event(s) : Cleveland Summer Arts Festival;
    Annual, June-Aug., May Festival of Contemporary
    Music;
    Annual, May, Summer Pops Concerts; Annual, June-
    July

•**CLEVELAND HEIGHTS, City; Cuyahoga County; Pop. 56,438;
Area Code 216; Zip Code 44118; Elev. 915'; 10 m. E of Cleveland
on an Appalachian Plateau above Lake Erie in NE Ohio; Inc.,
village 1903, city 1921.**

A small crossroads with a country store or two in the 1870's, Cleveland Heights became one of Cleveland's most popular suburbs (along with Shaker Heights) in the early 20th Century. Today it remains so. Over the years, its beautiful large houses situated in wooden hills and its close proximity to Cleveland has attracted some of Ohio's most prominent residents. Among the trees, there are lakes, landscaped lawns, and beautiful parks. *John D. Rockefeller* donated his summer residence here to the city in the 1930's for the creation of Forest Hills Park, a year-round recreation facility. Its park system also includes Cain Park which is known for its outdoor amphitheatre. The city government is a city-manager form, while there is no industry or railroad.

Mayor - Marjorie B. Wright 321-0100

•CLEVES, Village; Hamilton County; Pop. 2,094; Area Code 513; Zip Code 45002; SW Ohio; Just N of the Ohio River and E of the Miami River, to the W of Cincinnati; Suburban, with some industry. The village was named for early proprietor *John Cleves Symmes*.

Mayor - Patrick Wadsworth 547-0575

•CLIFTON, Village; Clark and Greene Counties; Pop. 182; Area Code 513; Zip Code 45316; on the little Miami River in SW central Ohio; a recreational area; was named for the cliffs that surround the Little Miami River.

•CLINTON, Village; Summit County; Pop. 1,277; Area Code 216; Zip Code 44216; NE Central Ohio, just SW of Akron; Near the Chippewa River in a residential - recreational area.

•CLINTON COUNTY, SW Ohio; Area 410 sq. miles; Pop. 34,603; County seat - Wilmington; Est. February 19, 1810; Named for *George Clinton*, first and third governor of New York and Vice President (1805-12); Hilly land, fed by many streams and small rivers; Farming.

•CLOVERDALE, Village; Putnam County; Pop. 304; Area Code 419; Zip Code 45827; NW Ohio; Near the Ottawa River.

•CLYDE, City; Sandusky County; Pop. 5,489; Area Code 419; Zip Code 43410; Elev. 682'; N Ohio; *Sherwood Anderson*, born in Camden, Ohio, in 1876, poet and interpreter of small-town life in the Middle West spent most of his boyhood in Clyde.

During the War of 1812, an officer under *General William H. Harrison*, passing through, drove a stake into the ground here and said: "At this spot I shall build my future home, which shall be the nucleus of a thriving town". Years passed, and a squatter built a hut on the site. Then, in 1820 the soldier returned and by means of a barrel of whisky – which accomplished many things in those days –recovered his chosen land. Today Clyde is known for cabbages and melons, strawberries and cherries, its milling, canning and cutlery-making.

Lee Stanley, creator of the comic strip, Our Town, was born at Clyde. So was *James Albert Wales* (1852-86), wood engraver, cartoonist for Puck, and chief artist and one of the founders of Judge.

Agriculture - Grain, truck and varied farming.
Industry/Mfg. includes- Household applainces, paint and plastics.
Mayor - Patrick Wadsworth- 547 0575

•COAL GROVE, Village; Lawrence County; Pop. 2,630; Area Code 614; S Ohio; On the Ohio River across from Ashland, Kentucky; Named for the abundance of coal mines in the area.

Mayor - Bernard T. McKnight- 532 7447

•COALTON, Village; Jackson County; Pop. 639; Area Code 614; Zip Code 45621; S central Ohio; Named for the mining in the region; Nearby is the Leo Petroglyph State Memorial, with several carvings into a flat sandstone, made by prehistoric Indians.

•COLDWATER, Village; Mercer County; Pop. 4,220; Area Code 419; Zip Code 45828; 30 m. SW of Lima in W Ohio; W of Grand Lake St. Marys; Named for the several cool streams which branch off from the Wabash River and Beaver Creek here.

Agriculture - Grain, hogs, cattle and varied farming.
Industry/Mfg. includes- Clothing, machine shops.
Mayor - Maurice G. Cron- 678 4881

74

•COLLEGE CORNER, Village; Butler and Preble Counties; Pop. 364; Area Code 513; Zip Code 45003; SW central Ohio; On Indiana state line, approx. 6 m. NW of Miami University in Oxford.

•COLUMBIANA, Village; Columbiana County; Pop. 4,987; Area Code 216; Zip code 44408; Elev. 1,138'; 15 m. S of Youngstown in E Ohio.

First called Dixonville for its founder, *Joshua Dixon*, was laid out in 1805. During the early decades of the nineteenth century the Pittsburgh Wooster stagecoach line passed through the town and taverns flourished along Main Street. Later the manufacture of agricultural machinery and carriages were the principal industries. *Harvey S. Firestone* (1868-1938) was born here. The current name is derived from combining Columbus and Anna.

> *Agriculture* - Dairy, fruit and varied farming.
> *Industry/Mfg. includes* - Dairy products,
>   building supplies, coal mining.
> *Mayor* - Richard D. Simpson- 482 2173

•COLUMBIANA COUNTY, E Ohio; Area 534 square miles; Pop. 113,572; County seat Lisbon; Est., March 25, 1803; Named for *Christpher Columbus* and Anna; in a hilly region; Bordered to SE by Ohio River.

•COLUMBUS. City; Fairfield & Franklin Counties; Pop. 564,871; Area Code: 614; Elev. 760.

Columbus is 97 m. NE of Cincinnati on the Scioto in River in Central Ohio. It is spread over 40 square miles in the rolling Scioto Valley near the geographic center of the state. Named in honor of *Christopher Columbus.* The name was suggested by the *Honorable Joseph Foos* who was a Senator from Franklin County in 1816.

Columbus was born as Ohio's capital. When the state was only a few years old, it sought a centrally located site for its statehouse. The seat of government had wandered from Chillicothe to Zanesville and back again, but neither town was considered ideal. Among leading bidders was Franklinton, now a part of Columbus' West Side, then a frontier village established in 1797 by *Lucas Sullivant*, a surveyor from Virginia. In 15 years Franklinton had become an important trading center, rough and ungainly, but determined, ambitious, and eager to be the capital. A group of promotors, *Lyne Starling, John Kerr, Alexander McLaughlin*, and *James Johnson*, proposed that the site be the "high bank east of the Scioto River directly opposite the town of Franklinton." They agreed to lay out a town and to convey to the State two tracts of 10 acres each for a capitol and a penitentiary. The two buildings were to be erected by the promoters at a cost not exceeding $50,000. After much wrangling this plan was accepted by the legislature on February 14, 1812.

The syndicate immediately started operations in a 1,200-acre tract of wilderness, swamps, and bogs, title to which the four men held jointly. The original platting provided for what are now Broad and High Streets and for several intersecting lanes. The name Columbus was adopted by the legislature on February 22 at the suggestion of *Joseph Foos*. Four months later, as congress declared war on Great Britain, the first public sale of lots was held, prices ranging from $200 to $1,000 each.

At the end of 1812 the population of the village was 300. In three years it increased to 700. The syndicate erected a modest two story brick capitol in the southwest corner of the 10-acre square, and a penitentiary several hundred yards to the southwest. The work had been delayed by the War of 1812, but both buildings were ready for occupancy within four years. In December 1816, legislators rode in to hold their first session in the new building. One of their acts at this session was to make Columbus a full-fledged borough. The first municipal election, held in the Columbus Inn, made *Jarvis Pike* mayor and president of the council.

As Columbus steadily grew, it absorbed Franklinton, from which the county seat was moved to the east side of the river in 1824. Small manufacturing concerns were started, schools were established, a market house was built, and Columbus forged ahead of the older towns of central Ohio despite serious handicaps. Chief of these was a series of fever and cholera epidemics that threatened to depopulate the village. When the large swamps, fed by springs only a few blocks from the center of the village, were finally drained, the epidemic subsided and the capital resumed normal growth.

What Columbus lacked most was easy transportation, and this need was soon met by canal and turnpike. The Ohio and Erie Canal passed a few miles east of Columbus, but was connected with it by a feeder canal opened with much fanfare on September

23, 1831, when the Governor Brown made the trip up from Circleville. Three days later Columbus welcomed, with parades, speeches, and banquets, the *Cincinnati* and the *Red Rover,* first boats to make the entire trip through the canal from Lake Erie to the capital. The canal was hailed as a great boon to commerce. It provided a much-needed and cheap outlet for agricultural products and opened the way for the importing of manufactured goods from the East.

The National Road reached Columbus two years later (1833). For a decade *William Neil* had been operating a famous stagecoach system radiating from Columbus, carrying travelers as far as Washington, D.C., on the east and St. Louis on the west. Now speedier express coaches thundered into Columbus from the East, volume of traffic increased greatly, and local inns became the most popular centers of business and social life. The glamour of the canal and overland traffic continued barely a score of years before giving way to the steam roads. On February 22, 1850, a steam engine, pulling a few flat cars, chugged out of Columbus on the Columbus and Xenia Railroad and made its maiden trip of 54 miles to Xenia in three hours and five minutes. The railroad officials who rode on the flat cars were enthusiastic over this record speed and the possibilities for the future.

By 1860 the population of Columbus was nearly 20,000. With the outbreak of the Civil War, the capital became an important military center. Several large camps were established in and near the town. Camp Chase, the most important, occupying a tract of 160 acres that is now a residential section on the extreme West Side, was the largest Confederate prison camp in the North. Of the many prisoners who died there, 2,260 are buried in a cemetery maintained by the federal government at the edge of the former camp site. Fort Hayes had its beginning as an arsenal during the Civil War. By the end of the war Columbus was firmly established as the state's principal mobilization point for military forces, a distinction it has since maintained.

Postwar prosperity brought a general expansion of business and industrial activity in the capital. Six new banking houses were organized, the city's first building and loan company began to function, and Columbus capital built two railroads, the Hocking Valley and the Columbus and Toledo. By 1872, five railroads, almost entirely financed with Columbus money, were doing a thriving business. This period also brought many civic improvements, including extension of streetcar service, paving of High Street, and construction of the city's first waterworks system. The legislature reflected the growing interest of the State in education by establishing the Ohio State University in 1873.

During the horse-and-buggy era the city boasted 18 factories that had a combined annual output of 20,000 carriages and wagons. By 1900, the availability of electricity and natural gas and a great web of electric inter-urban lines radiating from the capital made Columbus the leading industrial and commercial city of central Ohio. The city then began an intensive development of its civic resources, including the launching of a vast program to harness the Scioto River and to beautify its banks. But hardly was the program under way when the river went on its rampage in 1913, flooded the valley, took more than 100 lives, made 20,000 homeless, and caused property damage of nearly $9,000,000 in the Columbus area. When the flood subsided the river channel was widened, levees, retaining walls, and bridges were built, and the way was paved for the development of the civic center on the river front.

The worst of Columbus's sporadic labor disputes was the streetcar strike in 1910, which saw rioting, dynamiting of cars, one death, and numerous injuries. Columbus walked while the strke continued throughout the summer, and many attempts at arbitration failed. Troops were called out, and the National Guard patrolled the streets for weeks. The end of the strike in October brought few concessions from the railway company.

When World War I broke out, troops crowded into the city, and Fort Hayes was expanded to care for 8,000 men. More than 16,000 men and women from Columbus and Franklin County went into service, and many of the city's plants were converted to the manufacture of war materials.

Civic improvement was resumed after the war. Port Columbus, the municipal airport, was laid out and transcontinental air service was inaugurated with Columbus as an important terminal; the principal units of the civic center were built or started; and Ohio Stadium, one of the largest in the country, was finished.

As the twentieth century progressed, so did Columbus. The city limits pushed further outward from 50 to almost 150 square miles as more and more people moved in. Today's Columbus is a leader in mass communications, such as cable television, magazines and newspapers. A carefully-planned civic center includes an avenue of the flags of the 50 states, the city hall, departments of state building, federal building, LeVeque-Lincoln Tower, Ohio State Library and Ohioana Library, where a repository of books by Ohioans or about Ohio is located, along with collections of music clippings, photographs and other items relating to Ohio and its history. Many buildings in Columbus commemorate historical happenings simply by their existence: The Old Post Office on State and Third Streets was built in 1887, and re-dedicated in 1907 by *President William A. Taft* ; Trinity Episcopal Church, built in 1831, still serves as a house of worship for hundreds who love the stained-glass peacefulness of its interior; the Franklinton area west of the Scioto River from downtown Columbus was a settlement before Ohio reached statehood in 1803 and many old buildings still remain. For prehistory many visit the Olentangy Indian Caverns just north of Columbus, which were formed millions of years ago by an underground river. Wyandot Indians used these caverns much later as a haven from the weather and warring Indians.

More history is in the making for 1992, when some citizens' groups wish to hold an exposition commemorating the 500th anniversary of Columbus' discovery of America. The Development Commitee for Greater Columbus estimates about 21 million people will attend the six-month-long World's Exposition, on a 144-acre site near downtown and bordering the Scioto River.

POINTS OF INTEREST

OHIO STATE CAPITOL
Greek Revival style, stands in 10 acre park, cornerstone laid 1839; completed 1861; *Henry Walter* of Cincinnati architect.

MY JEWELS MONUMENT
Corner of the capital; a group of bronze statues including *Ulysses S. Grant, William T. Sherman, Philip H. Sheridan, Edwin M. Stanton, James A. Garfield, Salmon P. Chase,* and *Rutherford B. Hayes,* all Ohioians.

COLUMBUS GALLERY OF FINE ARTS
Principal art center of Columbus; modified Italian Renaissance style; designed by *Richard, McCarty and Bulford* of Columbus (1931).

Industry/Mfg. includes- Varied trade, manufacturing
and services.
Higher Education - Bliss College;
Capital University;
Columbia College of Art;
Franklin University;
Ohio College;
Ohio State University
Daily Newspaper - Citizen-Journal 34 S. Third St.
Dispatch 34 S. Third St.

•COLUMBUS GROVE, Village; Putnam County; Pop. 2,313
NW central Ohio; Trading center for a large, sparsely
populated farming region and lumber.

•COMMERCIAL POINT, Village; Pickaway County; Pop.
316; Area Code 614; Zip Code 43116; S central Ohio; Name
describes the small trading facilities in this farm
community.

•CONESVILLE, Village; Coshocton County; Pop. 451; Area
Code 614; Zip Code 43811; E central Ohio; On the Muskingum River in a hilly region.

•CONGRESS, Village; Wayne County; Pop 178; Area Code
216; NE central Ohio.

•CONNEAUT, City; Ashtabula County; Pop. 13,835; Area
Code 216; Zip Code 44030; Elev. 650'; NE corner of the State
on Lake Erie in NE Ohio. At the mouth of Conneaut Creek.
Its name is an indian word variously interpreted to
mean "fish", or "snow place", or it may be a corruption of
gunniate, which means "it is a long time since they have
gone". On July 4, 1796, *Moses Cleaveland,* surveyor for the
Connecticut Land Company, stopped here briefly with 50
New Englanders, but the site remained unsettled until 1799
when *Thomas Montgomery* and *Aaron Wright* appeared.
The natural harbor, around which Conneaut's
livelihood still centers, early attractd shipping of all kinds,
causing the village to grow rapidly. Millions of tons of coal
and ore are transshipped yearly from its docks, the coal to
the upper Great Lakes, the ore to the steel mills in eastern
Ohio and Pennsylvania.

Daily Newspaper - News Herald 182 Broad St.

•**CONTINENTAL**, Village; Putnam County; Pop. 1,179; Area Code 419; Zip Code 45831; NW Ohio; 25 m. W of Lima.

Agriculture - Soybeans, sugar beets and varied farming.

•**CONVOY**, Village; Van Wert County; Pop. 1,140; Area Code 419; Zip Code 45832; NW central Ohio; Rural community, just off U.S. Highway 30.

•**COOLVILLE**, Village; Athens County; Pop. 649; Area Code 614; Zip Code 45723; SE Ohio; Rural community on the Hocking River; Former coal mining area. The village was named after *Simon Cooley* the father of pioneer and settler, *Asahel.*

•**CORNING**, Village; Perry County; Pop. 789; Area Code 614; Zip Code 43730; SE central Ohio; In the Wayne National Forest.

•**CORTLAND**, Village; Trumbull County; Pop. 5,011; Area Code 216; Zip Code 44410; 15 m. NE of Warren on Mosquito Lake in NE Ohio; Camping, boating facilities. Named by the Company Railroad that came through here in the 1800's. The place was originally known as Baconsburgh for *Enos Bacon* who owned a store here in 1829.

•**CORWIN**, Village; Warren County; Pop. 276; Area Code 513; No Zip Code; Rural area in SW Ohio.

•**COSHOCTON**, City; Seat of Coshocton County; Pop. 13,405; Area Code 614; Zip Code 43812; Elev. 770'; SE central Ohio; On a plateau southeast of confluence of the Walhonding and Tuscarawas Rivers.
    The town's name was probably taken from one of two Delaware Indian names: Cush-og-wenk, meaning "black bear town", or Coshoc-gung, meaning "union of waters". Until 1830, when the Ohio and Erie Canal was built through the town, it had no outlet for its produce, but by 1865 the railroads made possible the developement of the coal fields in this vicinity. In 1887 *J.F.Meek* built an advertising-novelty plant that became the town's leading industry.

Agriculture - Varied farming.
Industry/Mfg. includes- Clothing, paper products, beverages, coal mining.
Daily Newspaper - Tribune 115 N. Sixth Street
Mayor - Daniel L. Moody- 622 1373

•COSHOCTON COUNTY, E central Ohio; Area 562 sq. miles; Pop. 36,024; County seat Coshocton; Est., January 31, 1810; Named for Delaware Indian word meaning "union of the waters", or "black bear town'; Hilly farmland countryside, cut through by the Tuscarawas and Walhonding Rivers as well as many small streams.

•COVINGTON, Village; Miami County; Pop. 2,610; Area Code 513; Zip Code 45318; 5 m. W of Piqua in SW Ohio; on Stillwater Creek.

Agriculture - Grain, cattle and varied farming.
Industry/Mfg. includes- Dairy products.
Mayor - Donald E. Garman- 473 2102

•CRAIG BEACH, Village; Mahoning County; Pop. 1,657; Area Code 216; On a widened area of the Mahoning River, W of Youngstown.

•CRAWFORD COUNTY, N central Ohio; Area 404 sq. miles; Pop. 50,075; County seat Bucyrus; Est., February 12, 1820; Named for *William Crawford* U.S. Secretary of the Treasury at the time of county founding; Sandusky River flows through the county, which is generally flat and covered by farmlands.

•CRESTLINE, City; Crawford County; Pop. 5,406; Area Code 419; Zip Code 44827; 10 m. W of Mansfield on the Sandusky River in N central Ohio; The name comes from the watershed locatd here. Crestline was important railroad junction in the early days.

•CRESTON, Village; Wayne County; Pop. 1,828; Area Code 216; Zip Code 44217; NE Central Ohio; Set among crested hills near the Chippewa River.

•CRIDERSVILLE, Village; Auglaize County; Pop. 1,843; Area Code 419; Zip Code 45806; 10 m. S of Lima in W central Ohio; in a farming region.

•**CROOKSVILLE**, Village; Perry County; Pop. 2,766; Area Code 614; Zip Code 43731; 10 m. S of Zanesville in SE central Ohio; clay deposits in the region make this a ceramics-making center.

Mayor - Jmaes W. Carmen- 982 2656

•**CROWN CITY**, Village; Gallia County; Pop. 513; Area Code 614; Zip Code 45623; 25 m. S of Gallipo, is in S Ohio; on bluffs above the Ohio River.

•**CUMBERLAND**, Village; Guernsey County; Pop. 461; Area Code 614; Zip Code 43732; E central Ohio; 21 m. SE of Zanesville in a coal mining area. *James Bay* was the first settler here in 1821 and his wife suggested the name.

•**CUSTAR**, Village; Wood County; Pop. 254; Area Code 419; Zip Code 43511; 17 m. SW of Bowling Green in NW Ohio; rural.

•**CUYAHOGA COUNTY**, N Ohio; Area, 456 sq. miles; Pop. 1,498,295; County seat Cleveland; Est., February 10, 1807; Named for an Indian word meaning "crooked"; Bordered to N by Lake Erie, and criss-crossed by rivers such as the Cuyahoga and Rocky, this county is mainly industrialized, with its focus at Cleveland; The decline of the steel industry in recent years had led to an exodus of hundreds of thousands of people from this once-booming area, although some revitalization is underway.

•**CUYAHOGA FALLS**, City; Summit County; Pop. 43,710; Area Code 216; Zip Code 442 + zone; 5 m. N of Akron in NE Ohio; has residential areas and small industries making metal goods, medical appliances, tools, molds and dies, wire, lumber, chemicals, and furniture; Named because it lies along a rapids area of the Cuyahoga River.

Industry/Mfg. includes- Medical equipment,
lumber, chemicals
Mayor - Richard J. Quirk- 923 9921

•**CUYAHOGA HEIGHTS**, Village; Cuyahoga County; Pop. 739; Area Code 216; Zip Code (with Cleveland); S suburb of

Cleveland, at a higher elevation than the city; Near the
Cuyahoga River.

•CUYAHOGA RIVER, River; Geauga, Portage, Summit
Counties; The river flows SW then turns abruptly N and
runs into Lake Erie at Cleveland. The Little Cuyahoga
River is received near Akron.

•CYGNET, Village; Wood County; Pop. 646; Area Code 419;
Zip Code 43413; 10 m. S of Bowling Green in central Ohio.

●DALTON, Village; Wayne County; Pop. 1,357; Area Code 216;
Zip Code 44618; 7 m. W of Massillon in NE central Ohio.

●DANVILLE, Village; Knox County; Pop. 1,132; Area Code 419;
Zip Code 43014; N central Ohio.

●DARBY CREEK, Creek; Central Ohio; Flows S approx. 60 m.
from E Logan County to confluence with the Scioto River at
Circleville; Irrigates a large flat farmlands area. The creek was
named after the Wyandot Indian *Chief Darby*.

●DARBYDALE, Village; Franklin County; Pop. 825; Area Code
614; Central Ohio; on Darby Creek; just SW of the Columbus
metropolitan area.

●DARBYVILLE, Village; Pickaway County; Pop. 282; Area
Code 614; about 25 m. S of Columbus, S central Ohio; along Darby
Creek; was named after a Wyandot Indian *Chief Darby*.

●DARKE COUNTY, W Ohio; Area 605 sq. miles; Pop. 55,096;
County seat Greenville; Est., January 3, 1809; Named for
William Darke, Indian fighter, Revolutionary War Major, and
member of the federal constitutional convention; cut through by
Stillwater River; Bordered to W by Indiana state line; Site of
many Indian wars during the 1790's. (See Greenville).

●DAYTON, City; Seat of Montgomery County; Pop. 203,588;
Area Code 513; Zip Code 454 + zone; in SW Ohio; spreads over a
great flood plain and into the surrounding hills of the Miami
Valley, 50 miles N of Cincinnati at the forks of the Great Miami

River. Four streams draining the upper valley unite in the heart of Dayton: The great Miami itself coming down through the city from the northeast; the Stillwater River flowing in from the north to join the Great Miami a half-mile or so above the Main Street Bridge; the Mad River entering the enlarged stream from the east. Named for the early landowner *Johnathan Dayton*, who plotted the town in 1795.

Dayton has a rich past that goes back to the time following the Treaty of Greenville (1795) when four Revolutionary War soldiers, *General Arthur St.Clair*, *General James Wilkinson*, *Colonel Israel Ludlow*, and *Johnathan Dayton* contracted with *John Cleves Symmes* for the purchase of 60,000 acres at the place where the Mad River flows into the Miami. This region was a notable center of Indian life; for decades the Miami Valley had been a thoroughfare for the Indians on their seasonal journeys from Lake Erie to Kentucky, and for the armies of the whites, led by such frontier heroes as *George Rogers Clark*, *Simon Kenton*, *Daniel Boone*, and *Anthony Wayne*.

In November 1795 *Colonel Israel Ludlow* surveyed the town plot in preparation for settlement. When spring came, three parties set out for the site from Cincinnati. After 10 days of rowing and poling their clumsy pirogues up the Miami, the first party, consisting of six men and several women and children, arrived on April 1, 1796. Others soon followed. The newcomers were warned by friendly Indians against floods at the junction of the rivers, but they thought only of the Great Miami as an avenue to market. Moreover, the site was level, rich, and well timbered, and there were bottom lands of wild white clover, wild rye, and blue grass: such a place was worth the risk. At first, however, the prodigality of the land meant little, for markets were far away. For several years the inhabitants lived very poorly.

By 1709 Dayton was a cluster of nine cabins, a blockhouse which served as a school, a distillery, sawmill, lime kiln, and a Presbyterian church. In the same year the first cargo, including grain, pelts, and 500 venison hams, moved down the Miami bound for Cincinnati and the New Orleans market.

When Ohio became a state in 1803, Dayton began dressing up formally; it became the Montgomery County seat, and two years later an incorporated town. In 1805, likewise, its public library, the first in the state, was incorporated. There was plenty of excitement, too, in this year, when Dayton had its first flood, and the titles of its town lots were placed in jeopardy because

Symmes, the original purchaser of the tract, did not complete his payments, and land titles reverted to the Government. The resolute settlers struck a bargain with the government, held on to their land, and began building levees against the river.

Dayton's first two decades were consumed largely in cutting trees, building houses, distilling corn whisky, grinding grain, curing pork, and building boats. During 1809-10 two keelboats were built in the road in front of the courthouse to ply the Miami-Loramie route to Lake Erie. Transportation in these pre-canal days reached a climax in 1825 when a late March freshet carried down the Miami River 30 boats heavily laden with cargoes of pork, flour, and whisky bound for New Orleans. Before the year was out, work on the Ohio canal system was begun between Dayton and Cincinnati, and the first section of the Miami and Erie Canal was opened in 1829. At daybreak of Sunday, January 25, cannons boomed and crowds cheered. The Governor Brown, the first canal packet on the new canal, had arrived from Cincinnati. In the afternoon the Forrer came, at dark the General Marion, and during the night General Pike. Each new arrival was greeted in gala style. Ten years later the canal had reached Piqua, and Dayton's principal plants, four cotton mills, several iron foundries, two gun-barrel factories, and carpet, chair, clock, and soap factories turned out more products for new customers.

In 1840, when Whig Presidential candidate *Harrison* came to Dayton for an "endorsing convention," the turnpike and canal poured an estimated 100,000 people into Dayton, then a town of 6,067. In 1851 the Mad River and Lake Erie Railroad was opened to Dayton, linking it with the growing lake-port towns. Daytonians watched wide-eyed and wondered at the marvelous wagon "without horses in front." The canal was through to Lake Erie in 1845, and two years later the telegraph had come to town. Citizens began to feel that Dayton was headed for big things. They built new factories such as the railroad car works, destined to become Dayton's first big industry. They planned an elaborate courthouse, "the most costly and elegant in Ohio," and had it and the city's first high school completed in 1850. The population was then 11,000, and the city had added to its industries two hydraulic races, oil and paper mills, and a wheel factory. By 1854 the Dayton and Springfield and Dayton and Western Railroads were completed, and tracks were laid for horse-car service.

During the Civil War Dayton was active in the anti-

86

administration Copperhead movement, led by a local congressman, *Clement L. Vallandigham.* Mobs of pro-Unionists and Copperheads pelted one another with bricks and stones. The *Dayton Journal,* ardent champion of the Administration, and the *Dayton Empire,* supporter of Vallandigham and States' rights, waged a war of abuse. On November 1, 1862, *J.F.Bollmeyer,* editor of the *Empire,* was shot down on the street, touching off two years of rioting and blood-spilling. In May 1863 a mob of Copperheads wrecked the Journal office. Vallandigham was forcibly arrested the following night on the charge of giving comfort and aid to the enemy, and was banished from the Union.

The war boomed Dayton's industries; agricultural machinery and railroad cars became its major products. After the Turner Opera House fire in 1869 focused thought on the town's hopelessly inadequate cisterns and wells, a waterworks system was installed by the Holly Manufacturing Company. Several generations were to drink "Holly Water." The town reached a population of 30,000 in the 1870's. *James Ritty* invented the "mechanical money drawer" in 1879, but the early cash registers excited only laughter among Daytonians, who were amused at the alarm bell that rang whenever the drawer was opened - a very useful device, however, as storekeepers soon discovered, in keeping clerks out of the petty cash. In the meantime, *Barney and Smith* in their great car sheds were nurturing the idea of assembly-line production and precision craftsmanship, innovations which were later taken up by *John Patterson* and made the basis on which mass-production cash-register manufacture was developed.

The rivers went over the levees again in 1883, and Dayton once more set about building the banks higher. The following year *John Patterson* came to Dayton and bought *James Ritty's* cash register company for $6,500; the next day he tried to sell it back for half price. He found no takers, and buckled down to make the money box pay. Following the practice of the car works, he insisted on fine, accurate workmanship. He searched for artisans and drew them to Dayton with high wages. In 1886 Patterson built a new factory with walls of 9—percent glass and thus introduced the "daylight factory;" a new standard of working conditions was set by this radical building, and a new style of American architecture created. By 1890, with the car works carrying 4,000 on the pay roll and National Cash Registers beginning to ring all over the country, Dayton's population had increased to 61,220.

A centennial celebration was held in 1896. Speeches and pageantry expressed the wonder of Dayton's 100 years. But the genuine marvel had hardly begun, for in 1898, the year a local boy fired the first shot in the Spanish-American War, *Wilbur and Orville Wright* were still tinkering with an idea. And while the Wright brothers worked in their bicycle shop, the beloved Black poet, *Paul Laurence Dunbar*, "the sweetest singer of his race," was operating an elevator in a downtown office building and writing Oak and Ivy. Dayton's industries were expanding but there was little for the frail Dunbar. The car works were bending wood to "palace cars" and coal gondolas, and around the livery stable and the blacksmith shop there was talk of the horseless carriage. A local inventor, *Dr. L.E.Custer*, built an electric runabout in 1899; three years later as many as four "gasoline buggies" could be seen on the streets in the course of a few hours. In this year *Barney Oldfield*, in the "Old 999," his pioneer racing car, got his start as one of the racing immortals by winning a local exhibition match. The Main Street Bridge, one of the first concrete bridges, was arched over the Miami in 1903, and in no time at all Dayton, getting accustomed to mechanical magic, was seeing its local-made Stoddard-Dayton, Speedwell, and Big Four automobiles wheeling over the new bridge for a test spin.

In the interim the Wright brothers had continued their experiments with kites and gliders, read every book in the Dayton public library pertaining to aerodynamics, built a wind tunnel (first in the world), and developed their own science of flying. They discovered the use of the aileron, the invention that made their fragile flying machine the world's first successful heavier-than-air craft after its flight at Kitt Hawk, North Carolina, on December 17, 1903.

Another mechanic, *Charles F. Kettering*, came to Dayton fresh from college in 1906, and got a job at the cash register plant. Here he developed a quick-starting electric motor for the cash register. Three years later he quit this job and retired to a woodshed to fashion a gadget that became known as the automobile self-starter. In 1910 he sold a big order to the Cadillac Motor Company, and with *E.A.Deeds* started the Dayton Engineering Laboratories Company (Delco). The next year the *Wright brothers*, who had become world-famous, established an experimental airplane factory here.

Then came catastrophe. Early on Tuesday, March 25, 1913, following a five-day downpour in which 10 inches of rain had fallen, the muddy waters of the Great Miami rolled over the levees with the most disastrous flood in the city's history. By 8:15 a.m. all communication lines were dead. Bridges were washed out, fires broke out everywhere, and explosions inflamed the sky. Houses were lifted from their foundations and carried down the river. Flood water climbed to second-story windows and thousands of people were marooned on house tops. On Thursday night the wind changed, blowing the fires back over the burned areas. Then the waters began to recede, and by Friday morning citizens were able to get down on the streets again. The flood had taken 361 lives and destroyed property worth more than $100,000,000.

Dayton citizens at last saw the futility of trying to keep the rivers within their channels by use of levees, and they began a movement to gain full protection against future floods. In 60 days popular subscription had raised $2,000,000. *Arthur E. Morgan* was commissioned to draw up a comprehensive plan of flood protection. A special Conservancy Act of 1915, the Miami Conservancy District was established. Finally, on November 25, 1916, the official plan, a combination of retarding basins and channel improvements, was approved. The actual work began on January 1, 1918, and was completed four years later at a cost of $32,000,000. During the critical months following the flood when need of effective city government was most acute, Dayton became the first large American city to adopt the commission-manager form of government.

The damage the flood had caused was soon repaired. At Delco a flourishing self-starter business was supplemented by ignition-system production. In 1916 the company became a part of the General Motors organization. Kettering and Deeds then organized the Delco-Light Company to make farm electric-light systems. In 1919 this concern was also absorbed by General Motors, and shortly thereafter the manufacture of electric home refrigerators was begun. Throughout the Nation the trade name "Frigidaire" came to mean "electric ice box."

Dayton experienced the urban crisis that hit many larger U.S. cities during the 1950's and '60s as many residents moved out

89

to the suburbs. Urban riots in the late 1960's brought in the National Guard, and many were left homeless after slum clearance and urban renewal projects took over. However, increasing federal and state funds have helped somewhat to provide relief programs for the underpriveleged.

POINTS OF INTEREST

DAYTON ART INSTITUTE - created by *Edward B. Green*

Buffalo, N.Y.; completed 1928.
PAUL LAURENCE DUNBAR MUSEUM - Opened 1938, has Dunbar
library, the poet's manuscripts and memorbilia.

Industry/Mfg. - Varied manufacturing trade and
services
Higher Education - St. Leonard College, Defiance
College, University of Dayton, Wright State
University
Mayor - James McGee 225-5145
Daily Newspaper - The Beavercreed Daily, 1342 N.
Fairfield Rd.
Chamber of Commerce - Suite 200, 111 W. 1st Street
Community Event(s) : Westminister Festival of
Religious Arts; Annual, May, A World A'Fair; Annual, June

● **DEER PARK**; City; Hamilton County; Pop. 6,745; Area Code 513; Zip Code 45236; 10 m. NE of Cincinnati in SW corner of Ohio; in a hilly area; Residential suburb.

Mayor - Francis R. Healy 791-1081

● **DEERSVILLE**, Village; Harrison County; Pop. 109; Area Code 216; Zip Code 44693; E Ohio; In a region of small lakes; Rural.

● **DEFIANCE**, City; Seat of Defiance County; Pop. 16,810; Area Code 419; Zip Code 43512; Elev. 712'; 40 m. NW of Lima in NW Ohio; At the joining of the Auglaize and Maumee Rivers. Named for Fort Defiance.

The French were here in 1760, trading with the Indians. As white settlers encroached more and more upon Indian hunting grounds, the uneasy Indians gathered under *Pontiac* and threatened reprisals. *General "Mad Anthony" Wayne* led his army to the site of Defiance on August 6, 1794, referring to the place as "the grand emporium of the hostile Indians of the West." Wayne named the place after he "defied" the English or the Indians to take it. When *General William Henry Harrison*, com-

90

mander of the Army of the Northwest, arrived here in 1812 he found Wayne's old fort in ruins and too small for his purpose. He built a larger fort and named it Fort Winchester for the officer placed in charge.

Growth was spurred by the activity along the Wabash and Erie and the Miami and Erie Canals, which joined near here to form a single waterway to Toledo. By the time canals were outmoded, Defiance had become the stable little industrial-agricultural city it is today.

The site of *Pontiac's* birthplace is believed to be on the north bank of the Maumee River, opposite the site of Fort Defiance. The son of an Ottawa father and Ojibwa mother, *Pontiac* (c.1720-79) became the chief of the Otawa, Potawatomi, and Ojibwa. He realized that the Indians would be driven from their lands by the English unless agressive action was taken. To that end he bent all his energy and organizing genius. Encouraged by the French, *Pontiac* in 1762 banded together nearly all the Indian tribes from Lake Superior to lower Mississippi for a united effort against the English. *Pontiac's* Conspiracy took place in 1763-4 when the inflamed tribesmen captured nine of the 12 fortified posts they attacked, massacred their garrisons, and spread fear and trembling among all the English settlements west of the Alleghenies. But *Pontiac* could not take the key for at Detroit, an aid from the French never materialized; finally he acknowledged defeat. He signed a treaty of peace with the English at Oswego, New York, in July 1766, and returned to his home on the Maumee, later going west to die at the hands of a paid assassin of his own race.

Between Defiance and the Indiana Line US 24 runs along the antic twistings of the Maumee River, penetrating a sparsely settled countryside of black loam.

This section of the state, now well drained, cleared of timber, and yielding bumper crops of corn, was the last to be settled. In 1830 not more than 3,000 people lived in the area lying west of Toledo and north of the Maumee; in 1850 its development was just beginning. There was a reason: from Perrysburg through Defiance to northwestern Indiana, and from southern Michigan through Bryn to the dune region west of Toledo, extended the Black Swamp – a pear-shaped wasteland 120 miles long and from 20 to 40 miles wide, thickly forested and filled with malarial bogs and pools of water. Through this desolated tract, which even the Indians avoided, ran a single foot trail; but immigrants gave it a wide berth as they pushed on toward Indiana or Illinois. Trees in the swamp appeared like a blue wall on the horizon; and an early surveyor made this entry in his journal: "water! water! water! tall timber! deep water! Not a blade of grass growing, nor a bird to be seen."

A few struggling villages made their appearance in the area during the early decades of the nineteenth century, but not until the late 1830's and early 1840's, when the Wabash and Erie and the Miami and Erie Canals were built along the Maumee river, did an incentive arise for husbanding the swampland. Extensive reclamation work was carried on during the latter half of the century as farming proved a profitable undertaking on this virgin soil; new towns arose and old ones grew larger. Today the only reminders of the blight that once infested the region are the parallel rows of drainage ditches running across the fields like strings on a harp.

Agricultur - Dairy, poultry, truck, cattle and varied farming
Industry/Mfg. - Electronics, auto parts, dairy products
Mayor - Ken Amsbaugh 784-2101
Daily Newspaper - The Crescent News, PO Box 229
Chamber of Commerce - 615 W. Third St.
Community Event(s) : Johnny Appleseed Festival; Annual, September

● **DEFIANCE COUNTY**, NW Ohio; Area 412 sq. miles; Pop. 39,987; County seat Defiance; Est., March 4, 1845; Named for Fort Defiance, built here in 1794 by *General Anthony Wayne* and his men on their Indian-fighting expedition; Activity centered around the Maumee River, which runs across the county; This section of the state, now well drained, cleared of original timber and yielding bumper crops of corn, was the last to be settled, since it was once covered with swamps and floodlands.

● **DE GRAFF**, Village; Logan County; Pop. 1,358; Area Code 419; Zip Code 43318; 12 m. SW of Bellefontaine in W central Ohio; in a hilly region of farmlands.

● **DELAWARE**, City; Seat of Delaware County; Pop. 18,760; Area Code 614; Zip Code 43015; Elev. 900'; central Ohio.

Early in the nineteenth century, the Indians had been drawn to the site. The Mingo had a settlement called Pluggy's Town; the Delaware Indians, for whom the city and the county are named, also had a village here. A sulphur spring which they called Medicine Waters seems to have been the attraction. *Moses*

Byxbe arrived in 1804 and laid out a town on the east side of the Olentangy; it was soon abandoned. In 1807 *Joseph Barber* built the first house on the present site and opened a tavern in it. Delaware was platted in the following year.

Agriculture - Varied farming
Industry/Mfg. - Bottles, applicances, cement blocks
    auto parts
Mayor - Donald E. Wuertz 363-1965
Daily Newspaper - The Gazette, 18 E. William Street
Chamber of Commerce - 27 W. Winter

● **DELAWARE COUNTY**, Central Ohio; Area 450 sq. miles; Pop. 53,840; County seat Delaware; Est., February 10, 1808; Named for the Delaware Indian tribe, which once lived in this region; Hilly region, with the Scioto, Olentangy, Alum, and Big Walnut Rivers flowing through; Mostly farmlands, with some N suburbs of Columbus in S county.

● **DELLROY**, Village; Carroll County; Pop. 368; Area Code 614; Zip Code 44620; 30 m. S of Canton on the N tip of Atwood Lake in E Ohio.

● **DELPHOS**, City; Allen and Van Wert Counties; Pop. 7,314; Area Code 419; Zip Code 45833; Elev. 750'; 10 m. NW of Lima in NW Ohio.
    Platted in 1845 by *Otto and Ferdinand Brederick,* Delphos for years was larger than either of its neighbors, Lima or Van Wert, because of the traffic on the Miami and Erie Canal and because it was crossed by the Pennsylvania Railroad. With the decline of the canal and the advent of railroads in other communities, Delphos' growth slowed down.

Agriculture - Grain, truck and varied farming
Industry/Mfg. - Lumber, machine shop, dairy products
    quarrying, farm equipment
Mayor - Ralph Wagner 692-9961
Daily Newspaper - The Herald, 405 N. Main
Chamber of Commerce - Commercial Bldg.

● **DELTA**, Village; Fulton County; Pop. 2,886; Area Code 419; Zip Code 43515; Approx. 25 m. W of Toledo in NW Ohio; a stock raising area.

93

• **DENNISON**, Village; Tuscarawas County; Pop. 3,398; Area Code 614; Zip Code 44621; Elev. 908'; 30 m. S of Canton in E Ohio; owes its founding to the Pittsburgh, Columbus & St. Louis Railroad, whose officers selected the site in 1864 for division shops midway between Pittsburgh and Columbus; Named for *William Dennison*, a Civil War governor of Ohio.

Mayor - Eugene Hart 922-2067

• **DESHLER**, Village; Henry County; Pop. 1,870; Area Code 419; Zip Code 43516; NW Ohio; 20 m. NW of Findlay in a grain and dairy farming region; Mail boxes and auto parts are made in this village's small factories, and an egg processing plant is near town.

• **DEXTER CITY**, Village; Noble County; Pop. 173; Area Code 614; Zip Code 45727; 21 m. N of Marietta; SE Ohio; off U.S. Highway 77; Hilly coal mining area.

• **DILLONVALE**, Village; Jefferson County; Pop. 912; Area Code 614; Zip Code 43917; E Ohio; A few miles W of the Ohio River in a rural area.

• **DONNELSVILLE**, Village; Clark County; Pop. 219; Area Code 513; Zip Code 45319; W central Ohio; 7 m. W of Springfield; Farming center.

• **DOVER**, City; Tuscarawas County; Pop. 11,526; Area Code 614; Zip Code 44622; Elev. 900'; E Ohio.

The only collector's port for the Ohio and Erie Canal in Tuscarawas County, the town was once called Canal Dover. In 1807 the settlement was laid out on ground owned by *Jesse Slingluff* and *Christian Deardorff*, German settlers from Pennsylvania.

Like many other towns in this section of Ohio, Dover's industrial and commercial development began with the construction of the Ohio and Erie Canal. Among the early industries were flour mills, salt works, a brick plant, and several foundries.

Mayor - Guy M. Smith 343-7725
Chamber of Commerce - PO Box 487

●DOYLESTOWN, Village; Wayne County; Pop. 2,493; Area Code 216; Zip Code 44230; NE central Ohio; Just SW of Akron in a residential area.

Mayor - David Holvey 658-6933

●DRESDEN, Village; Muskingum County; Pop. 1,646; Area Code 614; Zip Code 43821; 20 m. S of Coshocton on the Muskingum River in E central Ohio.
Dresden was named by the landowners that were initially from Philadelphia in 1817. Dresden was originally the site of an Indian settlement in 1764, located on the Creek and was named Wakatomika.

Agriculture - Fruit, grain and varied farming
Industry/Mfg. - Cement, dairy products, coal mining, oil

●DUBLIN, Village; Delaware and Franklin Counties; Pop. 3,855; Area Code 614; Zip Code 43017; Elev. 805'; Central Ohio; on the W bank of the Scioto River; Laid out in 1818 by *John Shields*, forebearer of the organizers of the Sheilds Brothers' Circus.
Dublin was chosen as the capital of the state by a commission appointed for that purpose, but political forces nullified its selection. The village is named after the city of the same name in Ireland that was the home of the surveyor *John Sheilds*.

●DUNKIRK, Village; Hardin County; Pop. 954; Area Code 419; Zip Code 45836; 20 m. S of Findlay in NW central Ohio; a farming area.

●DUPONT, Village; Putnam County; Pop. 308; Area Code 419; Zip Code 45837; NW Ohio.

•EAST CANTON, Village; Stark County; Pop. 1,721; Area Code 216; Zip Code 44730; Elev. 1,050'; 5 m. E of Canton in NE Ohio; Industries such as brick, tile, and ceramics are derived from the clay deposits in the region. Founded in 1805 and was originally named as Osnaburg, the name was changed to East Canton in 1918.

Industry/Mfg. - Ceramic and dairy products

•EAST CLEVELAND, City; Cuyahoga County; Pop. 36,957; Area Code 216; Zip Code 44112; Elev. 730'; NE Ohio; Suburb of Cleveland with no connection with the village formerly known by that name.

The original East Cleveland was annexed by Cleveland in 1872, and the name disappeared from the map until 1892 when neighboring Collamer, with other land to the east, became East Cleveland Hamlet; in 1911 the village became a city.

Mayor - Wallace D. Davis 681-5020

•EASTLAKE, City; Lake County; Pop. 22,104; Area Code 216; Zip Code 44094; NE Ohio; 20 m. NE of Cleveland on Lake Erie shoreline; Expensive residential area.

Mayor - Morris Becker 951-1416
Chamber of Commerce - 35475 Vine St.

•EAST LIVERPOOL, City; Columbiana County; Pop. 16,687; Area Code 216; Zip Code 43920; Elev. 686'; 20 m. N of Steubenville in E Ohio; Lies along an elbow of the Ohio River at a point where Pennsylvania, Ohio, and West Virginia meet.

This city of pottery and brick plants, foundries, machine shops, and breweries got its start in 1798 when *Thomas Fawcett*, of Ireland, ended his journey down the Ohio River and built a cabin for his family. Other settlers – Dutch, Welsh, Scotch, English, and German – arrived, and the growing village was called St. Clair by its founder. The first residents called it Fawcett's Town, and it kept this name until 1860, when Liverpool was substituted because many of the inhabitants had come from the English pottery city. Later the name was changed to East Liverpool.

Industry/Mfg. - Ceramic and paper products, coal mining, oil, chemicals
Higher Education - Kent State University
Mayor - Howard A. Tullis 385-3381

96

Daily Newspaper - The Review, 210 E. Fourth Street
Chamber of Commerce - 516 Market St.
Community Event(s) : Tri-State Pottery Festival;
 Annual, June

•**EAST PALESTINE**, City; Columbiana County; Pop. 5,306; Area
Code 216; Zip Code 44413; Elev. 1,015'; 20 m. S of Youngstown in E
Ohio; Est., in 1828 by *Thomas McCalla* and *William Grate.*

It is surrounded by rich deposits of coal, fire clay, building
stone, oil, and brick shales --natural resources upon which the
local industries depend. Manufactured products include pottery
ware, electrical refractories, automobile tires and tubes, electric
wire devices, and high-pressure steel tanks. In recent years hor-
ticulture has become important; more than 500,000 fruit trees
cover the hilltops of Columbiana County.

Agriculture - Truck farming
Industry/Mfg. - Clay products, coal mining, dairy
 products
Mayor - Wayne Nulf 426-4345
Daily Newspaper - The Leader, 78 N. Market Street
Chamber of Commerce - PO Box 106

•**EAST SPARTA**, Village; Stark County; Pop. 867; Area Code
216; Zip Code 44626; NE Ohio; 10 m. S of Canton in a dairy farming area.

•**EATON**, City; Seat of Preble County; Pop. 6,839; Area Code 513;
Zip Code 45320; Elev. 1,040'; 20 m. W of Dayton in SW Ohio; was
founded in 1806 and named after *General William Eaton,* hero of
the Tripolitan War of 1805. The community relies on the highly
productive farm country here.

Agriculture - Tobacco, wheat and varied farming
Industry/Mfg. - Clothing, metal products, nurseries
Mayor - Eric W. Daily 456-5561

•**EDGERTON**, Village; Williams County; Pop. 1,815; Area Code
419; Zip Code 43517; 40 m. NE of Fort Wayne, Indiana in NW
Ohio; a grain and stock raising area on the St. Joseph River; is
named for a land developer of this area of the state, *Alfred P.
Edgerton.*

97

Agriculture - Varied farming
Industry/Mfg. - Grain milling, auto parts, lumber
Chamber of Commerce - PO Box 238

•**EDISON**, Village; Morrow County; Pop. 504; Area Code 614; Zip Code 43320; Central Ohio; 15 m. E of Marion; Rural.

•**EDON**, Village; Williams County; Pop. 947; Area Code 419; Zip Code 43518; NW Ohio; 40 m. NE of Fort Wayne.

Agriculture - Soybean, grain and varied farming
Industry/Mfg. - Campers
Chamber of Commerce - Box 104

•**ELDORADO**, Village; PREBLE County; Pop. 509; Area Code 513; Zip Code 45321; SW OHIO; 15 M. S of Greenville; near the Indiana state line.

•**ELGIN**, Village; Van Wert County; Pop. 96; Area Code 419 Zip Code 45838; W Ohio; Rural farming community.

•**ELIDA**, Village; Allen County; Pop. 1,349; Area Code 419; Zip Code 45807; NW Ohio; 7 m. NW of Lima in a farming area.

•**ELMORE**, Village; Ottawa County; Pop. 1,271; Area Code 419; Zip Code 43416; N Ohio; On the Portage River, just off the Ohio Turnpike (U.S. 80).

•**ELMWOOD PLACE**, Village; Hamilton County; Pop. 2,840; Area Code 513; Zip Code 45216; SW Ohio; On Mill Creek just N of Cincinnati city center; Suburban; hilly land.

Mayor - Emmitt L. Spears 242-0563
Chamber of Commerce - 6019 Vine St.

•**ELYRIA**, City; Seat of Lorain County; Pop. 57,504; Area Code 216; Zip Code 440 + zone; Elev. 730'; N Ohio; Lies at and around the confluence of the east and west branches of the Black River, 25 m. SW of Cleveland. Probably the first white person to live on the site of Elyria was *Colonel James Smith*, who was brought to Ohio as an Indian captive in 1755. Settlement began in 1817 when *Herman Ely*, a New Englander, acquired 12,500 acres around the falls of the Black River, where he constructed a dam, gristmill, sawmill, and log house. The name was derived by combining Ely with ria, because his wife's name was Maria. By 1819 a town was in the making; mills and factories sprang up along the river. Later Elyria prospered as the retail and marketing center for a fertile area producing grapes, dairy products, cattle, and fruits; the city today is an important retail and industrial city.

Industry/Mfg. - Machine shop, sporting goods, furnaces, auto parts, plastics, chemicals.
Mayor - Marguerite E. Bowman 322-1819
Daily Newspaper - The Chronicle-Telegram, 225 East Ave.
Chamber of Commerce - PO Box 68, 356 Second Street

•EMPIRE, Village; Jefferson County; Pop. 484; Area Code 614; Zip Code 43926; E Ohio; On the Ohio River approx. 13 m. N of Steubenville; small port.

•ENGLEWOOD, City; Montgomery County; Pop. 11,329; Area Code 513; Zip Code 45322; Elev. 922'; 10 m. NW of Dayton in SW Ohio; Englewood is a Mennonite and Dunkard community whose Germanic character is readily apparent in its churches, its solid dwellings, the features of its residents, and their lingering accent. The town was settled by descendants of a Mennonite group *William Penn* had invited to Pennsylvania.

Mayor - James M. McGraw 836-5106

•ENON, Village; Clark County; Pop. 2,597; Area Code 513; Zip Code 45323; W Ohio; 10 m. SW of Springfield.

•ERIE COUNTY, N Ohio; Area 264 sq. miles; Pop. 79,655; County seat Sandusky; Est., March 15, 1838; Named for Erie Indians, who once lived in western New York, from a name meaning "cat"; Bordered to N by Lake Erie; Huron River flows N through county; Vegetable and fruit farming along level lakefront; Industry centered around Sandusky.

•EUCLID, City; Cuyahoga County; Pop. 59,999; Area Code 216; Zip Code 44117; Elev. 648'; on Lake Erie in N Ohio; suburb of Cleveland, first settled in 1798, was named for the Greek mathematician by surveyors in the party of *Moses Cleaveland.*

Mayor - Tony J. Sustarsic 731-6000
Chamber of Commerce - 333 Babbitt Rd.

•**EVENDALE**, Village; Hamilton County; Pop. 1,954; Area Code 513; Zip Code (with Cincinnati); SW Ohio; 15 m. N of Cincinnati; Residential.

•**FAIRBORN**, City; Greene County; Pop. 29,702; Area Code 513; Zip Code 45324; 10 m. NE of Dayton in SW Ohio; the name came from the two towns Fairfield and Osborn in 1950.

Agriculture - Varied farming
Industry/Mfg. - Cement and dairy products
Mayor - Herbert H. Carlisle 879-1730
Daily Newspaper - The Herald, One Herald Square
Chamber of Commerce - 333 Babbitt Rd.

•**FAIRFAX**, Village; Hamilton County; Pop. 2,222; Area Code 513; SW Ohio; N of Cincinnati; a residential area.

•**FAIRFIELD**, City; Butler County; Pop. 30,777; Area Code 513; Zip Code 45014; 20 m. N of Cincinnati in SW Ohio; Adjacent to city of Hamilton in a heavily industrialized area.

Mayor - Clarence Phalen 867-5300
Chamber of Commerce - PO Box 6

•**FAIRFIELD COUNTY**, S central Ohio; Area 505 sq. miles; Pop. 93,678; County seat Lancaster; Est., December 9, 1800; Named for the flat meadows found by early settlers here; Hocking River flows across county.

•**FAIRLAWN**, City; Summit County; Pop. 6,100; Area Code 216; Zip Code 44313; NE central Ohio; Residential area on the Cuyahoga River, just N of Akron.

Mayor - Joseph A. Hartlaub 666-8875
Chamber of Commerce - 137 S. Main

•**FAIRPORT HARBOR**, Village; Lake County; Pop. 3,357; Area Code 216; Zip Code 44077; Elev. 581'; 30 m. NE of Cleveland in NE Ohio on Lake Erie, 1 m. N of Painesville; Lake town whose principal industries are fishing, salt, and iron ore shipment. Fairport was established and named by (third) *Gov. Samuel Huntington* in 1812. Later Harbor was added as a description of the location.

Site of the Fairport Marine Museum, in the former lighthouse keepers home, adjacent to the old lighthouse, built in 1871.

Mayor - Delbert Lintala 352-3620

•FAIRVIEW PARK, City; Cuyahoga County; Pop. 19,311; Area Code 216; Zip Code 44126; NE Ohio; 10 m. SW of Cleveland city center; Residential.

Mayor - Joseph M. Gaul 333-2200

•FARMERSVILLE, Village; Montgomery County; Pop. 950; Area Code 513; Zip Code 45325; SW central Ohio; 15 m. SW of Dayton.

•FAYETTE, Village; Fulton County; Pop. 1,222; Area Code 419; Zip Code 43521; Elev. 821'; NW Ohio; Grain and livestock shipping center which lies at the western edge of an ancient glacial lake.

Agriculture - Grain and varied farming
Industry/Mfg. - Auto chassis, animal feed

•FAYETTE COUNTY, SW central Ohio; Area 406 sq. miles; Pop. 27,467; County seat Washington Court House; Est., February 19, 1810; Named for *Marquis de Lafayette*, general in the Revolutionary War, of French origin; Paint Creek flows across county; Stock raising important; Rich glacial soils make the county one of the most productive in the state.

•FELICITY, Village; Clermont County; Pop. 929; Area Code 513; Zip Code 45120; SW Ohio; 5 m. N of Ohio River; Rural trading center.

•FINDLAY, City; Seat of Hancock County; Pop. 35,594; Area Code 419; Zip Code 45840; Elev. 777'; 41 m. S of Toledo in NW Ohio; was laid out in 1821 by *Joseph Vance* and *Elnathan Cory*, and named for Fort Findlay, one of the outposts built here under the direction of *General Hull* during his march to Detroit in the War of 1812.

In the midst of rich farming territory, Findlay competed with other county towns as a trade center, and became the county seat in 1828. Unaware of the treasures in gas and oil that lay beneath its foundations, the town struggled along for several decades. In 1836 *Richard Wade* struck a gas pocket while digging a water well, but thought of it merely as a phenomenon with which to entertain visitors. Two years later, *Daniel Foster* found gas on his farm and sensibly piped it into his house for heating purposes. For years *Dr. Charles Osterlin* tried unsuccessfully to interest the state in the possibilities of natural gas for fuel; after the Civil War he and a few friends organized the Findlay Natural Gas Company, and, with a pittance for capital, they began to exploit the immediate vicinity. They struck a rich vein of gas and oil on Osterlin's farm by drilling 1,648 feet through Trenton limestone. In January 1886, the great Karg well came in with a tremendous roar and a 100-foot flame that could be seen at night for 50 miles. The boom was on, and a forest of derricks soon covered the countryside. Findlay began to grow in a wave of speculatin such as Ohio had never known. Its population soared from 5,000 to almost 20,000 in a single year. New industries, anxious to feed upon the cheap fuel, deluged the town - glass factories, potteries, brick and tile kilns, tube, nail and rolling mills appeard overnight. Hundreds of people made fortunes from real estate and leases.

Agriculture - Varied farming
Industry/Mfg. - Auto parts, appliances, electronics,
    plastics, limestone quarrying
Higher Education - Findlay College
Mayor - Donald s. Renninger 422-1012
Daily Newspaper - The Courier, 701 W. Sandusky St.
Chamber of Commerce - 118 E. Sandusky St. PO Box 923

•FLETCHER, Village; Miami County; Pop. 498; Area Code 513; Zip Code 45326; W central Ohio; 14 m. NE of Troy in a farming region.

•FLORIDA, Village; Henry County; Pop. 294; Area Code 419; Zip Code 294 + zone; NW Ohio.

•FLUSHING, Village; Belmont County; Pop. 1,266; Area Code

614; Zip Code 43977; Approx. 40 m. SW of Steubenville in E Ohio in a former coal mining area. The village was named for the English meaning Dutch Vlissinger, a place in Holland. The place was platted by *Jesse Foulke* in 1813.

•**FOREST**, Village; Hardin County; Pop. 1,633; Area Code 419; Zip Code 45843; NW central Ohio.

•**FOREST PARK**, City; Hamilton County; Pop. 18,675; Area Code 513; Zip Code 454 + zone; Approx. 20 m. N of downtown Cincinnati in a hilly, forested area in SW central Ohio; Residential.

Mayor - Cletus McDaniel 825-7752

•**FORT JENNINGS**, Village; Putnam County; Pop. 538; Area Code 419; Zip Code 45844; NW Ohio; Rural region, crossed by the Auglaize and Ottawa Rivers.

•**FORT LARAMIE**, Village; Shelby County; Pop. 977; Area Code 419; Zip Code 45945; 10 m. W of Sidney on the Loramie Creek where it empties into Lake Loramie in W central Ohio.
    The lake covers 1,950 acres adjacent to this village. Named for the fort built by *Gen. Anthony Wayne* during his anti-Indian campaign. The fort was destroyed in 1812, 18 years after it was built. A store operated by *Peter Loramie,* a French-Canadian trader, stood on the site in 1769. When *George Rogers Clark* and his mounted men swept through western Ohio in 1782 to quiet the troublesome Indians, the store was destroyed and its contents auctioned off to Clark's soldiers.

•**FORT RECOVERY**, Village; Mercer County; Pop. 7,370; Area Code 419; Zip Code 45846; W Ohio; On the Wabash River near the Indiana state line.
    A rural trading center, Fort Recovery is the site of *Gen. Arthur St.Clair's* defeat in 1791, and of *General Anthony Wayne's* "recovery" of the area in 1793, after the erection of a fort here. A state park now marks the site with a rebuilt fort and stockade built by the state Historical Society.

•**FORT SHAWNEE**, Village; Allen County; Pop. 4,541; Area Code 419; NW Ohio; nearby is the Shawnee State Forest, the largest forested area in Ohio, covering 33,410 acres. The timber consists of second-growth native softwoods and hardwoods. Rabbits, skunks, squirrels, and other small animals, as well as some deer and bear, live here. *James Flint*, British traveler, ate breakfast at a tavern in this vicinity in 1818 and said later that deer were so plentiful they sold at $1 apiece. The highest points in the forest are the five observaton towers, each 72 feet above the ground.

Mayor - Harry E. Baber 991-2015

•FOSTORIA, City; Seneca County; Pop. 15,743; Area Code 419; Zip Code 44830; Elev. 780'; N Ohio.

Two rival settlements, Rome and Risdon, were started on the site in 1832 and were united in 1854. Because *C.W.Foster* had much to do with local development in the real-estate, merchandising, and banking fields, the community was named for him. His son, Charles, served as governor of Ohio from 1880 to 1884.

Agriculture - Grain, cattle and varied farming
Industry/Mfg. - Auto parts, grain mmilling, beverages
Mayor - George W. Peeler 435-8282
Daily Newspaper - The Review-Times, 113 E. Center
St. Drawer
Chamber of Commerce - 121 N. Main St.

•FRANKFORT, Village; Ross County; Pop. 1,008; Area Code 614; Zip Code 45628; Elev. 740'; S. Ohio; Site of one of several Shawnee villages in western Ohio known as *Chillicothe* (Ind. village). The local chillicothe was plundered and burned by *Simon Kenton* in 1787 following Shawnee raids on towns in northern Kentucky.

Mayor - Daniel C. Moore 746-9921
Chamber of Commerce - 10 W. Fourth St.

•FRANKLIN COUNTY, Central Ohio; Area 538 sq. miles; Pop. 869,109; County seat Columbus; Est., March 30, 1803; Named for *Benjamin Franklin*, Colonial publicist and Revolutionary War figure; Scioto, Olentangy and Big Walnut Rivers flow through area; Some truck farming around the outer perimeters, of the Columbus metropolitan area, which takes up most of the county.

•FRAZEYBURG, Village; Muskingum County; Pop. 1,025; Area

Code 614; Zip Code 43822; 15 m. N of Zanesville in a hilly region in SE central Ohio; was named for *Samuel Frazey* who bought Knoxville, TN.

•**FREDERICKSBURG**, Village; Wayne County; Pop. 511; Area Code 216; Zip Code 44627; 10 m. S of Wooster in NE central Ohio.

•**FREDERICKTOWN**, Village; Knox County; Pop. 2,299; Area Code 614; Zip Code 43973; 20 m. S of Mansfield in a farming region in central Ohio.

Cement mixers, plastic goods, lamps, and metal products are made in Fredericktown factories.

Agriculture - Grain, cattle and varied farming
Industry/Mfg. - Cement products, dairy products

•**FREEPORT**, Village; Harrison County; Pop. 525; Area Code 614; Zip Code 43973; E Ohio; On Stillwater Creek in a rural farming and recreational area.

•**FREMONT**, City; Seat of Sandusky County; Pop. 17,834; Area Code 419; Zip Code 43420; 45 m. W of Cleveland on the Sandusky River in N Ohio; named for the explorer *John C. Fremont.*

Noteworthy during the War of 1812, when it was the site of Ft. Stephenson, Fremont was successfully defended by *Maj. George Croghan* and a small force of 165 in comparison to the British-Indian attackers with a much larger contingent. The Birchard Public Library now stands at the scene of the battle.

There were formerly three villages in the area: Bollsville, Free City and Croghansville. Lower Sandusky was formed in 1829 from the villages. The name was changed in 1849 to Fremont.

President Rutherford B. Hayes and his wife are buried in Spiegel Grove, their former homesite.

Agriculture - Sugar beet, and truck farming
Industry/Mfg. - Plastics, medical supplies.
   household appliances, iron casting, foam rubber,
   boxes
Mayor - Richard D. Maier 332-2591
Daily Newspaper - The News-Messenger, 111 S. Arch St.,
   PO Box 311
Chamber of Commerce - 316 W. State St.

•**FRIENDSHIP**, Village; Scioto County; Pop. (Rural); Area Code 614; Zip Code 45630; Elev. 530'; S. Oiho; had its beginning in the early years of the past century when *Major John Belli* built his home, Belvidere, near the mouth of Turkey Creek.

•**FULTON**, Village; Morrow County; Pop. 378; Area Code 614; Zip Code 43321; 40 m. N of Columbus in a rural area along Alum Creek in central Ohio.

•**FULTON COUNTY**, NW Ohio; Area 407 sq. miles; Pop. 37,741; County seat Wauseon; Est., February 28, 1850; Named for *Robert Fulton*, inventor of the first successful steamboat, which sailed up the Hudson River in 1807.

•**FULTONHAM**, Village; Muskingum County; Pop. 281; Area Code 614; Zip Code 43738; SE central Ohio; is named for *Lyle Fulton*, postmaster of Uniontown. For postal reason "ham" was added.

•**GAHANNA**, City; Franklin County; Pop. 186001,398; Area Code 614; Zip Code 43230; 5 m. NE of Columbus along the Big Walnut Creek in central Ohio; Suburban - residential; named for the Indian word "ghannah" meaning three united in one.

> *Agriculture* - Grain, poultry and varied farming
> *Industry/Mfg.* - Dairy products, grain milling
>   machine shops
> *Mayor* - Charles A. Leavitt 471-2411

•**GALENA**, Village; Delaware County; Pop. 358; Area Code 614; Zip Code 43021; Central Ohio on the Hoover Reservoir N of Columbus; Recreational facilities.

•**GALION**, City; Crawford County; Pop. 12,391424; Area Code 419; Zip Code 44833; Elev. 1,169'; 15 m. W of Mansfield in N central Ohio; Settled by German Lutherans from Pennsylvania in 1831.

The place was laid out by *Michael and Jacob Ruhl*. Galion remained rural in character until the middle of the century when several large railroad repair shops, buggy works, breweries, flour mills, and other factories were located here. Toward the end of the century a Galion man, *C. H. North*, inventor of improvements now embodied in the telephone organized a company for the manufacture of telephone equipment and made Galion for many years a pioneering center for this industry. In recent years the nature of the industries has changed.

Agriculture - Varied farming
Industry/Mfg. - Electronics, auto bodies, metal
   products
Mayor - Donald E. Yunker 468-1857
Daily Newspaper - The Inquirer, 378 N. Market St., PO
   Box 648
Chamber of Commerce - Credit Bureau Bldg., Public
   Square, PO Box 374

•GALLIA COUNTY, S Ohio; Area 471 sq. miles. Pop. 30,098; County seat Gallipolis; Est., March 25, 1803; Name is a derivative of the Latin word for France; Gaul; Bordered to E by Ohio River and partly designated as the Wayne National Forest; Originally settled by French; Hilly region, site of some prehistoric Indian burial mounds.

•GALLIPOLIS, City; Seat of Gallia County; Pop. 5,576; Area Code 614; Zip Code 45631; on the Ohio River, 30 m. NE of Ironton in S Ohio near the West Virginia border. Gallipolis was established in 1790. It was the third settlement in Ohio. It's founders were the Ohio Company of Associates for the French Royalists. The name means "City of the Gauls." Incorporated as a village, 1842; as a city, 1865.

Agriculture - Tobacco, cattle and varied farming
Industry/Mfg. - Concrete, animal feed, dairy products,
   furniture, motors.
Daily Newspaper - The Times-Sentinel, 825
   Third Ave.
Chamber of Commerce - 16 State St.

•GAMBIER, Village; Knox County; Pop. 2,056; Area Code 614; Zip Code 43022; 5 m. E of Mount Vernon on the Walhonding River in N central Ohio; named for *Lord James Gambier*, an English Admiral.

•GANN, Village; Knox County; Pop. 173; Area Code 614; Central Ohio.

•**GARFIELD HEIGHTS**, City; Cuyahoga County; Pop. 33,380; Area Code 216; Zip Code 441 + zone; NE Ohio, S suburb of Cleveland bordered to the W by the Cuyahoga River- Ohio Canal; Residential, with some industry.

Mayor - R. A. Stachewicz 475-1100

•**GARRETTSVILLE**, Village; Portage County; Pop. 1,769; Area Code 216; Zip Code 44231; 20 m. W of Warren in NE Ohio; named for *Col. John Garrett* who was the first settler here.

Agriculture - Varied farming
Industry/Mfg. - Electronics, auto tires, dairy
   products, lumber
Chamber of Commerce - PO Box 1

•**GATES MILLS**, Village; Cuyahoga County; Pop. 2,236; Area Code 216; Zip Code 44040; 15 m. E of Cleveland, outside of the busy metropolitan area in NE Ohio; named for *Halsey Gates* who settled here in 1812.

•**GEAUGA COUNTY**, NE Ohio; Area, 407 sq. miles; Pop. 74,474; County seat Chardon; Est., December 31, 1805; Name is derived from an Indian word meaning "raccoon"; Cuyahoga River flows through; Highlands, with many creeks feeding fruit orchards and maple groves.

•**GENEVA**, City; Ashtabula County; Pop. 6,655; Area Code 216; Zip Code 44041; Elev. 685'; 10 m. SW of Astabula in NE Ohio; named for Switzerland town.

    Founded in 1805, Geneva has extensive greenhouses and aviaries and a large farm implement factory. In Evergreen Cemetery, Eastwood St., stands the *Platt R. Spencer* Monument. Spencer (1800-64) founded business schools in 44 American cities and created the Spencerian penmanship system.

Agriculture - Truck, poultry farming
Industry/Mfg. - Beverages, hardware wheels, Resort
   Area
Mayor - William D. Shea 466-4675
Daily Newspaper - The Star Beacon, 23 S. Forest St.
Community Event(s) : Grape Jamboree; Annual, September

•GENEVA-ON-THE-LAKE, Village; Ashtabula County; Pop. 1,634; Area Code 2116; Zip Code 44043; N of the city of Geneva in NE Ohio, on Lake Erie shoreline.

•GENOA, Village; Ottawa County; Pop. 2,213; Area Code 419; Zip Code 43430; N Ohio; 15 m. S of Lake Erie shoreline and 20 m. SE of Toledo.

Industry/Mfg. - Automobiles and related products
Chamber of Commerce - 405 West St.

•GEORGETOWN, Village; Seat of Brown County; Pop. 3,467; Area Code 513; Zip Code 45121; SW Ohio near the Ohio River.
It was surveyed in 1819 and named for Georgetown, Kentucky. During the latter half of the nineteenth century, the town was an important distributing point for the tobacco grown in the area.

Agriculture -Tobacco, hogs, and varied farming
Industry/Mfg. - Granite works, grain milling, dairy
   products
Mayor - Joseph C. Rose 378-6400
Chamber of Commerce - PO Box 24

•GERMANTOWN, Village; Montgomery County; Pop. 5,015; Area Code 513; Zip Code 45327; 15 m. SW of Dayton in SW central Ohio; a grain farming region.
Early settlers of German descent gave this town its name after the same town name in Pennsylvania.

Agriculture -Tobacco, grain and varied farming
Industry/Mfg. - Building materials, aluminum castings,
   meat packing
Mayor - Ralph E. Moler 855-6567
Chamber of Commerce - PO Box 212

•GETTYSBURG, Village; Darke County; Pop. 545; Area Code 513; Zip Code 45328; Central Ohio; Rural community named after the city in Pennsylvania.

•GIBSONBURG, Village; Sandusky County; Pop. 2,479; Area Code 419; Zip Code 43431; N Ohio; 24 m. SE of Toledo.

Agriculture - Grain, cattle and varied farming
Industry/Mfg. - Oil, limestone, dairy products
Mayor - David L. Souder 637-3166
Chamber of Commerce - 415 W. Yeasting St.

•GILBOA, Village; Putnam County; Pop. 220; Area Code 419; Zip Code 45847; NW Ohio.

•GIRARD, City; Trumbull County; Pop. 12,517; Area Code 216; Zip Code 44420; Elev. 866'; NE Ohio; named for *Stephen Girard*, philanthropist and founder of Girard College at Philadelphia, Pennsylvania.

It was settled about 1800, but remained static until the Ohio and Erie Canal was completed. The advent of the railroads and the utilization of near-by coal deposits by several local factories gave further impetus to the growth of the community.

Mayor - N.J.Tiny E'Eramo Jr. 543-3879
Chamber of Commerce - 15 E. Liberty St.

•GLANDORF, Village; Putnam County; Pop. 746; Area Code 419; Zip Code 45848; NW central Ohio, along the Ottawa River; named by the early settlers of German descent for the town in Germany.

•GLENDALE, Village; Hamilton County; Pop. 2,368; Area Code 513; Zip Code 45246; 15 m. N of Cincinnati in SW Ohio, outside of the metropolitan area in a hilly region; Residential.

•GLENMONT, Village; Holmes County; Pop. 270; Area Code 216; Zip Code 44628; NE central Ohio; 22 m. S of Wooster.

•GLENWILLOW, Village; Cuyahoga County; Pop. 492; Area Code 216; Zip Code (with Cleveland); 15 m. SE of Cleveland city center; Rural-residential area outside of the metropolitan area.

•GLORIA GLENS PARK, Village; Medina County; Pop. 435; Area Code 216; N Ohio.

•GNADENHUTTEN, Village; Tuscarawas County; Pop. 1,320; Area Code 614; Zip Code 44629; Elev. 835'; 10 m. S of New Philadelphia on the Tuscarawas River in E central Ohio.

Near town is the Gnadenhutten State Park, where 96 Christian Indians were massacred by white men in 1782. They are buried in a mound inside the park. A group of Christian Indians led by *Joshua*, a Mohican elder, came here in 1772 and founded this town, calling it after the German word for "tents of grace," which they had learned from Moravian missionaries. The little community held on until 1781 when a white renegade, *Elliott* and two Delaware chiefs forced the Gnadenhutten Indians to move to the Sandusky plains. When their supplies ran low the next winter, however, a large group returned to Gnadenhutten to salvage what they could of the crops remaining in the fields.

At the same time an expedition under *Captain David Williamson* left Pennsylvania for Gnadenhutten, and arrived just before the Indians left for Sandusky. Gnadenhutten was pillaged and burned and the Indians killed.

•GOLF MANOR, City; Hamilton County; Pop. 4,317; Area Code 513; SW Ohio; Residential development just N of downtown Cincinnati; In a hilly area; named for the golf facilities in the city.

Mayor - Michael S. Schwarts 531-7491

•GORDON, Village; Darke County; Pop. 230; Area Code 513; Zip Code 45329; W Ohio; 15 m. SE of Greenville in a corn farming region; Near Indiana state line.

•GRAFTON, Village; Lorain County; Pop. 2,231; Area Code 216; Zip Code 44044; N Ohio, along the Black River just S of Elyria; Auto parts and machines are made in this town, and many residents commute to work in Elyria or Lorain.

•GRAND RAPIDS, Village; Wood County; Pop. 962; Area Code 419; Zip Code 43522; NW Ohio; Along the Maumee River, 7 m. W of Bowling Green; Residential area, with a large state park nearby.

•GRAND RIVER, Village; Lake County; Pop. 412; Area Code 216; Zip Code 44045; NE Ohio; 2 m. S of Lake Erie shoreline and just W of the Grand River's mouth; mostly residential.

•GRAND ST. MARYS LAKE, Lake; W Ohio; Approx. 10 m. long

and 3 m. wide at widest point; State's largest interior lake, with 33 m. of shoreline.

This lake was created in 1845 when the Wabash River was dammed to provide water for 60 miles of the Miami and Erie Canal. Best known for its fishing, and stocked regularly with crappies, bluegills, and bass, Lake St. Marys attracts thousands of visitors annually, particularly in the spring and summer. Cottages, camps and pleasure resorts line most of the lakeshore.

•GRANDVIEW HEIGHTS, City; Franklin County; Pop. 7,420; Area Code 614; Zip Code (with Columbus); Central Ohio; On the Olentangy River, just W of downtown Columbus; Hilly area overlooking the Capitol building and the city's buildings; Residential.

Mayor - Lawrence E. Pierce 488-3159

•GRANVILLE, Village; Licking County; Pop. 3,851; Area Code 614; Zip Code 43023; Elev. 960'; 10 m. W of Newark in a rich farming area in central Ohio; named for the town in Massachusetts.

Fiberglass and chemicals are made in Granville. Denison University is located on a horseshoe-shaped hill in town. It was founded in 1853 by Baptists and serves about 900 students. Before the National Road was cut across Ohio, Granville was as important a trading center as Columbus. Many early nineteenth century homes grace the town's street.

Agriculture - Soybeans, grain and varied farming
Industry/Mfg. - Dairy products, chemicals
Higher Education - Denison University

•GRATIOT, Village; Licking and Muskingum Counties; Pop. 227; Area Code 614; Zip Code 43740; off U.S. Highway 70, 10 m. W of Zanesville in SE central Ohio. The place is named for *General Charles Gratiot* who was a chief of Army engineer that built a National Road between Columbus in Zanesville.

•GRATIS, Village; Preble County; Pop. 809; Area Code 513; Zip Code 45330; SW Ohio; Community of corn farmers near Twin Creek.

•GRAYSVILLE, Village; Monroe County; Pop. 112; Area Code

112

614; Zip Code 45734; SE Ohio in the E Wayne National Forest; Many creeks run through this area, branches of the Little Muskingum River; The hilly region here was once mined for coal.

•GREAT MIAMI RIVER, River; Logan and Indian Lakes Counties; W Ohio; The River is 160 miles in length and flows S into the Ohio River in SW Ohio.

•GREEN CAMP, Village; Marion County; Pop. 475; Area Code 614; Zip Code 43322; Central Ohio; On the Scioto River where it branches off the Little Scioto River; Former Indian camp.

•GREENE COUNTY, SW Ohio; Area 415 sq. miles; Pop. 129,769; County seat Xenia; Est., March 24, 1803; Named for *Nathanael Greene*, American Revolutionary War general; Purebred stock raising is important here; Former Miami and Shawnee Indian lands.

•GREENFIELD, City; Seat of Highland County; Pop. 5,034; Area Code 614; Zip Code 45123; 20 m. W of Chillicothe along Paint Creek in S Ohio. The name describes the locality.

> *Agriculture* - Grain, cattle and varied farming
> *Industry/Mfg.* - Sports equipment, footwear, plastic products
> *Daily Newspaper* - The Times, 345 Jefferson St., Box 118
> *Chamber of Commerce* - PO Box 58

•GREENHILLS, City; Hamilton County; Pop. 4,927; Area Code 513; Zip Code 45218; Elev. 968'; SW Ohio, N suburb of Cincinnati, first developed in 1937 by the Federal Works Project Administration.

•GREEN SPRINGS, Village; Sandusky and Seneca Counties; Pop. 1,568; Area Code 419; Zip Code 44836; N Ohio; 10 m. SE of Fremont.

•GREENVILLE, City; Darke County; Pop. 13,002; Area Code 513; Zip Code 45331; Elev. 1,020'; 30 m. NW of Dayton in W Ohio.
Ohio's richest area in general farming and second richest in corn. Site of Fort Greenville, built in 1793. Once the home of

Tecumseh, Shawnee Indian chief. The place is named for *Gen. Nathaniel Greene.*

> *Agriculture* - Tobacco soybeans and varied farming
> *Industry/Mfg.* - Sportswear, cement, plastics, meat
>   packing, medicines, gravel
> *Daily Newspaper* - The Advocate, PO Box 220
> *Chamber of Commerce* - PO Box 237, 813 E. Main St.
> *Community Event(s)* : Annie Oakley Days; Annual,
>   July

•**GREENWICH**, Village; Huron County; Pop. 1,458; Area Code 216; Zip Code 44837; Elev. 1,031'; N Ohio; in a large farming area. Named for Greenwich, CT. The early settlers came from Massachusetts and Connecticut.

> *Agriculture* - Grain, cattle and varied farming
> *Industry/Mfg.* - Lumber, dairy products, plastics,
>   wood products
> *Chamber of Commerce* - 28 E. Main St.

•**GROVE CITY**, City; Franklin County; Pop. 16,793; Area Code 614; Zip Code 43123; Elev. 835'; Central Ohio; Just S of Columbus; Formerly a truck gardening village, settled largely by German immigrants, Grove City is now a growing residential suburb. Named by *William F. Bruck* for the description of the area. The land was first owned by *John Smith* in 1852 and was laid out by *William F. Bruck* who was *John Smith's* son-in-law.

> *Agriculture* - Grain, cattle and varied farming
> *Industry/Mfg.* - Electronics, building materials,
>   trucks

•**GROVEPORT**, Village; Franklin County; Pop. 3,286; Area Code 614; Zip Code 43125; Central Ohio; Between the Hocking River and Big Walnut Creek, SE of Columbus city center; Former canal port. Nearby is Rickenbacker Air Force Base.

First named Wert's Grove by *Jacob Wert* in 1843 for the walnut groves here. A year later, nearby, *John Rareysport*, a great horse trainer, started a settlement. In 1846 the names were combined.

•**GROVER HILL**, Village; Paulding County; Pop. 486; Area Code 419; Zip Code 45849; NW Ohio; 20 m. SW of Defiance; Rural center.

•**GUERNSEY COUNTY**, E Ohio; Area 528 sq. miles; Pop. 42,024; County seat Cambridge; Est., January 31, 1810; Named for the Isle of Guernsey, one of the Channel Islands owned by Great Britain; Coal mining is important here; The National Road, used by westward-moving pioneers in the mid-eighteenth century, once crossed this county.

•**GYPSUM**, Unincorporated Village; Ottawa County; Pop. (Rural); Area Code 216; Zip Code 43433; Elev. 579'; N Ohio.
Virtually all of the adult population here is employed in the large mines and plants.

•**HAMDEN**, Village; Vinton County; Pop. 1,010; Area Code 614; Zip Code 45634; S Ohio; 38 m. S of Lancaster, near the small Lake Alma, with camping facilities.

•**HAMERSVILLE**, Village; Brown County; Pop. 688; Area Code 513; Zip Code 45130; SW Ohio; 35 m. SE of Cincinnati.

•**HAMILTON**, City; Seat of Butler County; Pop. 63,189; Area Code 513; Zip Code 450 + zone; 20 m. N of Cincinnati in SW Ohio. It lies on the Great Miami River; named after *Alexander Hamilton*.
In the 1790's the city was called Fairfield and Fort Hamilton. This fort served *Generals St.Clair* and *Anthony Wayne* in their activities against the Indians.
The city became an industrial center after its combining with Rossville (1854) and with the completion of the Miami and Erie Canal which served the area.
The settlement began as an outpost of Fort Washington in 1791, when *General St.Clair* notified squatters and Indians of his arrival from Cincinnati by firing a salvo from his two pieces of artillery. His force immediately began building Fort Hamilton, which was not only a refuge during the first surprise attack by the Indians a few weeks after its completion, and a garrison post in Wayne's campaign of 1793-94, but also a headquarters for trade and homesteading.
In December 1794, *Colonel Israel Ludlow* platted the town, naming it Fairfield. But the garrison was removed in 1796, and the site temporarily abandoned except by a few followers of the army. In 1802 the plat was recorded, and by 1803, when Ohio

became a State, a permanent settlement was under way. The town, named Hamilton in honor of the fort, became the seat of Butler County.

The government-owned lands in the west bank of the river were then sold at auction, giving the residents an opportunity to own the lands on which they had settled. The western side, which became known as Rossville (1804), communicated with the other bank by ferry and existed as a separate community until 1854, when it became part of Hamilton. A peculiar characteristic of Rossville's architecture, possibly showing the French influence received from the river trade in New Orleans, appeared in the many grilled balconies which still cling to the buldings.

Early days were spent in the production of necessities, and in crude trade. With the coming of high water, flatboats, filled with great stores of products, including whisky, were floated to Cincinnati and other markets. Yet the freshets were dangerous, and the flood of 1805 almost washed away the cluster of homes.

In 1807 arrived the first physician, *Dr. Daniel Millikin*, who founded a family succession of medical men. When incorporated in 1810, Hamilton had a population of 210 people, and Rossville 84. In 1812 political council fires were lighted in Wigwag No.9, Hamilton headquarters of Tammany Hall, a secret society that dominated politics in the town until 1816. The Miami Intelligencer appeared in 1814, a jail was constructed in 1815, and three years later a great toll bridge costing $25,000 was built across the river to connect Hamilton and Rossville.

The Miami and Erie Canal, completed from Dayton to Cincinnati in 1827, ran east of Hamilton, but a wharf basin, hollowed out at what is now Court Street, brought shipping to the center of the city.

Upon completion of the Hamilton "Hydraulic" in 1852, the town had the best water-power plant west of the Allegheny Mountains; it changed from a dozing midwestern village into an alert industrial center. Growing industries stimulated the construction of hydraulic races; and the water power brought many more factories into the city. In *A Boys Town, William Dean Howells,* who as a youngster ran errands here for his father's print shop, talks about the excellent swimming provided by the races.

With the canal, the basin, and the hydraulic system completed, Hamilton became a well-equipped industrial center. The first railroad, the Cincinnati, Hamilton, and Dayton, arrived in 1851. In 1884 new reservoirs for the town's water supply were completed, bringing a cheap pure water supply. As in most cities, quick growth brought an era of lawlessness, which was endured until 1875, when a police force was established and a rigidly just government inaugurated. On September 19, 1895, as the climax of a great celebration of the occasion, city-owned electric lights fed by a municipal plant were turned on.

•HAMILTON COUNTY, SW corner, Ohio; Area 414 sq. miles; Pop. 873,136; County seat Cincinnati; Est., January 2, 1890; Named for *Alexander Hamilton*, Revolutionary war soldier and U.S. Secretary of the Treasury under *President Washington*. Bordered to S by Ohio River; Hilly countryside, dominated by Cincinnati metropolitan area. (See Cincinnati).

•HAMLER, Village; Henry County; Pop. 625; Area Code 619; NW Ohio; 20 m. E of Defiance; Rural trading community.

•HANCOCK COUNTY, NW Ohio; Area 532 sq. miles; Pop. 64,581; County seat Findlay; Est., February 12, 1820; Named for *John Hancock*, first signer of the Declaration of Independence; Blanchard river flows through county.

•HANGING ROCK, Village; Lawrence County; Pop. 353; Area Code 614; Zip Code 45635; Elev. 550'; S Ohio; At the end of the crescent formed by the Ohio River; Almost a continuation of Ironton.
    It takes its name from the cliff of sandstone 400 feet high, the top of which juts out over the wall like the cornice of a house. The village, founded in 1820.

•HANOVER, Village; Licking County; Pop. 926; Area Code 614; central Ohio.

•HANOVERTON, Village; Columbiana County; Pop. 490; Area Code 216; Zip Code 44423; E Ohio; 25 m. E of Canton.

•HARBOR VIEW, Village; Lucas County; Pop. 164; Area Code 419; Zip Code 43434; NW Ohio; Just E of Toledo across the Maumee River at its mouth at Maumee Bay; Suburban development, with boating facilities in the bay.

•**HARDIN COUNTY**, NW central Ohio; Area 467 sq. miles; Pop. 32,719; County seat Kenton; Est., February 12, 1820; Named for *John Hardin*, Revolutionary war soldier and Indian fighter in the frontier; Gradually rising farming country, cut through by the Scioto, Blanchard and part of the Ottawa Rivers; Rural.

•**HARPSTER**, Village; Wyandot County; Pop. 239; Area Code 419; Zip Code 43323; NW central Ohio; 8 m. S of Upper Sandusky in a rural farming region.

•**HARRISBURG**, Village; Franklin County; Pop. 363; Area Code 614; Zip Code 43126; 15 m. SW of Columbus, outside of the metropolitan area in central Ohio.

•**HARRISON**, Village; Hamilton County; Pop. 5,855; Area Code 513; Zip Code 45030; Elev. 820'; SW Ohio; Named for *Gen. William Henry Harrison*.
　　The first settlers came here before 1800, but the town was not formally laid out until 1813.

•**HARRISON COUNTY**, E Ohio; Area 401 sq. miles; Pop. 18,152; County seat Cadiz; Est., January 2, 1813; Named for *William H. Harrison* ; Site of the Clendening and Tappan Reservoirs, dammed areas of the Stillwater and Tuscarawas Rivers, respectively.

•**HARRISVILLE**, Village; Harrison County; Pop. 324; Area Code 614; Zip Code 43974; E Ohio; 13 m. NW of the Ohio River at Martin's Ferry; Rural.

•**HARROD**, Village; Allen County; Pop. 506; Area Code 419; Zip Code 45840; NW Ohio; 13 m. E of Lima.

•**HARTFORD**, Village; Licking County; Pop. 444; Area Code 614; Zip Code 44424; E central Ohio; Rural. Named for the city in Connecticut. In 1798 this land was deeded to *Ephriam Root* and *Urial Holmes*.

•**HARTVILLE**, Village; Stark County; Pop. 1,772; Area Code 216; Zip Code 44632; 12 m. NE of Canton in NE Ohio.

•**HARVEYSBURG**, Village; Warren County; Pop. 425; Area

Code 513; Zip Code 45032; 29 m. SE of Dayton along Caesar's Creek in SW Ohio. Named for *George Harvey* and was platted in 1815.

•HASKINS, Village; Wood County; Pop. 568; Area Code 419; Zip Code 43525; 8 m. NW of Bowling Green, near the S banks of the Maumee River in NW Ohio; Residential area.

•HAVERHILL, Village; Scioto County; Pop. (Rural); Area Code 614; Zip Code 45636; Elev. 550'; S Ohio.

This village is all that is left of the community that thrived around the Ohio Furnace after the Civil War. It stands on a 400-acre tract of land, a part of the large grant given by the federal government to 92 of the ill-fated French immigrants who settled Gallipolis. The French called it Burrsburgh in honor of *Aaron Burr*, but failed to develop it. It was later sold to New Englanders who named it for Haverhill, Massachusetts.

•HAVILAND, Village; Paulding County; Pop. 219; Area Code 419; Zip Code 45851; NW Ohio; Rural.

•HAYDENVILLE, Village; Hocking County; Pop. (Rural); Area Code 614; Zip Code 43127; Elev. 710'; S central Ohio; Founded in 1852 as an "ideal town" by *Peter Hayden*, first to recognize the economic possibilities of the coal and clay deposits in the vicinity.

•HAYESVILLE, Village; Ashland County; Pop. 518; Area Code 216; Zip Code 44838; Elev. 1,244'; N central Ohio.

Hayesville got its start by means of a jug of whiskey. In 1830, *Linus Hayes*, tavern owner, and the *Reverend John Cox* laid out the village, and advertised the sale of lots for a certain day. Buyers came, but failed to buy. Cox then passed a jug of whisky among the crowd, and by sundown every lot was taken. In Hayesville *William McKinley* pleaded his first law case. *Atlee Pomerene*, United States Senator from Ohio, *William L. Strong*, mayor of New York City, and *Dr. Henry S. Lehr*, founder of Ohio Northern University, all studied here at Vermillion Institute.

•HEATH, City; Licking County; Pop. 6,969; Area Code 614; Zip Code 43055; S central Ohio; Just W of Newark; Residential suburb with some high technology businesses.

•**HEBRON**, Village; Licking County; Pop. 2,035; Area Code 614; Zip Code 43025; S central Ohio; 9 m. SW of Newark on a branch of the Licking river.

•**HELENA**, Village; Sandusky County; Pop. 307; Area Code 419; Zip Code 43435; N Ohio; 10 m. W of Fremont in a vegetable farming area.

•**HEMLOCK**, Village; Perry County; Pop. 197; Area Code 614; Zip Code 43743; SE central Ohio; In central Wayne National Forest; Recreational facilities.

•**HENRY COUNTY**, NW Ohio; Area 416 sq. miles; Pop. 28,383; County seat Napoleon; Est., February 12, 1820; Named for *Patrick Henry*, governor of Virginia and Revolutionary War advocate; Cut through by a wide area of the Maumee River; Rolling farmlands.

•**HICKSVILLE**, Village; Defiance County; Pop. 3,742; Area Code 419; Zip Code 43526; 20 m. W of Defiance, just W of the Indiana state line in NW Ohio. Named for *Henry W. Wicks* who laid out this town in 1836 with a New York state group named "American Land Co."

•**HIGGINSPORT**, (alt. GINSPORT), Village; Brown County; Pop. 343; Area Code 513; Zip Code 45131; SW Ohio; On the Ohio River across from Kentucky; Near Georgetown; Small port town, which was dependent for a centrury upon the Chesapeake and Ohio station across the river at Augusta, Kentucky. Named for *Robert Higgins* who in 1894 settled here.

•**HIGHLAND**, Village; Highland County; Pop. 284; Area Code 614; Zip Code 45132; S central Ohio; 11 m. N of Hillsboro. Descriptive name.

•**HIGHLAND COUNTY**, S Ohio; Area 549 sq. miles; Pop. 33,477; County seat Hillsboro; Est., February 18, 1805; Named by early settlers for the many large hills in the area; Sparsely settled farming region.

•**HIGHLAND HEIGHTS**, City; Cuyahoga County; Pop. 5,739; Area Code 216; NE Ohio; Suburb of Cleveland; Hilly terrain.

•**HILLIARD**, City; Franklin County; Pop. 8,008; Area Code 614; Zip Code 43026; S central Ohio; W of Columbus; Residential community with some farming. Named for the man who laid out this place in 1853.

Mayor - R.A.Reynolds 876-7361

•**HILLS AND DALES**, Village; Stark County; Pop. 281; Area Code 216; NE Ohio.

•**HILLSBORO**, City; Seat of Highland County; Pop. 6,356; Area Code 614; Zip Code 45133; Elev. 1,129'; S Ohio.

South of Hillsboro are fine stands of hardwood –gnarled oak, walnut, silver beech, pines, and cedars. As early as 1863, *General James Loudon* pointed out that the most profitable crop to be obtained from the limestone soil near the Ohio River was tobacco.

Agriculture - Grain, cattle and varied farming,
  tobacco
Mayor - D. Dean Hill 393-3447
Daily Newspaper - The Press-Gazette, Box 40, 209 S.
  High St.
Chamber of Commerce - 126 S. High St.

•**HIRAM**, Village; Portage County; Pop. 1,360; Area Code 216; Zip Code 44234; Elev. 1,260'; 20 m. NW of Warren in a dairy and fruit-raising area in NE Ohio.

Hiram College was founded here in 1850 by the Disciples of Christ, *James Garfield* entered the school in 1851, worked as a janitor to pay his tuition, and graduated as valedictorian of his class two years later. In 1857-59, Garfield was principal of the school. *Vachel Lindsay* also attended classes here before beginning his wanderings on which he traded rhymes for bread.

•**HOCKING COUNTY**, S central Ohio; Area 421 sq. miles; Pop. 24,304; County seat Logan; Est., January 3, 1818; Named for the Hocking River, which in turn was taken from a Delaware Indian word Hockhock, meaning "gourd," or "bottle," since the river "bottles up" as it winds through this county; Partially designated as the Wayne National Forest, coal, oil and gas deposits have variously developed the county's economy; Several caves set aside as state parks in W county.

•HOCKING RIVER, River; SE Ohio and NW West Virginia; Flows S and SE approx. 80 miles from Fairfield County. Ohio to Ohio River, S of Parkersburg, W Virginia; Runs through part of the Wayne National Forest.

Sometimes brightly stained with the red copperas waters from coal mines, the Hocking River is surrounded by hills which yield rich mineral deposits.

•HOLGATE, Village; Henry County; Pop. 1,315; Area Code 419; Zip Code 43527; NW Ohio; 11 m. S of Napoleon.

Agriculture - Varied farming

•HOLLAND, Village; Lucas County; Pop. 1,048; Area Code 513; Zip Code 43528; 10 m. SW of downtown Toledo in NW Ohio; Suburban development.

•HOLLANSBURG, Village; Darke County; Pop. 339; Area Code 513; Zip Code 45332; W Ohio; 13 m. SW of Greenville, just W of the Indiana state line.

•HOLLOWAY, Village; Belmont County; Pop. 459; Area Code 614; Zip Code 43985; E Ohio; 40 m. SW of Steubenville near the Piedmont Reservoir. Named for the Holloway family from Virginia in 1827. *Issac Holloway* platted the town in 1883.

•HOLMES COUNTY, NE central Ohio; Area 424 sq. miles; Pop. 29,416; County seat Millersburg; Est., January 20, 1824; Named for *Andrew H. Holmes*, Major in the War of 1812, who was killed at Fort Mackinac, Michigan in 1814; Settled by Pennsylvania Dutch and Amish-Mennonites.

•HOLMESVILLE, Village; Holmes County; Pop. 436; Area Code 216; Zip Code 44633; 11 m. S of Wooster along Killbuck Creek in NE central Ohio; Rural. Named after the County which was named for *Major Holmes.*

•HOOVER RESERVOIR, Lake; Central Ohio; Approx. 8 m. long, an extension of the Big Walnut River, just N of the city of Columbus; For water use within the city, and some recreational uses.

122

•**HOPEDALE**, Village; Harrison County; Pop. 857; Area Code 614; Zip Code 43976; E Ohio; 19 m. W of Steubenville.

•**HOYTVILLE**, Village; Wood County; Pop. 315; Area Code 419; Zip Code 43529; 18 m. NW of Findlay in NW Ohio.

•**HUBBARD**, City; Trumbull County; Pop. 9,245; Area Code 216; Zip Code 44425; Elev. 935'; NE Ohio; 10 m. N of Youngstown, just W of the Pennsylvania state line; Suburban, with many of the same steel industries as other cities in the area.

This town was named for *Nehemiah Hubbard*, who purchased the surrounding township in 1801. Fifty years later, the town turned to manufacturing, but when the local coal was exhausted in 1880, business dragged until about 1900 when steel gained demand.

Agriculture - Varied farming
Industry/Mfg. - Heavy machinery and equipment
Mayor - Arthur U. Magee 534-3090
Chamber of Commerce - PO Box 177

•**HUDSON**, Village; Summit County; Pop. 4,615; Area Code 216; Zip Code 44236; Elev. 1,409'; 10 m. NE of Akron in NE Ohio.

Hudson was the first settlement in Summit County, as evidenced by old homes built in the Greek Revival style lining heavily foliaged streets. In the newer sections of town, sheet metal, construction machinery and fireworks are made, but most of the town is residential.

In 1799, *David Hudson* and a group from Connecticut settled this site, and the village was later on the stage route between Pittsburg and Cleveland. *John Brown*, an abolitionist, spent part of his youth here.

Mayor - John W. Rogers 650-1799
Chamber of Commerce - 134 N. Main

•**HUNTING VALLEY**, Village; Cuyahoga and Geauga Counties; Pop. 786; Area Code 216; NE Ohio.

•**HUNTSVILLE**, Village; Logan County; Pop. 489; Area Code 513; Zip Code 43324; W Ohio; 7 m. NW of Bellefontaine, just S of Indian Lake; Quiet farming community.

•HURON, City; Erie County; Pop. 7,123; Area Code 216; Zip Code 44839; Elev. 599'; 10 m. ESE of Sandusky in N Ohio; at the mouth of the Huron River, has a natural harbor that made communications with the interior of Ohio comparatively easy a century ago. It quickly rose to prominence during the first decades of the nineteenth century, then plunged into a destetude from which it is only now emerging. The harbor caught the eye of the French, and a trading post seems to have stood here about 1749. An American trader, *B.F.Flemond*, appeared in 1805. Rapid settlement followed the improvement of the harbor, and shipping made the town prosper. A new industry, shipbuilding, gave further impetus to Huron's feverish saga. In a few decades the population exceeded 2,000. But the cholera epidemic of 1834 killed many residents and caused others to flee, and when the completion of the Huron-Milan canal diverted shipping and building to Milan, the town's propelling force was lost. Decades passed before fishing, and later coal and iron ore transshipping, and finally the tourist business restored Huron to some semblance of its former self.

Agriculture - Grain and varied farming
Industry/Mfg. - Concrete, chemicals, boats. Resort
    Area
Mayor - George Sheard 433-5000
Chamber of Commerce - PO Box 43
Community Event(s) : Water Festival; Annual, July

•HURON COUNTY, N Ohio; Area 497 sq. miles; Pop. 54,608; County seat Norwalk; Est., February 7, 1809; Named for the Indian tribe which once frequented this region; Cut through by Hruon and Vermillion Rivers.

•IBERIA, Village; Morrow County; Pop. (Rural); Area Code 614; Zip Code 43325; Elev. 1,155'; Central Ohio; Site of the defunct Ohio Central. *Warren G. Harding* was a student here from 1879 to 1882.

•INDEPENDENCE, City; Cuyahoga County; Pop. 8,165; Area Code 216; Zip Code 44131; NE Ohio; Just S of Cleveland along the old Ohio Canal; Industrial suburb.

Mayor - Anthony Bontempo 524-4131

•**INDIAN LAKE**, Lake; W central Ohio; Approx. 5 m. wide, with 61 small islands; Designated as a state park in 1891.

Once the home of the Wyandot, Roundhead, and Cherokee, Indian Lake is one of the most popular recreational areas in W central Ohio; attracting nearly a million visitors each summer. The lake was formerly a small natural lake, and was expanded to a reservoir in the 1850's to supply water for the Miami and Erie Canal.

Cottagers and other resorters enjoy boating, golf, tennis, swimming, and baseball in the resort towns and beaches along the lakeshore. Duck hunting is permitted in season.

•**IRONDALE**, Village; Jefferson County; Pop. 535; Area Code 614; Zip Code 43932; 4 m. W of the Ohio River in E Ohio; in an iron ore district; Declining population. Originally known as Pottsdale for *Samuel Potts.* Secondly, named Huntersville for *John Hunter* who was the manager of the coal company that revived the town in 1816. Current name, given in 1869, comes from Pioneer Iron Co. for the substance that is mined here.

•**IRONTON**, City; Seat of Lawrence County; Pop. 14,290; Area Code 614; Zip Code 45638; Elev. 547'; S Ohio; On the Ohio River across from the Kentucky state line; Founded in 1848.

After iron ore was discovered here in 1826, *John Means* built a charcoal furnace to turn the ore into pig iron. The Virginian's furnace was the first of its kind north of the Ohio River. In 1834, *John Campbell* moved into the Ironton area and constructed the Mount Vernon Furnace, a new furnace he invented which would soon change the industry. Campbell founded the city in 1848. During and after the Civil War, Ironton's iron industry continued to grow, but during the Great Depression following the First World War, the industry came to a close.

•**ITHACA**, Village; Darke County; Pop. 130; Area Code 513; Zip Code (Rural); W Ohio; Farming community 15 m. S of Greenville.

•**JACKSON**, City; Seat of Jackson County; Pop. 6,675; Area Code 614; Zip Code 45640; Elev. 670'; S Ohio; Platted in 1817 and 1819, and grew rapidly after the coming of the railroad in 1853. Named after *Gen. Andrew Jackson.*

•**JACKSON CENTER**, Village; Shelby County; Pop. 1,310; Area Code 513; Zip Code 45334; 15 m. NE of Sidney in W Ohio. Named for *Andrew Jackson*.

•**JACKSON COUNTY**, S Ohio; Area 419 sq. miles; Pop. 30,592; County seat Jackson; Est., January 12, 1816; Named for *Andrew Jackson*, U.S. President (1829-37), and War of 1812 hero; Originally settled by Welsh.

•**JACKSONBURG**, Village; Butler County; Pop. 58; Area Code 513; Zip Code 43933; SW Ohio.

•**JACKSONTOWN**, Village; Licking County; Pop. (Rural); Area Code 614; Zip Code 43030; Elev. 1,013'; S central Ohio; Named for *Andrew Jackson*.
Here stands the Manuel Custer Conestoga Wagon, built in 1821 by the father of *General George A. Custer* and used by the family in their travels across the country.

•**JACKSONVILLE**, Village; Athens County; Pop. 651; Area Code 614; Zip Code 45740; 15 m. N of Athens in central Wayne National Forest in SE central Ohio; Hunting trading post. Named for *Andrew Jackson*.

•**JAMESTOWN**, Village; Greene County; Pop. 1,702; Area Code 513; Zip Code 45335; Elev. 1,053'; SW Ohio; Rich farming country amidst high table lands; The town was rebuilt along Victorian lines after a devastating tornado in 1844. Named for Jamestown, VA.

•**JEFFERSON**, Village; Seat of Ashtabula County; Pop. 2,952; Area Code 216; Zip Code 44047; Elev. 700'; NE corner of Ohio; 10 m. S of Ashtabula. Named for *Thomas Jefferson*.
Named by *Gideon Granger*, the Postmaster General in *President Thomas Jefferson's* cabinet, Jefferson village is primarily a dairy farming community, but chemicals are also produced here. The first national platform for the Republican Party was written in Jefferson by a local attorney, *Joshua R. Giddings*. Giddings' law partner was *Benjamin F. Wade*, a United States Senator and abolitionist who served as acting vice president during *Andrew Johnson's* impeachment proceedings.

•JEFFERSON, Village; Madison County; Pop. 4,448; Area Code 614; Zip Code 43162; SW central Ohio; 15 m. W of Columbus in a truck farming area; Along Little Darby Creek. Named for *Thomas Jefferson.*

•JEFFERSON COUNTY, E Ohio; Area 411 sq. miles; Pop. 91,464; County seat Steubenville; Est., July 27, 1797; Named for *Thomas Jefferson,* author of the Declaration of Independence, President of the U.S., and Vice President at the time the county was founded; Bordered to E by Ohio River.

•JEFFERSONVILLE, Village; Fayette County; Pop. 1,252; Area Code 614; Zip Code 43128; SW central Ohio near Paint Creek; Rural trading community. Named for *Thomas Jefferson.*

•JENERA, Village; Hancock County; Pop. 302; Area Code 419; Zip Code 45841; 12 m. S of Findlay in NW central Ohio; Farming region.

•JEROMESVILLE, Village; Ashland County; Pop. 582; Area Code 419; Zip Code 44840; N central Ohio; Along the Vermillion River, approx. 10 m. SE of Ashland.
     This peaceful rural trading center was once the site of a Mingo Indian village visited by *Major Rogers* and his scouting party in 1761. The village was named for a French trader, *Jean B. Jerome,* who lived here.

•JERRY CITY, Village; Wood County; Pop. 512; Area Code 419; Zip Code 43437; NW central Ohio; 30 m. S of Toledo in a rural area.

•JERUSALEM, Village; Monroe County; Pop. 237; Area Code 614; Zip Code 43747; SE Ohio; In a hilly, rural area north of Woodsfield; Named, as were many towns in the area, for a Biblical city.

•JEWETT, Village; Harrison County; Pop. 972; Area Code 614; Zip Code 43986; E Ohio; 25 m. W of Steubenville in a coal mining area.

•**JOHNSTOWN**, Village; Licking County; Pop. 3,158; Area Code 614; Zip Code 43031; Elev. 1,166'; 20 m. NE of Columbus in N central Ohio. Named for *Capt. James Johnston* who was an early landowner.

In August 1926, a farmer digging in his garden uncovered the skeleton of a mastodon 8 feet high and 15 feet long. The Cleveland Museum of Natural History purchased it.

•**JUNCTION CITY**, Village; Perry County; Pop. 754; Area Code 614; Zip Code 43748; SE central Ohio; 18 m. E of Lancaster; On a railroad line transporting coal from local mines. Named for a railroad junction.

•**KALIDA**, Village; Putnam County; Pop. 1,019; Area Code 419; Zip Code 45853; 20 m. N of Lima in NW Ohio along the Ottawa River. Named for the Greek word meaning beautiful. The place was laid out for the seat of the justice for the county in 1834.

•**KELLEY'S ISLAND**, Island; S Lake Erie, off NE coast of N Ohio; Contained within Erie County; 2,888 acres, 7 m. wide at widest point.

Around 1800 the place was known as Cunningham's Island because a trader of that name lived here. For several decades the island was unoccupied save for a few squatters. But in 1833 the *Kelley brothers Irad and Datus,* acquired it, settled here, and began to exploit its resources, including its forest of red cedar. In 1846 an acre of grapes was planted as a commercial venture, wine was made in 1850, and in the following year the first wine cellar north of Cincinnati was built.

•**KENT**, City; Portage County; Pop. 26,164; Area Code 216; Zip Code 44240; 10 m. E of Akron on the Cuyahoga River in NE central Ohio; Residential with some metal industries.

Kent State University was founded as a state normal school here in 1910 and became a university in 1935. It is set on a wooded campus of 100 acres and most of its buildings are in a semi-circle on the crest of a slope. Here in 1970, several students observing an anti-war demonstration on campus were shot and killed by National Guardsmen, causing national outrage.

Industry/Mfg. - Cement products, sports equipment, plastic products

128

•**KENTON,** City; Seat of Hardin County; Pop. 8,605; Area Code 419; Zip Code 43326; Elev. 1,015'; 30 m. NE of Lima in NW central Ohio on the Scioto River; Named after *Simon Kenton,* an Indian fighter; Town was laid out in 1833.

Originally a farming center, Kenton became a railroad center and a major producer of iron products during the nineteenth century. Near the turn of the last century, its importance in these two areas began to fade as other communities became more important. Today, the production of machinery and toys are two of the towns biggest industries.

Agriculture - Grain and truck farming
Industry/Mfg. - Electronics, confection, plastics,
    dairy products. Limestone
Mayor - Parket J. Obenour 419 675-5292
The Times, 201 E. Columbus St.
Chamber of Commerce - 8 N. Main St.

•**KETTERING,** City; Montgomery County; Pop. 61,186; Area Code 513; Zip Code 454 + zone; SW Ohio; On the southern outskirts of Dayton; Named after *Charles F. Kettering* ; Incorporated, village 1952, city 1955.

Located in the heart of Miami valley, Kettering has grown rapidly in its two decades of existence. In the late 1950's there was only one factory here and the population was almost half its current size. A carefully planned community, there are now over 1,000 acres zoned for industrial use. In 1956, the city government was established by charter and is of the council- city manager form. Kettering College of Medical Arts is here. The city is named after *Charles F. Kettering,* an industrialist credited with inventing the self-starter for the automobile and a quick starting electric motor for cash registers.

Mayor - Charles F. Horn 296-2400
Chamber of Commerce - 40 Southmoor Cir.

•**KETTLERSVILLE,** Village; Shelby County; Pop. 199; Area Code 513; Zip Code 45336; W Ohio, in a rural area.

129

•**KILLBUCK**, Village; Holmes County; Pop. 937; Area Code 216; Zip Code 44637; Elev. 808'; NE central Ohio; First settled in 1811, was named for the Indian, *Killbuck*, who figured in the region's history.

The village is a trading and shipping center lying along Killbuck Creek to a point where the highway drops to the floor of the valley before resuming its climbing journey along the hills to the west.

•**KIMBOLTON**, Village; Guernsey County; Area Code 614; Zip Code 43749; 10 m. N of Cambridge along Wills Creek in E central Ohio. Initially named Liberty for the township. *Naphtali Lubbock*, who opened a store here became the town leader and when the name had to be changed for postal reasons Lubbock suggested his hometown in England.

•**KINGSTON**, Village; Ross County; Pop. 1,208; Area Code 614; Zip Code 45644; S central Ohio; 11 m. NE of Chillicothe in a rolling farmlands region.

•**KINSMAN**, Village; Trumbull County; Pop. (Rural); Area Code 216; Zip Code 44428; Elev. 940'; NE Ohio; At the tip of the Shenango River Reservoir.

New England in character, Kinsman was named for the original owner of the town site, *John Kinsman*, who arrived here in 1799. The simple, earnest existence of the village has been described by *Clarence Darrow* (1857-1938), in *Farmington* (1904), a novel of small-town life during the 1850's and 1860's.

•**KIPTON**, Village; Lorain County; Pop. 352; Area Code 216; Zip Code 44049; NE Ohio; 6 m. W of Oberlin; Rural.

•**KIRBY**, Village; Wyandot County; Pop. 158; Area Code 419; Zip Code 43330; NW central Ohio; Near Upper Sandusky in a rural area.

•**KIRKERSVILLE**, Village; Licking County; Pop. 626; Area Code 614; Zip Code 43033; 22 m. E of Columbus along a branch of the Licking River in central Ohio; Farming town.

•**KIRTLAND**, City; Lake County; Pop. 5,969; Area Code 216; Zip Code (with Euclid); Elev. 660'; a suburban residential village on the brow of a hill overlooking the East Branch of the Chargrin River.

Kirtland Temple, bears witness that the village was host to the first large gathering of the Mormons (1830). The place was organized in 1817 and named for *Turhanac Kirtland*. *Joseph Smith* and other followers from New York settled here in 1830. The Kirtland Temple was built here between 1833-36. The temple still stands here today and is an important architectural and historical landmark in the state.

Mayor - Wesley I Phillips 256-3332

•**KIRTLAND HILLS**, Village; Lake County; Pop. 506; Area Code 216; NE Ohio.

•**KNOX COUNTY**, Central Ohio; Area 531 sq. miles; Pop. 46,309; County seat Mount Vernon; Est., January 30, 1808; Named for *Henry Knox*, Revolutionary War soldier and U.S. Secretary of War (1789-95); Criss crossed by the Kokosing, Walhonding and Mohican Rivers as well as many small creeks; Hilly farm countryside.

•**LAFAYETTE**, Village; Allen County; Pop. 488; Area Code 419; Zip Code 45854; Elev. 1,013'; NW Ohio; Near Lima; Named for the French marquis who aided Washington in the Revolutionary War.

•**LAGRANGE**, Village; Lorain County; Pop. 1,258; Area Code 216; Zip Code 44050; N Ohio; 10 m. S of Elyria near the Black River.

•**LAKE COUNTY**, Pop. 212,801; Seat - Painesville; Est., March 6, 1940; 232 sq. miles; is named for the many lakes in the area.

•**LAKELINE**, Village; Lake County; Pop. 258; Area Code 216; Zip Code (with Cleveland); On Lake Erie in NE Ohio, just N of Cleveland; Residential.

•**LAKEMORE**, Village; Summit County; Pop. 2,744; Area Code 216; Zip Code 44250; NE Ohio; Just SE of Akron on the N tip of Springfield Lake; Residential suburb.

•**LAKESIDE-MARBLEHEAD**, Village; Ottawa County; Pop. 677; Area Code 419; Zip Code 43440; Elev. 580'; N Ohio; Across Sandusky Bay from city of Sandusky.

Marblehead is quarrying area founded in 1809 by *Benaiah Wolcott*. Lakeside is a summer camp operated by the Methodist Episcopal Church. The site was acquired in 1869 for religious camp meetings. In 1873, with the adoption of the Chautauqua idea, Lakeside began to develop into a vacation and recreational resort with an extensive program of youth conferences, training institutes, and conventions.

•**LAKEVIEW**, Village; Logan County; Pop. 1,089; Area Code 513; Zip Code 43331; W Ohio, on Indian Lake, 15 m. NW of Bellefontaine; Resort town with many summer-only residents.

•**LAKEWOOD**, City; Cuyahoga County; Pop. 61,963; Area Code 216; Zip Code 44107; Elev. 685'; NE Ohio; On Lake Erie; Largest of Cleveland's suburbs, was known as East Rockport until 1889 when its present name, descriptive of its setting along the wooded shore of Lake Erie, was adopted.

A city since 1911, Lakewood retains a residential character; industry is not encouraged.

At first, the settlement here was part of the Western Reserve. It was incorporated as a village in 1903, and quickly grew to its present high-density position.

Mayor - Anthony C. Sinagra 521-7580

•**LANCASTER**, City; Seat of Fairfield County; Pop. 34,953; Area Code 614; Zip Code 43130; Elev. 898'; S central Ohio; On the Hocking River Valley floor, 25 m. SE of Columbus.

In 1797 Zane's Trace came past the great sandstone eminence of Mount Pleasant, called Standing Stone by the Indians. The government gave *Ebenezer Zane* three sections of land upon completion of his conract for the trace, one of them on the banks of the Hocking River. In 1800 the settlement was named New Lancaster, because so many Lancaster, Pennsylvania, folk had been attracted to the site. The first newspaper (1809) was printed in German, the language used in the first school. As early as 1806 this cluster of log cabins was the county seat, and was ambitious of becoming the state capital. It was incorporated in 1831.

It was the birthplace of *W.T.Sherman* and *John Sherman*, 137 E. Main St., is a two-story frame house with a brick front. Built in 1811, it was occupied by the Sherman family until 1829. Orphaned in that year by the death of their father, *William Tecumseh Sherman* and *John Sherman* were adopted by *Thomas Ewing*, a family friend.

Agriculture - Grain and varied farming
Industry/Mfg. - Footwear, electronics, chemicals
Higher Education - Ohio University
Daily Newspaper - The Eagle-Gazette, 138 W. Chestnut St., PO Box 848
Chamber of Commerce - 203 Kresge Bldg.
Community Event(s) : Old Car Club Spring Festival: Annual, June

•**LA RUE**, Village; Marion County; Pop. 861; Area Code 614; Zip Code 43332; 13 m. W of Marion on the Scioto River in central Ohio. Named for land owner *William LaRue*. The Indiana and Bellefontaine Railroad was built here in 1851. The place expanded around Mr. LaRue's home.

•**LATTY**, Village; Paulding County; Pop. 261; Area Code 419; Zip Code 45855; W Ohio; 22 m. SW of Defiance in a quiet farming region.

•**LAURA**, Village; Miami County; Pop. 501; Area Code 513; Zip Code 45337; W central Ohio; 15 m. W of Troy; Rural.

•**LAURELVILLE**, Village; Hocking County; Pop. 591; Area Code 614; Zip Code 43135; S central Ohio; 33 m. SW of Lancaster in a hilly rural area.

•**LAWRENCE COUNTY**, S Ohio; Area 456 sq. miles; Pop. 63,849; County seat Ironton; Est., December 21, 1815; Named for *James Lawrence*, Navy commander who was killed during the War of 1812, when he issued the famous order, "Don't give up the ship;" Bordered to S by Ohio River; Part of the Wayne National Forest is in N county; Fruit orchards, coal mining, once mined for iron ore.

•**LAWRENCEVILLE**, Village; Clark County; Pop. 307; Area Code 513; W Ohio.

133

•**LEBANON**, City; Seat of Warren County; Pop. 9,636; Area Code 513; Zip Code 45036; Elev. 969'; 20 m. E of Hamilton in SW Ohio; was founded in 1803. Lebanon is the commercial center for the region between the two Miami Rivers. The Thomas Carwin House still stands in Lebanon. He was the politician that resided in this town. He was successively a member of the Ohio legislature, Governor of Ohio (see Biography), Secretary of the Treasury and Minister to Mexico under Lincoln. He is buried in the cemetery here.

> *Industry/Mfg.* - Building supplies, lumber, tools, steel
> *Mayor* - Eleanor C. Ullum 932-3060
> *Chamber of Commerce* - 204 Citizens Bank Bldg., PO Box 213
> *Community Event(s)* : Honey Festival; Annual, September

•**LEESBURG**, Village; Highland County; Pop. 1,019; Area Code 614; Zip Code 45135; Elev. 1,025'; SW central Ohio; 10 m. N of Hillsboro; Almost encircled by Lee's Creek.

Quakers from Pennsylvania migrated here shortly after its founding in 1802, and prior to 1900 it was the site of the annual meeting of the Society of Friends, attended by members of the sect from all parts of the United States.

> *Agriculture* - Grain farming, poultry, dairy
> *Industry/Mfg.* - Food processing, dairy products, tools and dies

•**LEESVILLE**, Village; Carroll County; Pop. 233; Area Code 614; Zip Code 44639; E Ohio.

•**LEETONIA**, Village; Columbiana County; Pop. 2,121; Area Code 216; Zip Code 44431; E Ohio; 20 m. SW of Youngstown in a residential area. Named for *William Lee* who laid out this place in 1867, he started coal and iron works here.

> *Mayor* - Dan J. Cullinan 427-6721

•**LEIPSIC**, Village; Putnam County; Pop. 2,171; Area Code 419; Zip Code 45856; 30 m. N of Lima in NW Ohio. Named by the settlers for their hometown in Germany.

Agriculture - Grain, poultry farming
Industry/Mfg. - Cement products, tools
Chamber of Commerce - 117 E. Main St.

•**LEWISBURG**, Village; Preble County; Pop. 1,450; Area Code 513; Zip Code 45338; Elev. 1,019'; 22 m. NW of Dayton in SW Ohio; Industrial center of a large agricultural region.

Agriculture - Tobacco, grain and varied farming
Industry/Mfg. - Cement products, boxes, limestone
Chamber of Commerce - 121 N. Commerce St.

•**LEWISVILLE**, Village; Monroe County; Pop. 285; Area Code 614; Zip Code 43754; SE Ohio; In a sparsely populated area in E Wayne National Forest; Camping trading post.

•**LEXINGTON**, Village; Richland County; Pop. 3,823; Area Code 419; Zip Code 44904; Elev. 1,180'; 10 m. SW of Mansfield in N central Ohio; Laid out in 1812, and named in honor of Lexington, Massachusetts.

Mayor - Donald L. Herbert 884-1329

•**LIBERTY CENTER**, Village; Henry County; Pop. 1,111; Area Code 419; Zip Code 43532; NW Ohio; 30 m. SW of Toledo.

•**LICKING COUNTY**, Central Ohio; Area 686 sq. miles; Pop. 120,981; County seat Newark; Est., January 30, 1808; Named for the salt licks in the area, once mined extensively; Cut through by the Licking River; Site of several prehistoric Indian mounds; Hilly countryside with industry centered near Newark and in W county, suburb of Columbus.

•**LICKING RIVER**, River; Central Ohio; Flows approx. 110 miles S and E through Knox and Licking counties to join the Muskingum River near Zanesville.

•**LIMA**, City; Seat of Allen County; Pop. 47,381; Area Code 419; Zip Code 458 + zone; Elev 878'; NW Ohio.

135

The Ottawa River, known locally as Hog Creek, flows through the city. Early settlers placed names in a hat, with the understanding that the last one drawn would be accepted for the new village. Another name origin is the *Hon. Patrick G. Goode* named the place after the city in South America.

Industry/Mfg. - Steel products, eclectronics, autos,
    metal parts, engines, motors, chemicals, plastics
Mayor - Harry J. Moyer 228-5462
Daily Newspaper - The News, 121 E. High St.
Chamber of Commerce - 53 Public Square

•**LIMAVILLE**, Village; Stark County; Pop. 164; Area Code 216; Zip Code 44640; NE Ohio; 5 m. N of Alliance on W tip of Berlin Lake.

•**LINCOLN HEIGHTS**, City; Hamilton County; Pop. 5,259; Area Code 513; Zip Code (with Cincinnati); SW Ohio; N suburb of Cincinnati, set amidst the hills encircling the city; Residential.

Mayor - Herman M. Dantzier 733-5900

•**LINDSEY**, Village; Sandusky County; Pop. 571; Area Code 419; Zip Code 43442; N Ohio; 30 m. SE of Toledo and approx. 10 m. W of Sandusky Bay.

•**LINNDALE**, Village; Cuyahoga County; Pop. 571; Area Code 216; N Ohio.

•**LISBON**, Seat of Columbia County; Pop. 3,159; Area Code 216; Zip Code 44432; Elev. 955'; 15 m. NW of East Liverpool in E Ohio; Founded in 1802, this village grew slowly into a major trading center for a coal mining and farming region.

•**LITHOPOLIS**, Village; Fairfield County; Pop. 652; Area Code 614; Zip Code 43136; 20 m. SE of Columbus in S central Ohio, near the source of the Hocking River. Named from the Greek word meaning stone city for the high-quality of stone found here. The Wagnalls Memorial and the Public Library are comprised of this stone. The town was laid out in 1814 by *Frederick Bougher*.

•**LITTLE HOCKING**, Village; Washington County; Pop. (Rural); Area Code 614; Zip Code 45742; Elev. 619'; SE Ohio; On the Ohio River.

In 1770, while making a tour of the Ohio Valley, *George Washington* and his companions camped near this spot.

•**LOCKBOURNE**, Village; Franklin County; Pop. 373; Area Code 614; Zip Code 43137; Central Ohio; Near Columbus along an old canal route. Initially named Eight Lock, was later combined with the last part of the founders name, *James Kilbourne.*

•**LOCKINGTON**, Village; Shelby County; Pop. 203; Area Code 419; SW corner of Ohio.

•**LOCKLAND**, City; Hamilton County; Pop. 4,292; Area Code 513; Zip Code 45215; SW Ohio; Just N of Cincinnati on Mill Creek; Suburban community.

•**LODI**, Village; Median County; Pop. 2,942; Area Code 216; Zip Code 44254; Elev. 927'; N Ohio.

Lodi lies in the heart of what was once a favorite hunting ground of the Wyandot and Shawnee Indians. Originally named Harrisville for the pioneer settler *James Harris* who settled here in 1811. Named after Bonaparte's Italian Campaign the Battle of Lodi because of the local argument of the name choice.

It is a distributing center for dairy products, fertilizers, onions, and celery. Facing the park is an Indian mound upon which *Judge Joseph Harris*, founder of Lodi, erected a house in 1824 that still stands.

> *Agriculture* - Fruit, grain and varied farming, sugar beets
> *Industry/Mfg.* - Cement products, iron works, boxes
> *Mayor* - Dale F. Hastings 948-1005

•**LOGAN**, City; Seat of Hocking County; Pop. 6,557; Area Code 614; Zip Code 43138; Elev. 728'; S Ohio; Named for the Mingo Chief; Lying on a rich agricultural plain in the lap of the Hocking hills.

It was founded in 1816 when *Governor Thomas Worthington* purchased a level tract near the Hocking Falls, platted the town, and set up mills. Two years later Logan was made the seat of Hocking County. The opening of the Hocking Canal to

Logan in 1840, and the completion of the Hocking Valley Railroad in 1869 were important milestones in the town's history.

Agriculture - Varied farming
Industry/Mfg. - Clay and paper products, well drilling
supplies. Resort Area
Mayor - Evans S. Hand Jr. 385-8393
Daily Newspaper - The News, 72 E. Main St.
Chamber of Commerce - 42 W. Hunter St., PO Box 838

•**LOGAN COUNTY,** W Ohio; Area 460 sq. miles; Pop. 39,155; County seat Bellefontaine; Est., December 30, 1817; Named for *Benjamin Logan,* Indian fighter and pioneer of Ohio and Kentucky; Part of Miami River flows through this county, which is mainly covered by hilly farmlands; Site of highest point in Ohio, Campbell Hill, at 1,550 feet elevation, as well as Indian Lake; Many caverns in area.

•**LONDON,** City; Seat of Madison County; Pop. 6,958; Area Code 614; Zip Code 43140; Elev. 1,046'; SW central Ohio.
In 1811, 100 acres were purchased from *John Murfin* to establish a village here. Incorporated in 1831, middle of the century London had extensive stockyards and a lively trade. The first stock sale was conducted in 1856. Stock sales are still held, on a smaller scale, each Thursday afternoon.

Agriculture - Grain, cattle and varied farming
Industry/Mfg. - Steel and dairy products
Mayor - Stephen E. Smith 852-1111
Daily Newspaper - The Madison Press, 30 S. Oak St.
Chamber of Commerce - 1 East High St.

•**LORAIN,** City; Lorain County; Pop. 75,416; Area Code 216; Zip Code 440 + zone; Elev. 610'; 25 m. W of Cleveland in N Ohio where Black River flows into Lake Erie; Incorporated as village of Charleston in 1836; recharted as town of Lorain in 1874. Named for the French *Lorraine* by *Judge Herman Ely* from his European travels.
Delaware Indians occupied the Black River area when Moravian missionaires and their Indian converts arrived here in 1787 looking for a place to settle. Although the site at the river's mouth could have provided a good home, the Delaware's presence forced the missionaries to look elsewhere. It wasn't un-

138

til 1807, two years after the Connecticut Land Company acquired the Connecticut Western Reserve, that a settlement arose. Est., by *Nathan Perry* and the *Azariah Beebe* family, the village was named "Mouth of Black River." With the launching of the sloop, General Howard, in 1819, shipbuilding became the settlement's largest industry and Lorain's reputation as a shipping center began. In 1836, during the height of the early boom years, Mouth of Black River was incorporated as the village of Charleston. The boom years lasted only a short while, however, as the city's importance declined after Cleveland was named as the terminus of the Ohio and Erie Canal and plans for a railroad were moved to Elyria. Without a major transportation connection with interior cities, Charleston could no longer compete with other booming Ohio towns. Times became so bad it lost its charter as a town. In 1872, the boom years began again. The Cleveland, Lorain and Wheeling Railroad was opened and the port city was finally connected to the steel towns of the south. The town was recharted as Lorain in 1874, having lost the name Charleston to another Ohio city.

The boom continued into the 1890's when the Johnson Steel Company moved from Pennsylvania to South Lorain. The high salaries *Tom L. Johnson* paid his employees attracted immigrant workers of many nationalities to Lorain. Today, Johnson is credited with much of the city's renewed growth.

In 1924, a devastating tornado swept through Lorain killing 79 people, injuring hundreds and destroying much of the city. With the reconstruction of the town, Lorain has grown into a major industrial and shipping center. Its numerous ethnic groups give it a cosmopolitan atmosphere.

Industry/Mfg. - Automobiles, apparel, electronics.
    Resort area
Mayor - Joseph J. Zahorec 244-3204
Daily Newspaper - The Journal, 1657 Broadway
Chamber of Commerce - 204 5th St.

•**LORAIN COUNTY**, N Ohio; Area 495 sq. miles; Pop. 274,909; County seat Elria; Est., December 26, 1822; Named for Lorraine, a region in France, by early settlers; Bordered to N by Lake Erie, and crossed by branches of the Black and Rocky Rivers; Well populated W suburbs of Cleveland; Site of several higher educational institutions and medium-sized towns.

•**LORDSTOWN**, Village; Trumbull County; Pop. 3,280; Area Code 216; NE Ohio.

•**LORE CITY**, Village; Guernsey County; Pop. 443; Area Code 614; Zip Code 43755; E Ohio; 10 m. SE of Cambridge.

•**LOUDONVILLE**, Village; Ashland County; Pop. 2,945; Area Code 216; Zip Code 44842; N central Ohio; Along the Black Fork of the Mohican River in a sparsely populated dairy and grain farming area. Named after *James Loudon*, Priest who laid out the town with *Stephen Butler* in 1814.

Loudonville is situated amidst some of Ohio's most beautiful hills and has become a recreation center because of its proximity to the forks of the Mohican River.

Agriculture - Grain, fruit and varied farming
Industry/Mfg. - Lumber, grain milling, dairy products
Mayor - M.D.Shilling 994-3214

•**LOUISVILLE**, City; Stark County; Pop. 7,873; Area Code 216; Zip Code 44641; 5 m NE of Canton in NE central Ohio; Residential and commercial business area. A land owner named *Henry Loutzenheiser* named the place after his son *Lewis Heald*.

Agriculture - Grain and varied farming
Industry/Mfg. - Clothing, dairy products, steel,
        plastics
Mayor - Maxine K. Imdorf 875-3321

•**LOVELAND**, City; Hamilton and Clermont Counties; Pop. 9,106; Area Code 513; Zip Code 45140; SW Ohio; 16 m. NE of Cincinnati on the Little Miami River; Named for *Colonel Loveland*.

Mayor - Ronald E. Binegar 683-0150
Chamber of Commerce - PO Box 111

•**LOWELL**, Village; Washington County; Pop. 729; Area Code 614; Zip Code 45744; SE Ohio; 11 m. N of Marietta along the Muskingum.

•**LOWELLVILLE**, Village; Mahoning County; Pop. 1,558; Area Code 216; Zip Code 44436; 5 m. SE of Youngstown in NE Ohio; On the Mahoning River at the Pennsylvania state line.

•**LOWER SALEM**, Village; Washington County; Pop. 110; Area Code 614; Zip Code 45745; SE Ohio, 15 m. NE of Marietta on the borders of the Wayne National Forest (E section); Rural trading community.

•**LUCAS**, Village; Richland County; Pop. 753; Area Code 419; Zip Code 44843; 10 m. SE of Mansfield in N central Ohio; an early-settled farming region. Named for *Robert Lucas*, who was a Governor of Ohio from 1832-1836. *John Tucker* laid out this place in 1836.

•**LUCAS COUNTY**, NW Ohio; Area 343 sq. miles; Pop. 471,741; County seat Toledo; Est., June 20, 1835; Named for *Robert Lucas*, twelth governor of Ohio (1832-36); Bordered to N by Maumee Bay of Lake Erie, and Michigan state line; Crossed by Maumee River; Mostly metropolitan areas, dominated by city of Toledo; (see Toledo).

•**LUCASVILLE**, Village; Scioto County; Pop. (Rural); Area Code 614;; Zip Code 45648; Elev. 550'; S Ohio; By the Scioto River.
    The village was founded in 1819 by *John Lucas* on land listed in the warrants received by his father, *William Lucas*, a Revolutionary War veteran. The founder's son, *Robert Lucas*, was governor of Ohio (1832-36) and territorial governor of Iowa (1838-41).

•**LUCKEY**, Village; Wood County; Pop. 895; Area Code 419; Zip Code 43443; NE central Ohio; Approx. 15 m. NE of Bowling Green along the Toussaint River.

•**LUDLOW FALLS**, Village; Miami County; Pop. 248; Area Code 513; Zip Code 45339; W Ohio.

•**LYNCHBURG**, Village; Highland County; Pop. 1,205; Area Code 614; Zip Code 45142; 15 m. NW of Hillsboro in S Ohio. Named by early settlers from Virginia for their original hometown.

•**LYNDHURST**, City; Cuyahoga County; Pop. 18,092; Area Code 216; Zip Code 44124; NE Ohio; Approx. 10 m. E of downtown

141

Cleveland in a residential area.

Mayor - Lester C. Ehrhardt 442-5777
Chamber of Commerce - PO Box 24119

•LYONS, Village; Fulton County; Pop. 596; Area Code 419; Zip Code 43533; NW Ohio; 50 m. W of Toledo, just S of the Michigan state line.

•MCARTHUR, Village; Seat of Vinton County; Pop. 1,912; Area Code 614; Zip Code 45651; Elev. 767'; S Ohio; In 1815, the village was at the junction of two wilderness roads. The community was platted the same year and named McArthurstown for *General Duncan McArthur*, later governor of Ohio. The place was incorporated in 1851 as McArthur.

•MCLURE, Village; Henry County; Pop. 694; Area Code 419; Zip Code 43534; NW Ohio; 15 m. W of Bowling Green in a rural-residential area near the Maumee River.

•MCCOMB, Village; Hancock County; Pop. 1,608; Area Code 419; Zip Code 45858; NW Ohio; 10 m. NW of Findlay in a farming area fed by several streams.

•MCCONNELSVILLE, Village; Seat of Morgan County; Pop. 2,018; Area Code 614; Zip Code 43756; Elev. 710'; 20 m. SE of Zanesville in SE Ohio on the Muskingum River; Est., in 1817 by *General Robert McConnel.*

For many years, McConnelsville's economy was closely linked with the prosperity of the Muskingum River. From the early nineteenth century to after the civil war, the towns along the Muskingum flourished. The Muskingum was McConnelsville's road to the rest of the country, and over this water roadway, it sent its industrial and agricultural products. Near the end of the nineteenth century the state's transportation network changed. Railroads and highways made the river traffic obsolete, and McConnelsville's economic growth came to an end.

One of McConnelsville's best known natives was *Frederick Dellenbaugh*, a member of the first expedition through the Grand Canyon.

Agriculture - Grain and truck farming
Industry/Mfg. - Window, furniture, gas, oil
Chamber of Commerce - PO Box 336

•MCDONALD, Village; Trumbull County; Pop. 3,744; Area Code 216; Zip Code 44437; NE Ohio, just S of Niles and Warren in the steel mill districts along the Mahoning River.

Mayor - Thomas Leskovac 545-5471

•MACEDONIA, City; Summit County; Pop. 6,571; Area Code 216; Zip Code 44056; NE Ohio; At a midpoint between Cleveland and Akron; Suburban-residential; Named for the ancient kingdom in Asia.

Mayor - Stuart W. Feils 468-1300

•MCGUFFEY, Village; Hardin County; Pop. 646; Area Code 419; Zip Code 45859; 10 m. W of Kenton in NW central Ohio on the N bank of the Scioto River; Rural; In 1833 the place was named after *John McGuffey,* landowner, by his heirs.

•MACKSBURG, Village; Washington County; Pop. 295; Area Code 614; Zip Code 45746; SE Ohio; Rural region formerly mined for coal.

•MADEIRA, City; Hamilton County; Pop. 9,341; Area Code 513; Zip Code 45243; SW Ohio; Approx. 15 m. NE of Cincinnati in a residential area.

•MADISON, Village; Lake County; Pop. 2,291; Area Code 216; Zip Code 44057; 15 m. SW of Ashtabula in NE Ohio; Nurseries are the main activity here, although some factories produce steel products; Just north of town is Madison-on-the-Lake, with resort and boating facilities on Lake Erie. Named for *President James Madison.*

Agriculture - Truck farming
Industry/Mfg. - Electronics, motors. Resort area
Chamber of Commerce - PO Box 4

143

•**MADISON COUNTY**, SW central Ohio; Area 464 sq. miles; Pop. 33,004; County seat London; Est., February 16, 1810; Named for *James Madison*, President of the U.S. (1809-17); Flat section of central Ohio farmlands; Crossed by Deer and Darby Creeks; Formerly covered in swamps, until land speculators established themselves near streams where the earth was well elevated and drained, laying the foundations for today's farming.

•**MAD RIVER**, River; Logan County; W central Ohio; flows S and SE to the Miami River near Dayton.

•**MAGNETIC SPRINGS**, Village; Union County; Pop. 314; Area Code 513; Zip Code 43036; W central Ohio; 33 m. NW of Columbus in a farming area.

•**MAGNOLIA**, Village; Carroll and Stark Counties; Pop. 986; Area Code 216; Zip Code 44643; 15 m. S of Canton along Sandy Creek in NE Ohio; *Richard Elson* founded the place in 1834. Here he built a Magnolia Mill, a type of flour. The town is actually named after the mill. He named the mill after the flower - magnolia - he admired from his travels in the southern states.

•**MAHONING COUNTY**, NE Ohio; Area 415 sq. miles; Pop. 289,487; County seat, Youngstown; Est., February 16, 1846; Name is Indian for "at the salt licks", along the Mahoning River and Mill Creek, among other streams in the region.

•**MAINEVILLE**, Village; Warren County; Pop. 307; Area Code 513; Zip Code 45039; SW Ohio; 30 m. NE of Cincinnati near the Miami River.

•**MALINTA**, Village; Henry County; Pop. 327; Area Code 419; Zip Code 43536; NW Ohio; 8 m. S of Maumee River and 38 m. W of Bowling Green; Rural.

•**MALTA**, Village; Morgan County; Pop. 956; Area Code 614; Zip Code 43758; SE Ohio; Across the Muskingum River from McConnelsville; Boating and fishing center.

•**MALVERN**, Village; Carroll County; Pop. 1,032; Area Code 614; Zip Code 44644; 16 m. SE of Canton on Sandy Creek in E Ohio; Named after the town in Pennsylvania by the two landowners,

Joseph Tidbald and *Lewis Vail*. The two men purchased the land on Dec. 1, 1829 from the General Land Office.

Agriculture - Fruit farming
Industry/Mfg. - Coal, clay and dairy products

•**MANCHESTER**, Village; Adams County; Pop. 2,313; Area Code 614; Zip Code 45144; Elev. 511'; S Ohio; On the Ohio River; the fourth white settlement in Ohio, founded in 1791 by *General Nathaniel Massie.*

The village was named after Manchester, England for this is where Gen. Massie's ancestors came from.

Agriculture - Poultry and varied farming
Industry/Mfg. - Lumber, clothing, dairy products

•**MANSFIELD**, City; Seat of Richland Conty; Pop. 53,927; Area Code 419; Zip Code 449 + zone; Elev. 1,240'; N central Ohio; Midway between Cleveland and Columbus on a branch of the Mohican River in the last foothills of the Appalachian Mountains; Incorporated town, 1828, city 1857.

It was established in 1808 under the direction of *Jared Mansfield*, Surveyor General of the United States. Shortly after Mansfield platted the town, *James Cunningham* became its first permanent resident. During the War of 1812, the settlement was threatened by Indian allies of the British Army. Hearing of the impending danger, *Johnny Appleseed* (John Chapman), an early resident, travelled 30 miles in the night to bring troops from Mt. Vernon. There is a monument here honoring Chapman for saving the settlement. Originally an agricultural community, Mansfield grew slowly. The completion of several railroads into the area in the 1840's, however, prompted the city's growth as a commercial center and attracted an influx of new residents. Although Mansfield grew steadily after the 1840's, it never boomed as other Ohio cities did. Yet its economy remained strong during the Great Depression of the 1930's while other cities faltered. Today its industry produces steel, automobile parts, electrical, gas, and plumbing equipment and numerous other goods.

In addition to Mansfield's long history as an economic center, it also has a long history in politics and the arts. During *President Lincoln's* years in office, Mansfield was one of his leading strongholds. The city was also a crossroads for the Underground Railroad during the Civil War.

Ohio's best known novelist, *Louis Bloomfield*, a Pulitzer Prize winner, resided in Mansfield for many years and used the city as a setting in his writing.

> *Industry/Mfg.* - Electrical and auto parts, electronics, tires
> *Mayor* - Richard A. Porter 526-2600
> *Daily Newspaper* - The News-Journal, 70 W. Fourth St.
> *Chamber of Commerce* - 33 Park Ave., West
> *Community Events* : Ohio Craftman's Festival; Annual, April, Ohio Winter Ski Carnival: Annual, February

•MANTUA, Village; Portage County; Pop. 1,041; Area Code 216; Zip Code 44255; 30 m. SE of Cleveland in NE Ohio on the Cuyahoga River. Named in honor of *Napoleon* who earlier conquered a town by the same name in Italy, by *John Leavitt.* The town was platted in 1798-99.

> *Agriculture* - Varied farming
> *Industry/Mfg.* - Plastic and dairy products

•MAPLE HEIGHTS, City; Cuyahoga County; Pop. 29,735; Area Code 216; Zip Code 44137; NE Ohio; SE suburb of Cleveland; Residential area named for the trees which line many of the streets.

> *Mayor* - Emil J. Lisy Jr. 662-6000

•MARBLE CLIFF, Village; Franklin County; Pop. 630; Area Code 614; central Ohio.

•MARBLEHEAD, Village; Ottawa County; Pop. 679; Area Code 419; Zip Code (with Sandusky); N Ohio; On the N tip of the Sandusky peninsula, 6 m. across the bay from the city of Sandusky.

> *Agriculture* - Fruit and truck farming
> *Industry/Mfg.* - Meat packing, limestone. Resort area

•MARENGO, Village; Morrow County; Pop. 329; Area Code 419; Zip Code 43334; N central Ohio; 25 m. N of Columbus along the Big Walnut Creek.

•**MARIEMONT**, Village; Hamilton County; Pop. 3,295; Area Code 513; Zip Code 45227; Elev. 650'; SW Ohio; Overlooking the Little Miami River; Laid out in 1922 on land owned by *Marie Emery* of Cincinnati.

Mayor - Arthur J. Davies 271-3246

•**MARIETTA**, City; Seat of Washington County; Pop. 16,467; Area Code 614; Zip Code 45750; Elev. 620'; SE Ohio; 45 m. SE of Zanesville where the Ohio and Muskingum Rivers merge; Named after *Queen Marie Antoinette* of France for her assistance in the American Revolution. First known as Aldelphia.

The earliest settlement in Ohio. Marietta was established in 1788 two years after the Ohio Company of Associates purchased 1.5 million acres of land in what is now southeastern Ohio. Under the leadership of *General Rufus Putnam*, a member of *George Washington's* staff, a party of 46 boat builders, surveyors and settlers came to the confluence of the two rivers to build Marietta in April, 1788. Within a few weeks, the first cabins had been built and a stockade erected. At the time, *Campus Martius*, as the stockade was called, was considered the strongest fortification in the United States. For several years, it housed *Arthur St.Clair*, the territorial governor, and served as a focal point for the city's social and politicl life. Over the years Marietta developed as an important river port and shipbuilding center. Today, the city's main industries are the production of metal alloys, office equipment and chemicals. Marietta College was established here in 1797.

Well-preservd earthworks have been uncovered near Marietta indicating that a town site exsisted here for perhaps a thousand years before the white settlers arrived.

Agriculture - Truck farming
Industry/Mfg. - Food packing, paint, plastics, chemicals, dairy products
Higher Education - Marietta College
Daily Newspaper - The Times, 700 Channel Lane
Chamber of Commerce - 310 Front St.
Community Event(s) - Mainstreams; Annual, April-May

•**MARION**, City; Seat of Marion County; Pop. 37,040; Area Code 614; Zip Code 43302; Elev. 986'; Central Ohio; Home of the steam shovel.

The town's birth is associated with digging. A steady diet of salt pork had produced an extreme thirst in three pioneers who, after a long journey from Upper Sandusky, found no water in this vicinity. *Jacob Foos,* one of the trio, dug a few feet into a moist place, discovered water in abundance, and named the spot, Jacob's Well. It is generally believed that the importance of Jacob's Well caused the legislature to select this community as county seat. The name of the community was changed in 1822 to honor *General Francis Marion* of Revolutionary War Fame.

Marion's most distinguished citizen was *Warren G. Harding* (1865-1923), 29th President of the United States. Born in nearby Corsica (now Blooming Grove), Harding came to Marion to engage in newspaper work. In 1884 he became owner and publisher of the Marion Star. Later he served in the Ohio senate, was Lieutenant Governor of Ohio, and United States Senator.

Industry/Mfg. - Heavy machinery, grain milling, rubber, paper, limestone
Mayor - Donald E. Quaintance 382-3123
Daily Newspaper - The Star, 150 Court St.
Chamber of Commerce - 206 S. Prospect St. PO Box 448

•MARION COUNTY, Central Ohio; Area 405 sq. miles; Pop. 67,974; County seat Marion; Est., February 12, 1820; Named for *Francis Marion,* Revolutionary War general, known as the "Swamp Fox" for his antics against British troops in his home state of South Carolina; Hilly countryside with heavily wooded areas, farms and rich muckland.

•MARSEILLES, Village; Wyandot County; Pop. 164; Area Code 419; NW central Ohio.

•MARSHALLVILLE, Village; Wayne County; Pop. 788; Area Code 216; Zip Code 44645; NE Ohio; 25 m. SW of Akron in a sparsely-populated area with small lakes nearby.

•MARTINSBURG, Village; Knox County; Pop. 240; Area Code 614; Area Code 43037; N central Ohio; 11 m. SE of Mt. Vernon; Rural.

•MARTINS FERRY, City; Belmont County; Pop. 9,331; Area Code 614; Zip Code 43935; Elev. 660'; E Ohio; Pushed against the

Ohio River by hills. In 1795, the town was laid out as Jefferson, in hopes of becoming the county seat, by *Absalom Martin*. This never happened. Later, in 1835, the place was known as Martinsville after *Ebenezer Martin*. The name was later changed by the post office to Martins Ferry.

Industry/Mfg. - Dairy products, steel boxes, furniture, coal.
Mayor - John Laslo 633-2678
Daily Newspaper - The Times-Leader, 200 South 4th St.
Chamber of Commerce - 407 Walnut St.

•**MARTINSVILLE**, Village; Clinton County; Pop. 539; Area Code 513; Zip Code 45146; SW Ohio; 10 m. S of Wilmington in a rural area.

•**MARYSVILLE**, City; Seat of Union County; Pop. 7,414; Area Code 419; Zip Code 43040; Elev. 999'; W central Ohio; Settled in 1816 by *Jonathan Summers*, and platted in 1820 by *Samuel Culbertson*, who named the village for his daughter Mary.

Marysville played a vital part in the Harrison-Van Buren Presidential contest of 1840.

Agriculture - Grain, poultry and varied farming
Mayor - Kenneth M. Kraus 642-6015
Daily Newspaper - The Journal-Tribune, 207 N. Main St.
Chamber of Commerce - 109 S. Main St.

•**MASON**, City; Warren County; Pop. 8,692; Area Code 513; Zip Code 45040; SW Ohio; 20 m. E of Cincinnati in a hilly residential area.

Mayor - Rea Boone 398-8010
Chamber of Commerce - PO Box 93

•**MASSILLON**, City; Stark County; Pop. 30,557; Area Code 216; Zip Code 44646; Elev. 1,030'; 10 m. W of Canton in NE central Ohio.

This city lies on both sides of the Tuscarawas River, in the midst of a rich agricultural region. It arose in 1826 near two small villages named Brookfield and Kendall (the latter a languishing Owenite community), after it became known that the Ohio and Erie Canal was to pass through Stark County. *James Duncan*

149

and *Ferdinand Hurxthal* laid out the town site which was named for *Jean Baptiste Massillon*, a celebrated French divine and Mrs. Duncan's favorite writer. On August 25, 1828, spectators lined the banks of the canal to greet, with blowing bugles and booming cannon, the Allen Trimble. Her coming signalized the opening of the Ohio and Erie Canal between Cleveland and Massillon, and Massillon's debut as a marketing and industrial town.

Industry/Mfg. - Rubber products, boxes, steel, clothing, paper
Mayor - Mark Ross 833-4625
Daily Newspaper - The Independent, 50 North Ave. NW
Chamber of Commerce - PO Box 508
Community Event(s) : Massillon Merchants' Sidewalk Festival; Annual, July, Ohio Artists and Craftsmen Show; Biannual, July-August

•MATAMORRAS, Village; Washington County; Pop. 1,172; Area Code 614; SE Ohio.

•MAUMEE, City; Lucas County; Pop. 15,747; Area Code 419; Zip Code 43537; NW Ohio; adjacent to and S of Toledo on the Maumee River; Early a trading post and fort (1680) later the British Ft. Miami (1764).

The present name is a variation of Miami. Maumee was platted in 1817 after the famous Indian war, Battle of Fallen Timbers, which occured nearby. Known as Waynesfield Township until 1838 when it became Maumee City. During the War of 1812, the Dudley Massacre involved the destruction of a large force of locals by the British. Today it is primarily a residential area.

Agriculture - Varied farming
Industry/Mfg. - Grain milling, auto bodies, limestone
Mayor - Arthur W. Buffington 890-8751
Chamber of Commerce - PO Box 3
Community Event(s) - German-American Festival; Annual, August

•MAUMEE BAY, Bay; NW Ohio; On Lake Erie's SW corner; N of Toledo; Fed by the Maumee and Ottawa Rivers; Portage area for vessels carrying coal, steel, and other industrial goods to and from other Great Lakes ports.

•MAUMEE RIVER, River; Ohio and Indiana; Flows approx. 175 miles NE from its confluence with the St. Joseph River at Fort

Wayne, Indiana to its mouth at Maumee Bay, Lake Erie, just N of Toledo, Ohio; Widened area is navigable for 12 miles from mouth of river; Rapids near Perrysburg; Industrial cities and villages line the river banks.

•**MAYFIELD**, Village; Cuyahog County; Pop. 3,577; Area Code 216; 15 m. E of Cleveland in NE Ohio; Residential.

Mayor - Robert G. Beebe 461-2210

•**MAYFIELD HEIGHTS**, City; Cuyahoga County; Pop. 21,550; Area Code 216; 15 m. E of Cleveland, just S of Village of Mayfield; Residential development.

Mayor - Ross C. Dejohn 442-2626

•**MECHANICSBURG**, Village; Champaign County; Pop. 1,792; Area Code 513; Zip Code 43044; W Ohio; 30 m. W of Columbus in a farming region.

•**MEDINA**, City; Seat of Medina County; Pop. 15,267; Area Code 216; Zip Code 44256; Elev. 1,086'; 20 m. NW of Akron in N Ohio.

Est. in 1818 by a *Captain Badger*, the town was originally known as Mecca named by the landowner *Elijah Boardman*. The reasoning for the name Mecca was that this very religous man *(Elijah Boardman)* from Connecticut considered this to be the end of the trail. Mecca is the Holy City in Saudi Arabia. The name was changed to Medina in 1825 for the ancient capital of Arabia. Another reasoning for the name is from Medina, New York.

Its large bee keeping industry has led some to call it the "sweetest town in America."

Agriculture - Poultry, and varied farming
Industry/Mfg. - Dairy products, aluminum, lumber
Mayor - August Eble 725-8881
Daily Newspaper - The Medina County, 885 W. Liberty St.
Chamber of Commerce - 120 N. Elmwood Ave.

•**MEDINA COUNTY**, N Ohio; Area 425 sq. miles; Pop. 113,150; County seat Medina; Est. February 18, 1812; Named for Medina, a city in the Near East which was a refuge for Mohammed after he fled from Mecca in 622; Parts of the Rocky, Black and Chip-

151

pewa rivers flow through this county; Mostly farmlands, with some residential-industrial areas near the Cleveland and Dayton metropolises.

•MEIGS COUNTY, SE Ohio; Area 436 sq. miles; Pop. 23,641; County seat Pomeroy; Est. January 21, 1819; Named for *Johathan Meigs*, Fourth governor of Ohio (1810-14) and U.S Postmaster General at time of county's founding; Bordered to S and E by Ohio River; Hilly plateau land, once heavily mined for coal; In 1880, when Ohio was the nation's third ranking bituminous coal state, Meigs County stood fifth among 30 coal-producing counties; Salt along the river used in chemical industries, but most of the county is now devoted to agriculture.

•MELROSE, Village; Paulding County; Pop. 315; Area Code 419; Zip Code 45862; Along the Auglaize River, approx. 20 m. S of Defiance; Former Indian hunting grounds.

•MENDON, Village; Mercer County; Pop. 749; Area Code 513; Zip Code 45862; W Ohio; Just S of the Saint Marys river in a rich farming area.

•MENTOR, City; Lake County; Pop. 42,065; Area Code 216; Zip Code 44060; Elev. 65'; NE Ohio, just S of the Lake Erie shoreline; Nurseries are the main industry.
   James A. Garfield, twentieth President of the U.S., was born in Mentor. His restored home and birthplace are in town, as is a small building used as a campaign office in 1880.

   Mayor - Gordon C. Hodgins 255-1100
   Chamber of Commerce - 7701 Reynolds Rd.

•MENTOR-ON-THE-LAKE, City; Lake County; Pop. 7,919; Area Code 216; Zip Code 44060; Just S of Lake Erie shoreline, and N of city of Mentor in a resort and tree nursery area.

   Mayor - Neil H. Crookshanks 257-7216

•MERCER COUNTY, W Ohio; Area 454 sq. miles; Pop. 38,334; County seat, Celina; Est. February 12, 1820; Named for *Hugh Mercer*, doctor and Revolutionary War general who died at the battle of Princeton in 1777; St. Marys and Wabash River flow through this area and feed Grand Lake St. Marys in E county; Former Indian lands, the site of *Arthur St.Clair's* defeat against them in 1791 at Fort Recovery (now a state park).

•**METAMORA**, Village; Fulton County; Pop. 556; Area Code 419; Zip Code 43540; NW Ohio; 20 m. W of Toledo, and just S of Michigan state line.

•**MEYERS LAKE**, Village; Stark County; Pop. 222; Area Code 216; Zip Code (Rural); NE central Ohio, near a lake by the same name.

•**MIAMI COUNTY**, W Ohio; Area 407 sq. miles; Pop. 90,381; County seat Troy; Est., January 16, 1807; Named for the Indian tribe which once frequented this region; and whose name signified the idea of "mother"; Cut through by Miami river.

Fields in the river valley here were once so lush that swine filled the air with the scent of anise, on which they fed, and cattle sometimes died of overeating; When the Erie Canal was built through the area, however, much of the herbage and wild game died away. A trip to Cincinnati down this canal through Miami County was an exciting honeymoon 150 year ago.

•**MIAMI RIVER**, River; W Ohio; Flows S approx. 160 miles from Indian Lake in Logan County to confluence with the Ohio River at SW corner of Ohio; Named for the Indian tribe which once lived along the water's edge.

Fields in the river valley are lush and productive. In the early 1800s, the water was diverted to form the Miami and Erie canal which traveled between Lake Erie and the Ohio River at Cincinnati. Today, the river is a transport waterway for the industries of several southwestern Ohio cities.

•**MIAMISBURG**, City; Montomery County; Pop. 15,304; Area Code 513; Zip Code 45342; Elev. 711' SW Ohio; On the Great Miami River, S of Dayton.

Laid out in 1818 by four Pennsylvania Dutchmen, it was known for years as Hole's Station, for *Zachariah Hole*, who had built a blockhouse on the site about 1800. With the establishment in 1840 of the Hoover and Gamble Compnay, manufacturers of reapers, the town's industries got under way.

The production of binders, which the firm later engaged in, led directly to the present-day manufacture of binder twine and cordage. Situated in the heart of the state's best tobacco-growing region, Miamisburg at the turn of the century supported ten tobacco warehouses (only three remain). Here the much-used Zimmer-Spanish tobacco was developed.

Mayor - Robert H. Mears 866-3303
Chamber of Commerce - Market Square Bldg.

•MIDDLEBURG HEIGHTS, City; Cuyahoga County; Pop. 16,219; Area Code 216; Zip Code (With Parma); 15 m. SW of Cleveland in a suburban-residential area.

•MIDDLEFIELD, Village; Geauga County; Pop. 1,997; Area Code 216; Zip Code 44062; NE Ohio; Near the Cuyahoga and Grand Rivers, 35 m. E of Cleveland near several lake recreation areas. Named this for its geographic location between Warren and Painesville.

•MIDDLE POINT, Village; Van Wert County; Pop. 709; Area Code 419; Zip Code 45863; NW Ohio; At the midpoint of a large bend in the Auglaize River, 8 m. E of Van Wert city.

•MIDDLEPORT, Village; Meigs County; Pop. 2,971; Area Code 614; Zip Code 45760; Elev. 564'; SE Ohio; 40 m. SW of Marietta. This port town shoulders with Pomeroy and might be mistaken for a continuation of it, except for the appearance of another business section.

Mayor - Fred L. Hoffman 992-2145

•MIDDLETOWN, City; Butler County; Pop. 43,719; Area Code 513; Zip Code 45042; SW Ohio; On the Miami River, 35 m. N of Cincinnati; Industries include paper and steel products. Named for its location between Dayton and Cincinnati.

In Middletown is the 60 acre Americana Amusement Park, with rides and games attracting many visitors from the Cincinnati metropolitan area.

Industry/Mfg. - Laser products, auto parts, boxes, steel.
Mayor - Stephen Tymcio 234-8811
Daily Newspaper - The Journal, Broad & First
Chamber of Commerce - Manchester Inn

•**MIDLAND**, Village; Clinton County; Pop. 365; Area Code 513; Zip Code 45148; SW Ohio; was once a thriving junction for the two branches of the Ohio and Baltimore Railroads.

•**MIDVALE**, Village; Tuscarawas County; Pop. 654; Area Code 216; Zip Code 44653; NE central Ohio; 6 m. S of New Philadelphia along Sugar Creek; Small farming center.

•**MIDWAY**, Village; Madison County; Pop. 339; Area Code 614; SW central Ohio.

•**MIFFLIN**, Village; Ashland County; Pop. 205; Area Code 216; N central Ohio.

•**MILAN**, Village; Erie and Huron Counties; Pop. 1,564; Area Code 216; Zip Code 44846; Elev. 602'; N Ohio; On a bluff overlooking the Huron River.

As early as 1787 *David Zeisberger* and his Indian followers settled temporarily near Milan. Again in 1804 a Moravian pastor came and established an Indian village which was called Pequotting. White settlers from Connecticut began to arrive a few years later, and the town was laid out in 1816 by *Ebenezer Merry.* By 1824, when enterprising citizens decide to make a shipping port of the village by running a canal to a point on the Huron River three miles away, thus permitting Lake Erie boats to come up to its back door. The *Thomas A. Edison* Birthplace, is a red brick house of two stores. Edison (1847-1931) spent only the first seven years of his life in Milan.

•**MILFORD**, Village; Clermont County; Pop. 5,227; Area Code 513; Zip Code 45150; SW Ohio; 12 m. NE of Cincinnati in an industrial area.

Agriculture - Fruit and varid farming
Industry/Mfg. - Tools and dies, concrete products, boxes
Mayor - Yvonne Haight 831-4192
Chamber of Commerce - 102 Main St.

•**MILFORD CENTER**, Village; Union County; Pop. 764; Area Code 419; Zip Code 43045; W central Ohio.

•**MILLEDGEVILLE**, Village; Fayette County; Pop. 162; Area Code 614; Zip Code 43142; S central Ohio, 38 m. SE of Dayton in a sparsely populated farmland region.

•**MILLER CITY**, Village; Putnam County; Pop. 168; Area Code 419; Zip Code 45864; 20 m. SE of Defiance in NW Ohio; Rural area. Originally named St. Nocholas when first laid out in 1882 for the landowner *Nicohlas Miller* and *Nicholas Noriot.* In 1890 was incorporated as Miller City in honor of Mr. Miller who was the leading resident.

•**MILLERSBURG**, Village; Seat of Holmes County; Pop. 3,247; Area Code 216; Zip Code 44654; Elev. 818'; NE central Ohio; The largest town in Holmes County; Named after *Charles Miller* who settled here in 1824 along with *Adam Johnson.*

Although Millersburg lies upon several slopes, its business section is generally level. Many of the residents are descendants of the so-called "Pennsylvania Dutch" who came here in large numbers after settlement began in 1816. Peculiarities of pronunciation are still evident here; bishop is "beeshop," district is "deestrict." Around the courthouse square are long hitching rails to which the Amish farmers tie their horses while they busy themselves with shopping.

> *Agriculture* - Grain and varied farming
> *Industry/Mfg.* - Dairy products, limestone, oil, coal
> *Mayor* - Robert R. Casey 674-1886
> *Chamber of Commerce* - PO Box 187
> *Community Event(s)* : Holmes County Antique Festival;
>   Annual, October

•**MILLERSPORT**, Village; Fairfield County; Pop. 844; Area Code 513; Zip Code 43046; S central Ohio; On SW tip of Buckeye Lake, in a recreational area; approx. 15 m. N of Lancaster; Camping and water sports facilities.

•**MILLVILLE**, Village; Butler County; Pop. 809; Area Code 513; SW Ohio.

•**MILTON CENTER**, Village; Wood County; Pop. 181; Area Code

419; Zip Code 43541; NW Ohio; Near Bowling Green in a rural area.

•MILTONSBURG, Village; Monroe County; Pop. 109; Area Code 614; SE Ohio.

•MINERVA, Village; Stark & Carroll Counties; Pop. 4,549; Area Code 216; Zip Code 44657; Elev. 1,050'; NE central Ohio on the Sandy River.

Minerva had some settlers from Maryland and Pennsylvania as early as 1802, but not until 1835, when Sandy and Beaver Canal was being built, did it become a town. It was named for the niece of *John Whitacre*, the founder. Minerva has several potteries and serves as a trading center for farmers.

Agriculture - Varied farming
Industry/Mfg. - Dairy products, electronics, tools and
   dies, lumber
Mayor - Walter L. Miller 868-5420
Chamber of Commerce - PO Box 279

•MINERVA PARK, Village; Franklin County; Pop. 1,618; Area Code 614; central Ohio.

•MINGO JUNCTION, City, Jefferson County; Pop. 4,834; Area Code 614; Zip Code 43938; E Ohio; On the Ohio River, just S of Steubenville; Small port.

Mayor - John L. Lewis 535-1511

•MINSTER, Village; Auglaize County; Pop. 2,557; Area Code 419; Zip Code 45864; W Ohio; On E shore of Loramie Lake, 33 m. SW of Lima in a rural-recreational area; Boating, camping and nature trails nearby.

Agriculture - Cattle and varied farming, grain
Industry/Mfg. - Heavy equipment, beverages, printing,
   dairy products
Chamber of Commerce - PO Box 128

•MOGADORE, Village; Portage & Summit Counties; Pop. 4,190; Area Code 216; Zip Code 44260; NE Ohio; Just E of Akron adjacent to a reservoir by the same name; Named after the city of the

157

same name in Morocco, North Africa. Residential suburb, with some industries which have moved here from downtown Akron.

Mayor - William R. Gallagher 628-4896

•**MOHICAN RIVER**, River; Central Ohio; Flows approx. 40 m. S from N Ashland County to confluence with the Walhonding River in Coshocton County; Two forks, fed by the Clear Fork Reservoir and the Charles Mills Reservoir.

Willows fringe this river valley; Grouse, woodpeckers, and Tanagers wing their way through the pine forests surrounding it, and ferns, trailing arbutus, huckleberry and creeping wintergreen grow in profusion during the summer.

•**MONROE COUNTY**, SE Ohio; Area 456 sq. miles; Pop. 17,382; County seat Woodsfield; Est., January 29, 1813; Named for *James Monroe*, President of the U.S. (1817-25), and U.S. Secretary of State when the county was formed; Bordered to E by Ohio River; Hilly region with many recreational facilities in the Wayne National Forest.

•**MONROE**, Village; Warren County; Pop. 4,256; Area Code 513; Zip Code 45050; SW Ohio; Approx. 30 m. N of Cincinnati in the great industrial area of between that city and Dayton. Named after *President James Monroe*.

Mayor - Seth Johnson 539-7374
Chamber of Commerce - PO Box 165

•**MONROEVILLE**, Village; Huron County; Pop. 1,329; Area Code 419; Zip Code 44847; N Ohio; 5 m. W of Norwalk in a fruit and vegetable farming area along the Huron River. Named after *President James Monroe*.

•**MONTEZUMA**, Village; Mercer County; Pop. 200; Area Code 419; Zip Code 45866; W Ohio; On the S shore of Grand Lake St. Marys, a recreational-boating lake; summer population swells this village.

•**MONTGOMERY**, City; Hamilton County; Pop. 10,088; Area Code 513; Zip Code 45242; SW Ohio; 15 m. NE of Cincinnati in a residential area; Some farming nearby produces corn, wheat and oats.

Mayor - Fred P. Young 891-2424
Chamber of Commerce - 7777 Sycamore St.

•MONTGOMERY COUNTY, SW Ohio; Area 459 sq. miles; Pop. 571,697; County seat Dayton; Est., March 24, 1803; Named for *Richard Montgomery*, Revolutionary War general, killed in Quebec in 1775; Site of part of the old Erie Canal along the Miami River.

•MONTPELIER, Village; Williams County; Pop. 4,431; Area Code 419; Zip Code 43543; Elev. 860'; 50 m. W of Toledo in NW Ohio on the St. Joseph River; Near Interstate Hwy 80. Stockraising area.

Mayor - David M. Anderson 485-5015
Chamber of Commerce - 302 W. Main St.

•MORAINE, City; Montgomery County; Pop. 5,325; Area Code 513; 5 m. S of Dayton in SW Ohio.

•MORELAND HILLS, Village; Cuyahoga County; Pop. 3,083; Area Code 216; Zip Code (with Cleveland Heights); 20 m. SE of Cleveland, in the residential outskirts of the Cleveland metropolitan area.

•MORGAN COUNTY, SE Ohio; Area 420 sq. miles; Pop. 14,241; County seat McConnelsville; Est., December 20, 1817; Named for *Daniel Morgan*, French and Indian War soldier and Revolutionary War general in Virginia; Muskingum River flows S through this sparsely populated county with some recreational areas.

•MORRAL, Village; Marion County; Pop. 454; Area Code 614; Zip Code 43337; Approx. 14 m. NW of Marion in a farming area in central Ohio. Named after *Samuel Morral* who owned the land here. The Toledo and Columbus Railroad ran through here at one time.

•MORRISTOWN, Village; Belmont County; Pop. 463; Area Code

614; Zip Code 43759; Elev. 1,510; E Ohio; Named after *Duncan Morrison* who was an early settler, first postmaster and Justice of the Peace. *William Chapline* and *John Zane* laid out the place in 1802.

•MORROW COUNTY, Central Ohio; Area 403 sq. miles; Pop. 26,480; County seat Mount Gilead; Est., February 24, 1848; Named for *Jeremiah Morrow*, ninth governor of Ohio (1822-26); Rolling farmlands.

•MORROW, Village; Warren County; Pop. 1,254; Area Code 513; Zip Code 45152; Elev. 640'; SW Ohio; Settled in 1844 and named for *Jeremiah Morrow*, Governor of Ohio from 1822 to 1826.

Rock quarries are in the vicinity. Steep hills and dense woods surround this pleasant little village which stands on the low flood plain of the Little Miami River.

•MOSCOW, Village; Clermont County; Pop. 324; Area Code 513; Zip Code 45153; Elev. 499'; SW Ohio; On the Ohio River; Was one of the first stations on the Underground Railroad.

It was a busy shipping point during the Reconstruction Period, and about 1900 produced large quantities of brandy. Prohibition, the decline of river traffic, and the growth of Cincinnati took most of the life out of the town. What was left was despoiled by the flood of 1937.

•MOSQUITO CREEK, Lake; Reservoir, NE Ohio; 10 m. N of Warren; Approx. 15 m. long and 2 m. wide; Surrounded by a 11,840 acre state park, with camping and water sports facilities; Formed by a damming of the Mosquito Creek.

•MOUND CITY GROUP, NATIONAL MONUMENT, Ross County; Southern Ohio; Authorized 1923; Occupies 67.50 acres; Prehistoric mounds.
•MOUNT BLANCHARD, Village; Hancock County; Pop. 492; Area Code 419; Zip Code 45867; 12 m. S of Findlay along east bank of the Blanchard River in NW Ohio; Farming community. Named for the Blanchard River. *Asa M. Lake* laid out the place in 1830

•MOUNT CORY, Village; Hancock County; Pop. 276; Area Code

419; Zip Code 45868; NW central Ohio; On elevated farmlands approx. 14 m. SW of Findlay.

•MOUNT EATON, Village; Wayne County; Pop. 289; Area Code 216; Zip Code 44669; NE central Ohio; 15 m. SW of Massillon in a hilly area.

•MOUNT GILEAD, Village; Seat of Morrow County; Pop. 2,911; Area Code 614; Zip Code 43338; Elev. 1,083'; was settled in 1817 by *Lewis and Ralph Hardenbrook.* Their farm was in the center of what was probably the largest tulip-tree forest in the state. The settlement was called Whetstone until 1824, when it was renamed Youngstown. In 1832 the name was changed again, this time by the Ohio legislature, to honor Mount Gilead, Virginia.

Agriculture - Grain, cattle and varied farming
Industry/Mfg. - Auto bodies, boxes, plastics, electronics
Mayor - Fred Wieland 946-3926
Chamber of Commerce - Civic Center, West Center St.
Community Event(s) : National Hunting and Fishing Day; Annual, September, Old Fashioned Days; Annual, October

•MOUNT HEALTHY, City; Hamilton County; Pop. 7,562; Area Code 513; Zip Code 45231; SW Ohio; 14 m. N of Cincinnati surrounding a large hill by the same name; Residential suburb.

Mayor - Howard G. Doerger 931-8840

•MOUNT ORAB, Village; Brown County; Pop. 1,573; Area Code 513; Zip Code 45154; SW Ohio; In a hilly region near Lake Grant; Farming and recreation.

•MOUNT PLEASANT, Village; Jefferson County; Pop. 616; Area Code 614; Zip Code 43939; E Ohio; 20 m. SW of Steubenville in one of the earliest-settled regions of Ohio; Site of an old Quaker meeting house.

•MOUNT STERLING, Village; Madison County; Pop. 1,623; Area Code 513; Zip Code 43149; SW central Ohio; On Deer Creek; 23 m. SW of Columbus.

Agriculture - Varied farming
Industry/Mfg. - Woolen and cotton goods, food
    packing
Chamber of Commerce - PO Box 62

•**MOUNT VERNON**, City; Seat of Knox County; Pop. 14,380; Area Code 614; Zip Code 43050; 35 m. NE of Columbus in central Ohio on the Kokosing River.

In 1805, the place was laid out by *Benjamin Butler, Joseph Walker*, and *Thomas Patterson*. These three men all hailed from Virginia in *George Washington's* county and named it after his hometown in Virginia. In 1897 a steel mill was built here by *Jacob Coxey*.

John Chapman, better known as *Johnny Appleseed*, owned three lots of land here. It is also the home of *Daniel Ducatur Emmett* (1815-1904), songwriter, best known as the author of "Dixie" and "Old Dan Tucker" which he wrote here at the age of 15.

Today the area is still primarily agricultural with petroleum production as an active industry.

Agriculture - Grain, cattle, and varied farming
Industry/Mfg. - Auto parts, bottles, windows, electronics, steel
Higher Education - Mt. Vernon Nazarene College
Mayor - Claude G. Schlosser 397-3917
Daily Newspaper - The News, PO Box 791
Chamber of Commerce - 51 Public Square, Joseph W. Street

•**MOUNT VICTORY**, Village; Hardin County; Pop. 667; Area Code 419; Zip Code 43340; NW central Ohio; 11 m. SE of Kenton among hilly farmlands.

•**MOWRYSTOWN**, Village; Highland County; Pop. 475; Area Code 614; Zip Code 46155; S central Ohio; 18 m. SW of Hillsboro in a quiet, sparsely populated farming area producing vegetables.

•**MUNROE FALLS**, Village; Summit County; Pop. 4,731; Area Code 216; Zip Code 44262; NE central Ohio; Just NE of Akron along the Cuyahoga river; Suburban.

Mayor - Gerald L. Hupp 688-7491

•**MURRAY CITY**, Village; Hocking County; Pop. 579; Area Code 614; Zip Code 43144; S central Ohio; In central Wayne National Forest, serving as a trading post for the recreational community.

•**MUSKINGUM COUNTY**, SE central Ohio; Area 667 sq. miles; Pop. 83,340; County seat Zanesville; Est., January 7, 1804; Named for the Muskingum River, which flows through this region, an Indian word meaning "near the river;" Coal-producing region; Ceramics and tile are also produced, an industry originating from the rich clay deposits along the Muskingum and Licking Rivers here.

•**MUSKINGUM RIVER**, River; E Ohio; Flows S and SE approx. 120 miles from the confluence of the Walhonding and Tuscarawas Rivers in Coshocton County to the Ohio River at Marietta.

Fertile fields lie near the river, while hills rise, often abruptly, from the floor of the river valley. Several flowering plants and sycamore trees bend gently along the water's edge. Barges transport industrial goods and ores down the river, which is navigable for 90 miles from its mouth, and was once the major transport route in the state. Settlers saw the first steamboat on the Muskingum on January 9, 1824, when the Rufus Putnam steamed up to what is now Zanesville. Several locks in the river control flooding and allow easier passage today. Fields of corn, melons, and tomatoes also spread out across the river bottom in summer.

Muskingum River Parkway, a 120 acre stretch of land along 80 miles of the River, has been set aside as a state park.

•**MUTUAL**, Village; Champaign County; Pop. 159; Area Code 513; W central Ohio; 6 m. E of Urbana; Grain farming trade center.

•**NAPOLEON**, City; Seat of Henry County; Pop. 8,614; Area Code 419; Zip Code 43545; Elev. 689'; NW Ohio.

Napoleon is the scene of an annual Schuetzenfest or target shooting contest. The town was named with Gallic pleasantry by a small group of Frenchmen who settled here in the midst of a preponderantly German population.

> *Agriculture* - Grain and varied farming
> *Industry/Mfg.* - Dairy products, auto parts, clay
> products

Mayor - Robert G. Heft 592-4010
Daily Newspaper - The Northwest-Signal, East Riverview,
    PO Box 567
Chamber of Commerce - 611 N. Perry St.

•NASHVILLE, Village; Holmes County; Pop. 211; Area Code
216; Zip Code 44661; NE central Ohio; 17 m. SW of Wooster in a
rural area; Named for the Tennessee city.

•NAVARRE, Village; Stark County; Pop. 1,343; Area Code 216;
Zip Code 44662; Elev. 940'; NE Ohio; Originally known as
Bethlehem in 1834 upon its being laid out. Later, named in honor
of *King Henry IV* of France and Navarre by the French speaking
wife of *James Duncan.*
    During the 1830's and 1840's the town had a number of dry
goods stores, grain warehouses, flour mills, and taverns;
farmers within a radius of 30 miles brought their produce here for
shipment to other points, principally by the Ohio and Erie Canal.

•NELLIE, Village; Coshocton County; Pop. 150; Area Code 614;
Zip Code (Rural); On the Walhonding River; aprox. 14 m. NW of
Coshocton city; Farmer community.

•NELSONVILLE, City; Athens County; Pop. 4,567; Area Code
614; Zip Code 45764; Elev. 1,044'; S Ohio; Originally known as
Englishtown, the town changed its name in 1824 to honor *Daniel
Nelson,* the settlement's most enterprising citizen.
    With completion of the Hocking Canal through the valley in
1841 and the Hocking Valley Railroad in 1869, shafts were sunk to
the nearby coal beds.

Mayor - Ralph Davis 753-1511
Chamber of Commerce - Box 276
Community Event(s) : Parade of the Hills; Annual,
    August

•NEVADA, Village; Wyandot County; Pop. 945; Area Code 419;
Zip Code 44849; NW central Ohio; 10 m. W of Bucyrus in a rich
farming area. Named in 1852 for the boundary of the Sierra
Nevada Mountains.

•NEVILLE, Village; Clermont County; Pop. 142; Area Code 513;
Zip Code 45156; Elev. 500'; SW Ohio; Founded in 1808; Named for

a Virginia officer in the Revolutionary War who was given 1,400 acres of land here; It was devastated by the 1937 Ohio River floods.

•NEW ALBANY, Village; Franklin County; Pop. 409; Area Code 614; Zip Code 43054; Central Ohio; 13 m. NE of Columbus on the outskirts of a vast farming region. Named for Albany, New York.

•NEW ALEXANDRIA, Village; Jefferson County; Pop. 410; Area Code 614; E Ohio.

•NEWARK, City; Seat of Licking County; Pop. 41,200; Area Code 614; Zip Code 43055; Elev. 836'; 35 m. E of Columbus where the North and Soth Forks of the Licking Rivers merge in central Ohio; Est., in 1802 by *General William Schenck,* the settlement was named after a New Jersey community.

For several years after it was platted, Newark grew slowly. By 1816, several taverns, log cabins and a few more elegant houses had sprung up on the city's wide streets. Although the Mary Ann charcoal furnace had already began producing iron ingots that year, it was not until 1832, when the Newark canal was completed, that the city began to grow rapidly. The town's population tripled within the next decade. In the early 1850's, three different railroad companies laid their tracks through Newark, further increasing its industrial importance. Industry was doing well in Newark in the late 1840's and early 1850's but the townspeople were having problems. In 1849 and 1854, cholera epidemics decimated much of the town's population. A large fire also destroyed some of the town in 1856. After the Civil War, more railroads came to Newark and its size continued to grow steadily. The economic depression of the 1930's hit the city hard.

Outside Newark is the site of a large earthwork of prehistoric mound builders. *Johnny Clem,* known in folklore as "the drummer boy of Shiloh," was a nine-year-old Newark resident when he ran away to fight in the Civil War.

Industry/Mfg. - Sports equipment, clay products, electronics, plastics, gas and oil
Mayor - Richard E. Baker 349-7185
Daily Newspaper - The Advocate, 25 W. Main Street
Chamber of Commerce - PO Box 702

•NEW ATHENS, Village; Harrison County; Pop. 440; Area Code 614; Zip Code 43981; E central Ohio; 7 m. S of Cadiz in a coal mining area.

•NEW BAVARIA, Village; Henry County; Pop. 135; Area Code 419; Zip Code 43548; NW central Ohio; 15 m. SE of Defiance in a farming area first settled by German immigrants.

•NEW BLOOMINGTON, Village; Marion County; Pop. 303; Area Code 614; Zip Code 43341; N central Ohio; On the Scioto River in the rich farmlands W of Marion.

•NEW BOSTON, Village; Scioto County; Pop. 3,188; Area Code 614; Zip Code 45662; S Ohio; On the Ohio River, 5 m. E of Portsmouth; Water power facilities and a port keep this town busy.

•NEW BREMEN, Village; Auglaize County; Pop. 2,393; Area Code 419; Zip Code 45869; W central Ohio; On the St. Marys River, between the recreational areas at Grand Lake and at Lake Loramie.

•NEWBURGH HEIGHTS, Village; Cuyahoga County; Pop. 2,678; Area Code 216; Zip Code 441–; NE Ohio; Just S of downtown Cleveland off the Willow Freeway (U.S.77); Bordered to W by the Cuyahoga River; Suburb, with some industries.

Mayor - Edmund D. Nowak 641-4650

•NEW CARLISLE, City; Clark County; Pop. 6,498; Area Code 513; Zip Code 45344; W central Ohio; 12 m. W of Springfield in a large farming district.

Agriculture - Varied farming
Mayor - Phil Cable 845-9493
Chamber of Commerce - PO Box 23

•NEWCOMERSTOWN, Village; Tuscarawas County; Pop. 3,986; Area Code 614; Zip Code 43832; Elev. 849'; E Ohio; On the site of the old Delaware capital of Gekelemukpechunk, lies near the Tuscarawas River.

It was to this place that the second wife of *Chief Eagle Feather* called "the newcomer" by his first wife, *Mary Harris,*

166

fled after circumstantial evidence pointed to her guilt in his murder. Settled in 1815 by the *Neighbor brothers* from New Jersey, it was called Neighbor Town for a time, but is said to have taken its final name from "the newcomer."

Agriculture - Varied farming
Industry/Mfg. - Bricks, tools and dies, plastics
Mayor - Robert G. Hall 498-6313
Chamber of Commerce - 123 N. Bridge St.

•**NEW CONCORD**, Village; Muskingum County; Pop. 1,860; Area Code 614; Zip Code 43762; 8 m. W of Cambridge in SE central Ohio; *Astronaut John H. Glenn, Jr.* spent most of his boyhood here.

Agriculture - Grain, cattle and vaired farming
Industry/Mfg. - Dairy products, quarrying
Higher Education - Muskingum College
Chamber of Commerce - W. Main St.

•**NEW HOLLAND**, Village; Fayette and Pickawy Counties; Pop. 783; Area Code 614; Zip Code 43145; 32 m. SW of Columbus in S central Ohio; Cannery and elevator here package the grains and vegetables grown on the surrounding farms.

Agriculture - Varied farming
Industry/Mfg. - Food packing, grain processing

•**NEW KNOXVILLE**, Village; Auglaize County; Pop. 760; Area Code 419; Zip Code 45871; W central Ohio; 14 m. SW of Wapakoneta in a farming area.

•**NEW LEBANON**, Village; Montgomery County; Pop. 4,501; Area Code 513; Zip Code 45345; Elev. 913'; 10 m. W of Dayton in SW Ohio; was a Dunkard village, reflects the character of its German-American citizens whose substantial homes are built close to the ground. It is difficult to associate this peaceful settlement with anything like rowdiness, but according to local histories there sprang up in New Lebanon and in Johnsville, during post-Civil War days, gangs of ruffians who fought constantly. A sensational murder and the burning of New Lebanon in 1876 are attributed to these warring gangs.

Mayor - Bernard W. Falldorf 687-1341

•NEW LEXINGTON, Village; Perry County Seat; Pop. 5,179; Area Code 614; Zip Code 43764; SE central Ohio; 19 m. SW of Zanesville. For over 150 years, coal has been mined in sites around New Lexington. It is also an agricultural center.

> *Agriculture* - Grain, cattle and varied farming
> *Industry/Mfg.* - Truck parts, dairy products, coal, oil, gas
> *Mayor* - Ottis Huffman 342-1633
> *Chamber of Commerce* - PO Box 104

•NEW LONDON, Village; Huron County; Pop. 2,449; Area Code 216; Zip Code 44851; 45 m. SW of Cleveland near the Vermillion River in N central Ohio.

This town, set amidst flat farmlands, is important in its manufacture of uniforms, building materials, truck and auto parts, and metal and rubber products. The newspaper, *Firelands Farmer* is distributed to local farmers.

> *Agriculture* - Varied farming
> *Industry/Mfg.* - Clothing, concrete, lumber, electronics, rubber products

•NEW MADISON, Village; Darke County; Pop. 1,008; Area Code 513; Zip Code 45346; W Ohio; 11 m. S of Greenville in a corn farming area.

•NEW MIAMI, Village; Butler County; Pop. 2,980; Area Code 513; E Ohio.

> *Mayor* - Eugene Mize 892-1141

•NEW MIDDLETOWN, Village; Mahoning County; Pop. 2,195; Area Code 216; Zip Code 4442; 12 m. SE of Youngstown in the great steel mill area near the Mahoning River valley in NE Ohio.

•NEW PARIS, Village; Preble County; Pop. 1,709; Area Code 513; Zip Code 45347; SW Ohio; 8 m. E of Richmond, Indiana; Farm trading center.

•NEW PHILADELPHIA, City; Seat of Tuscarawas County; Pop. 16,883; Area Code 614; Zip Code 44663; Elev. 901; E Ohio; Founded by *John Kinisely* in 1804.

From its earliest days the city has shown the influence of Moravian missionaries and of the Swiss-German immigrants from Pennsylvania.

Agriculture - Varied farming
Industry/Mfg. - Cement and clay products
Mayor - David Knisely 364-4491
Daily Newspaper - The Times-Reporter, 629, Wabash Ave.,
PO Box 667

•**NEW RICHMOND**, Village; Clermont County; Pop. 2,769; Area Code 513; Zip Code 45157; Elev. 510'; SW Ohio; is a union of two villages, one of which, Susanna, was planned and laid out by *Thomas Ashburn* in 1816.

In the 1837 flood, not a home, store, or factory escaped severe damage. In spite of repeated disasters, the people come back and clean up.

Mayor - Arthur H. Galea 553-4684

•**NEW RIEGEL**, Village; Seneca County; Pop. 329; Area Code 419; Zip Code 44853; N central Ohio; 10 m. SW of Tiffin in a rural area.

•**NEW ROME**, Village; Franklin County; Pop. 63; Area Code 614; Zip Code (Rural); Central Ohio; Farm trading center, 8 m. W of Columbus city center.

•**NEW STRAITSVILLE**, Village; Perry County; Pop. 937; Area Code 614; Zip Code 43766; Elev. 840'; SE central Ohio; 30 m. SE of Lancaster in a former coal mining area; central Wayne National Forest.

This village was laid out in 1870 by a mining company, and at one time had 2,500 residents. In 1884, striking miners set fire to the mine, and the subterranean flames may continue to burn for several hundred years unless abatement plans are successful.

•**NEWTON FALLS**, City; Trumbull County; Pop. 4,960; Area Code 216; Zip Code 44444; NE Ohio; On the Mahoning River, 10 m. W of Warren.

Mayor - Joseph J. Layshock 872-0806
Chamber of Commerce - PO Box 268

•**NEWTONSVILLE**, Village; Clermont County; Pop. 434; Area Code 513; Zip Code 45158; SW Ohio; 30 m. E of Cincinnati in a rural area.

•**NEWTOWN**, Village; Hamilton County; Pop. 1,817; Area Code 513; Zip Code 45244; SW Ohio; Just E of Cincinnati in the hilly suburban area surrounding that city.

•**NEW VIENNA**, Village; Clinton County; Pop. 1,133; Area Code 513; Zip Code 45159; SW central Ohio; 13 m. SE of Wilmington.

•**NEW WASHINGTON**, Village; Crawford County; Pop. 1,213; Area Code 419; Zip Code 44854; N central Ohio; 20 m. NW of Mansfield in a quiet farming area.

> *Agriculture* - Cattle, grain and varied farming
> *Industry/Mfg.* - Animal feed, dairy products, aluminum

•**NEW WATERFORD**, Village; Columbiana County; Pop. 1,314; Area Code 216; Zip Code 44445; E Ohio; 18 m. E of Salem, near the Pennsylvania border

•**NEW WESTON**, Village; Darke County; Pop. 184; Area Code 513; Zip Code 45348; W Ohio; 20 m. N of Greenville.

•**NEY**, Village; Defiance County; Pop. 379; Area Code 419; Zip Code 43649; NW Ohio; 10 m. NW of city of Defiance, in a rural area.

•**NILES**, City; Trumball County; Pop. 23,088; Area Code 216; Zip Code 44446; Elev. 912'; Just S of Warren in NE central Ohio.

Another iron and steel city, Niles was settled in 1806 by *James Heaton*, builder of the first gristmill and blast furnace in the vicinity. It was known as Heaton's Furnace until 1834, when it was named Nilestown for a Baltimore newspaper editor whom Heaton admired. Later the postmaster shortened the name.

William McKinley, twenty-fifth President, was born and raised here in a home preserved on Main Street.

> *Agriculture* - Truck farming
> *Industry/Mfg.* - Electronics, dairy products, steel
>   chemicals

170

Mayor - Arthur M. Doutt 652-3415
Daily Newspaper - The Times, 35 W. State St.
Chamber of Commerce - 44 S. Main

•**NOBLE COUNTY**, SE Ohio; Area 398 sq. miles; Pop. 11,310; County seat Caldwell; Est., March 11, 1851; Named for *James and Warren P. Noble,* early settlers here.

•**NORTH BALTIMORE**, Village; Wood County; Pop. 3,127; Area Code 419; Zip Code 45872; NW Ohio; 20 m. S of Bowling Green in a farming area. This village was once an active oil and gas drilling center. Few wells remain today, however.

Agriculture - Varied farming
Industry/Mfg. - Machine shop, quarrying, iron castings,
    rubber products, oil
Mayor - John W. Sterling 257-2394
Chamber of Commerce - 205 W. Maple St.

•**NORTH BEND**, Village; Hamilton County; Pop. 546; Area Code 513; Zip Code 45052; Elev. 510'; SW Ohio; On a bend in the Ohio River, 10 m. W of Cincinnati. Named after the northernmost bend in the Ohio River.

When *John Cleves Symond* founded this village in 1789, it became the fourth settlement in Ohio. It was the birthplace of *Benjamin Harrison,* twenty-third President (1889-93), grandson of *William H. Harrison,* who purchased a log and frame house here in the early nineteenth century.

•**NORTH BENTON**, Village; Mahoning County; Pop. (Rural); Area Code 216; Zip Code 44449; NE Ohio.

This is the site of the grave of *Chester Bedell,* marked by a life-size bronze male figure crushing under foot a scroll titled Superstition, and raising high another scroll inscribed Universal Mental Liberty. About *Charles Bedell* and his grave fantastic stories have circulated. Bedell (d. 1908) was the village agnostic, with a fierce hatred of ignorance and superstitution. Named after *Thomas Hart Benton.* North was added to Benton to differentiate it from two other Bentons in Ohio.

•**NORTH CANTON**, City; Stark County; Pop. 14,228; Area Code 216; Zip Code 447–; NE central Ohio; Just N of city of Canton;

171

Site of Walsh College; Suburban-residential, with some of the same industries as Canton.

Mayor - Dennis O. Grady 499-3464
Chamber of Commerce - 121 S. Main St.

•**NORTH COLLEGE HILL**, City; Hamilton County; Pop. 10,990; Area Code 513; Zip Code 45239; Elev. 712'; 10 m. N of Cincinnati in SW Ohio; Suburban.

The poets *Alice and Phoebe Cary* lived here as young girls. Today, their former home is a historic site.

Mayor - Joseph G. Binder 521-7413

•**NORTH FAIRFIELD**, Village; Huron County; Pop. 525; Area Code 419; Zip Code 44855; N central Ohio; Rural area, approx. 11 m. S of Norwalk.

•**NORTHFIELD**, Village; Summit County; Pop. 3,913; Area Code 216; Zip Code 44067; 20 m. S of Cleveland in NE Ohio; This growing residential area is set near Brandywine Falls, where a stream rushes over a shelf of rocks to a ledge 20 feet below. The first earlier settlers were from Massachusetts and named it after their hometown.

Mayor - N. Arch Milani- 467 7139

•**NORTH HAMPTON**, Village; Clark County; Pop. 421; Area Code 513; Zip Code 45349; W central Ohio; Rural farming center.

•**NORTH KINGSVILLE**, Village; Ashtabula County; Pop. 2,939; Area Code 216; Zip Code 44068; NE Ohio; Just S of the Lake Erie shoreline; Suburban.

•**NORTH LEWISBURG**, Village; Champaign County; Pop. 1,072; Area Code 513; Zip Code 43060; W central Ohio; Approx. 20 m. NE of Urbana.

•**NORTH OLMSTED**, City; Cuyahoga County; Pop. 36,486; Area Code 216; Zip Code 44070; NE Ohio; 15 m. W of Cleveland, just S of the Lake Erie shoreline; Suburban.

•**NORTH PERRY**, Village; Lake County; Pop. 897; Area Code

216; Zip Code (with Perry); NE Ohio, on Lake Erie shoreline 20 m. W of Ashtabula.

•NORTH RANDALL, Village; Cuyahoga County; Pop. 1,054; Area Code 216; Zip Code (with Randall); NE Ohio; Suburb of Cleveland.

•NORTH RIDGEVILLE, City; Lorain County; Pop. 21,522; Area Code 216; Zip Code 44039; N Ohio; N suburb of Elyria; Residential.

•NORTH ROBINSON, Village; Crawford County; Pop. 302; Area Code 419; Zip Code 44856; N central Ohio; 8 m. E of Bucyrus in a farming region.

•NORTH ROYALTON, City; Cuyahoga County; Pop. 17,671; Area Code 216; Zip Code 44133; NE Ohio; 20 m. S of Cleveland in a growing residential area.

•NORTH STAR, Village; Darke County; Pop. 254; Area Code 513; Zip Code 45350; Elev. 1,006'; 15 m. N of Greenville in W Ohio; Farming area.
     John Houston and *Heronimus Star* founded this town in 1844. Nearby is *Annie Oakley's* birthplace, a weatherboarded log cabin. She was an expert markswoman even as a child and earned money by killing game in this region.

•NORTHWOOD, Village; Wood County; Pop. 5,494; Area Code 419; Zip Code (with Toledo); NW Ohio; Across the Maumee River from Toledo in a residential area.

     Mayor - John R. Hageman- 693 9328

•NORTON, City; Summit County; Pop. 12,242; Area Code 216; Zip Code 44203; NE central Ohio; Residential suburb, just S of Akron and Barberton.

     Mayor - Walter C. Peterman- 825 7815

•NORWALK, City; Seat of Huron County; Pop. 14,358; Area Code 216; Zip Code 44857; Elev. 719'; N central Ohio; Founded in 1816 by *Platt Benedict*.
     It was named for the Connecticut town because many of its

settlers left that State to make homes here on their "Firelands" grants. During the 1830's and 1840's it ws widely known for its Norwalk Academy.

Agriculture -Truck farming
Daily Newspaper -The Reflector- 61 E. Monroe
Mayor - Walter C. Goodsite- 668 4159

•NORWICH, Village; Muskingum County; Pop. 170; Area Code 614; Zip Code 43767; Elev. 985'; ll m. NE of Zanesville in SE Ohio. Named by *Willie Harper* for the place where his gun was made - Norwich, England. He was originally going to name the town Cambridge and Zanesville.

The ravine behind the Presbyterian church in town is called Stumpy Hollow. In the nineteenth century, persons walking through the hollow at night allegedly encountered a headless creature which, they reported, left them speechless.

•NORWOOD, City; Hamilton County; Pop. 26,342; Area Code 513; Zip Code 452 + zone; SW Ohio; surrounded by the city of Cincinnati.

Originally known as Sharpsburg, and named after *John Sharp* an original resident. Current name given when it became a village in 1888. Growth of the railroads near the turn of the century spurred growth.

Mayor - Donald E. Prues- 631 2700

•OAK HARBOR, Village; Ottawa County; Pop. 2,678; Area Code 419; Zip Code 43449; N Ohio; On the Portage River, 11 m. W of Port Clinton.

Agriculture -Varied farming
Industry/Mfg. - Concrete products, food packing.
Mayor - William Bloom- 898 5561

•OAK HILL, Village; Jackson County; Pop. 1,713; Area Code 614; Zip Code 45656; 12 m. S of the city of Jackson, near the recreational area at Jackson Lake.

•OAKWOOD, City; Montgomery County; Pop. 9,372; Area Code 513; Zip Code (with Dayton); SW central Ohio; A suburb of Dayton in the industrial metropolitan area.

Mayor - C. F. Reidmuller- 298 0600

•OAKWOOD, Village; Cuyahoga County; Pop. 3,786; Area Code 216; Zip Code (with Cleveland); 15 m. SE of Cleveland in NE Ohio. Residential suburb.

•OAKWOOD, Village; Paulding County; Pop. 886; Area Code 419; Zip Code 45873; NW Ohio; On the Blanchard River, 15 m. S of Defiance.

•OBERLIN, City; Lorain County; Pop. 8,660; Area Code 216; Zip Code 44074; N Ohio; 20 m. SW of Cleveland. Has a primarily intellectual tradition. Incorporated: village 1846 and city 1960.

It was founded in 1832 by *Phillip P. Steward* and *Rev. John L. Shipward,* a Presbyterian minister from Elyria, Ohio. Oberlin Collegiate Institute was Est., (1834) and later became a college (circa 1851). Named after *Rev. Johann Friedrich Oberlin* it was one of the first colleges to admit Black students.

Charles Martin Hall (developer of a unique aluminum processing technique) was an Oberlin graduate.

It was also the home of the Anti-Saloon League (1893).

Higher Education -Oberlin College
Mayor - Carl Bruening- 775 1531

•OBETZ, Village; Franklin County; Pop. 3,095; Area Code 614; central Ohio.

Mayor - Ralph Hubner- 491 1080

•OCTA, Village; Fayette County; Pop. 74; Area Code 614; Zip Code (Rural); S central Ohio; community of farm families.

•OHIO CITY, Village; Van Wert County; Pop. 881; Area Code 419; Zip Code 45874; NW Ohio; 10 m. S of the city of Van Wert in a rural area.

•OHIO RIVER, River; starts in Pennsylvania by Pittsburgh and is formed by the Monogahelco and Allegheney Rivers. The river flows W and SW to form the boundaries of Ohio, West Virginia, Kentucky, Indiana and Illinois. The river empties in the Mississippi River near Cairo, Illinois in S Illinois.

Belle Riviere the French called it, "the beautiful river." It may have been so in 1670, when *LaSalle* is said to have claimed its discovery, and the French and English wrestled for it because of its strategic importance. The English finally won it in 1763, only to surrender it to the Americans 20 years later. With the passing of the Ordinance of 1787 part of the territory north of the river was opened to settlement; by overland trails and the Ohio River the Northwest Territory was invaded. Today, the Ohio seems majestic rather than beautiful as it sweeps around jutting headlands, through fertile bottoms, past scores of towns and cities and hundreds of sleepy villages, on its 967-mile journey from the confluence of the Allegheny and Monongahela Rivers at Pittsburgh to its junction with the Mississippi at Cairo, Illinois.

The Ohio is one of the great storied rivers of the United States. The routes of *Braddock, Washington, Boone, and Forbes* met it somewhere, and it was crossed by Zane's and Hannan's Traces and many Indian trails. North of its quiet shores the Indians made strenuous but futile efforts to stop the westward push of the white man. Strange characters drifted down its waters; *Johnny Appleseed,* the gentle planter of apple trees, and profane *Mike Fink,* the mighty riverman. *Aaron Burr* wove the subtle web of conspiracy about Blennerhassett Island. Up and down the river, Underground Railroad stations shunted hundreds of runaway Negroes towards Canada. *Morgan,* the Confederate raider, crossed it in 1863 and brought the Civil War to the back door of Indiana and Ohio. At various times, but especially in 1884, 1913, and 1937, raging floods brought destruction and death to dozens of towns and cities along the Ohio. *Pare Lorenz* has visited the floods in all their beauty and terror in his documentary film, The River.

•OLD WASHINGTON, Village; Guernsey County; Pop. 279; Area Code 614; Zip Code 43768; Elev. 1,010; E Ohio; formerly a rival of Cambridge but now content to stage the annual Guernsey County Fair. In July 1863, *General John Morgan,* the Confederate raider then being chased across Ohio by Union troops, stopped here for a quick snack. He left in a hurry but might just as well have stayed, since he was forced to surrender a few days later.

•OLENTANGY RIVER, River; Central Ohio; Flows approx. 80 m. from point in S Crawford County through fertile farmlands in central Ohio to confluence with the Scioto River at Columbus,; Widened by a dam at Delaware Reservoir, Delaware County.

•OLMSTED FALLS, City; Cuyahoga County; Pop. 5,868; Area

Code 216; Zip Code 44138; NE Ohio; 15 m. SW of Cleveland along Rocky Creek; Residential area, once a farming community.

Mayor - William P. Mahoney- 235 5550

•ONTARIO, Village; Richland County; Pop. 4,123; Area Code 419; Zip Code 44862; N central Ohio; Just W of Mansfield; Small manufactures include steel machinery, but the town serves mainly as a trade center for the many grain, fruit and vegetable farms in the area.

*Agriculture -*Varied Farming
Mayor - Charles K. Hellinger- 525 3818

•ORANGE, Village; Cuyahoga County; Pop. 2,376; Area Code 216; Zip Code (with Cleveland); Suburban-residential.

•ORANGEVILLE, Village; Trumbull County; Pop. 223; Area Code 216; Zip Code 44453; NE Ohio; On the Shenango River Reservoir, 25 m. NE of Warren on the Pennsylvania state line.

•OREGON, City; Lucas County; Pop. 18,675; Area Code 419; Zip Code 436 + zone; 10 m. E of Toledo in NW Ohio, just S of Maumee Bay in a fruit raising and residential area.

Mayor - Stephen J. Toth- 697 7045

•ORIENT, Village; Pickaway County; Pop. 283; Area Code 614; Zip Code 43146; On Darby Creek, 16 m. SW of Columbus in a truck farming area.

•ORRVILLE, City; Wayne County; Pop. 7,511; Area Code 216; Zip Code 44667; 44 m. S of Cleveland in NE central Ohio; In the large steel and metal manufacturing belt of Ohio.

Mayor - Howard E. Wade- 683 8715

•ORWELL, Village; Ashtabula County; Pop. 1,067; Area Code 216; Zip Code 44075; NE Ohio; 25 m. S of Ashtabula city.

•OSGOOD, Village; Darke County; Pop. 306; Area Code 513; Zip Code 45361; W Ohio; 25 m. NE of Greenville in a vast agricultureal region.

177

•OSTRANDER, Village; Delaware County; Pop. 397; Area Code 614; Zip Code 43061; Central Ohio; On the Scioto River about 20 m. N of Columbus city center; Rural.

•OTTAWA, Village; Seat of Putnam County; Pop. 3,874; Area Code 419; Zip Code 45875; Elev. 729'; NW Ohio; 20 m. N of Lime.
   The village was Est. in 1833, shortly after the last of the Ottawa Indians had been removed to their western reservations. At that time it was known as Tawa Town, for an Ottawa chief. When the town was platted, in 1834, it became Ottawa.

Agriculture -Grain and varied farming
Industry/Mfg. - Electronics, food packing, quarrying.
Mayor - Louis H. Macke- 523 5020

•OTTAWA COUNTY, N Ohio; Area 258 sq. miles; Pop. 40,076; County seat Port Clinton; Est., March 6, 1840; Named for the Indian tribe which once lived here, and also gave its name to a river in this state; Bordered to E by Lake Erie includes a large peninsula and several islands extending into the Great Lake; Fruit raising, gypsum mining and resort area; Flat stretches of fertile farmlands and marshes mark this county.

•OTTAWA HILLS, Village; Lucas County; Pop. 4,065; Area Code 419; NW Ohio.

Mayor - Keith Wilson- 536 1111

•OTTOVILLE, Village; Putnam County; Pop. 833; Area Code 419; Zip Code 45876; NW Ohio; On the Little Auglaize River, Approx. 18 m. SW of Ottawa. The place was named in 1845 for *Rev. John Otto Brederick* by *Elias Everett.*

•OTWAY, Village; Scioto County; Pop. 161; Area Code 614; Zip Code 46657; S Ohio; 18 m. NW of Portsmouth in the hilly lands above the Ohio River valley.

•OWENSVILLE, Village; Clermont County; Pop. 858; Area Code 513; Zip Code 45160; SW Ohio; 27 m. E of Cincinnati; Rolling countryside.

•OXFORD, City; Butler County; Pop. 17,655; Area Code 513; Zip Code 45056; SW Ohio; 25 m. SW of Dayton, Fourmile (Tallawanda) Creek runs along two sides.

As a township, Oxford was assigned by Congress to serve as an educational center for Ohio (1803). The first "McGuffey Readers" were written by *William Holmes McGuffey* while teaching at Miami University.

Oxford was planned even before the land had been surveyed and cleared by its first settlers. When the Ohio Legislature authorized the establishment of Miami University in 1809, it provided for the institution's support by using proceeds of land leases. *Joel Collins,* a surveyor living on Bull's Run, guided a committee of the board to the site now occupied by Harrison Hall. The university opened formally in the fall of 1824. Rome rent in the dormitory was $5 a year, and included servant's hire. Since *Robert Bishop,* the Scotch first president, thought a bell a sinful extravagance, the hours were marked by the notes of a bugle.

Associated with even the earliest days of the university were persons and events that were to exercise their influence far beyond the little town of Oxford. One of the first instructors was *William Holmes McGuffey,* whose name, during the nineteenth century, was synonymous with the first of the three R's in every little schoolhouse in the land. During his decade in Oxford, McGuffey compiled the first of the Eclectic Readers that some millions of Americans learned to think of as nearly on a par with the Bible among books. Each summer the confederated McGuffey Societies convene at Oxford. And it was in Oxford that three national fraternities had their beginnings; Beta Theta Pi (1839), Phi Delta Theta (1848), and Sigma Chi (1852). From Oxford's High Street the "Miami Triad" spread to almost every major campus in the country.

Meanwhile Oxford had decided, in 1830, that its 737 inhabitants comprised too large a settlement to be governed by county machinery. A petition for a charter was granted, and the following year a president, recorder, and three trustees were elected. The trustees began busily to devise ordinances. It became a crime for anybody more than three years old to play marbles in an alley, on the sidewalks, or on any of the public grounds. For the first offense the fine was 26 cents, the second 50 cents, and all susequent violations $1.

At the university the first president and *John W. Scott* were maturing an idea for higher education for women. Professor Scott went to College Hill (now part of Cincinnati) and inaugurated the plan, but in 1848 he returned to Oxford, bringing his school with him in an omnibus. Thus began the Oxford College for Women, which flourished for 80 years before it was absorbed by Miami University.

Through the years the town enlarged its fund of reminiscences. *John Scott's* daughter *Caroline* married a man who had just graduated at the head of his Miami class - a stubby, studius youth named *Benjamin Harrison.* Another Oxford lass, *Lottie Moon* left *General Ambrose E. Burnside* at the altar, and the legend grew that the man she subsequently married held a pistol at her side throughout the ceremony.

In 1855 the Western College for Women was established. What little industrial aspect Oxford had had gradually vanished, leaving the academic atmosphere virtually untainted. Early Oxford had built small places for making things: buggy, wagon, broom, drill and organ factories, and a distillery and cooperage, but the bad times following the Civil War killed them off. The same depression brought about the temporary closing of Miami University in 1873.

The year before, Oxford had closed its saloons, yielding to the exhortations and prayers of the temperance crusade. When one brave barkeeper held his liquor fortress by refusing to admit the crusaders, the ladies laid siege outside, praying mightily along the curb. Whereupon the proprietor came out with a sprinkling bucket, walked gravely down the row of bonnets, and watered their dry posies.

For 12 years livestock grazed over the broad, deserted campus, but in 1885 the State lent its support to the school and it reopened. The revitalizing force spread throughout the little town; in 1889 it acquired electric lights, in 1894 a water system, in 1902 telephones.

Agriculture -Varied farming.
Industry/Mfg. - Machine shops
Higher Education -Miami University
     Western College
Mayor - Stephan D. Snyder- 523 2171

•PAINESVILLE, City; Seat of Lake County; Pop. 16,391; Area Code 513; Zip Code 44077; Elev. 702'; 30 m. NE of Cleveland in NE Ohio; On a plateau overlooking the Grand River.

In 1805, *Henry Champion* laid the town out and named it for himself. There are several different name origins debated.

Some say it was named for *General Edward Paine* who was an officer in the Revolutionary War, who arrived here in the earlier 1800's and who the township is named after. Others claim it is named for *Col. Eleazer Paine* who hails from Connecticut.

Settled in the early nineteenth century by a group of Connecticut pioneers, Painesville is supported by its chemical and machinery industries. One of the early pioneers was *Jonathan Goldsmith,* an architect for the Western Reserve who lived here from 1811 until his death 36 years later. Several of the structures he designed remain here.

Higher Education -Lake Erie College
Daily Newspaper -Telegraph- 84 N. State St.

•**PALESTINE**, Village; Darke County; Pop. 213; Area Code 513; Zip Code 45352; W Ohio; Rural town named by religious settlers.

•**PANDORA**, Village; Putnam County; Pop. 977; Area Code 419; Zip Code 45877; NW Ohio; 18 m. NE of Lima in the corn and wheat belt of Ohio.

•**PARMA**, City; Cuyahoga County; Pop. 92,548; Area Code 216; Zip Code 441 + zone; 10 m. S of Cleveland in N Ohio; Incorporated, village in 1924, city in 1932.

A residential suburb of Cleveland, Parma was originally known as Greenbriar when New England immigrants began settling here prior to World War I. After a portion of the community broke away from Parma in 1912 to become Parma Heights, the city's economy became less dependent on agriculture. Its population has expanded rapidly since World War II.

Mayor - John Petruska- 886 2323

•**PARMA HEIGHTS**, City; Cuyahoga County; Pop. 23,112; Area Code 216; N Ohio; is a residential suburb of Parma.

Paul W. Cassidy- 884 9600

•**PARRAL**, Village; Tuscarawas County; Pop. 259; Area Code 614; Elev. 1,000'; E Ohio. In 1764 the peaceful meeting of a numer of Indian chieftains and the forces of *Colonel Henry Bouquet* occurred. After Pontiac's Conspiracy had failed, Bouquet and 1,500 armed men left Fort Pitt (Pittsburgh) and marched across eastern Ohio to confer with the Indian leaders. When the Indians made their appearance, they saw Scottish Highlanders, Royal Americans, Pennsylvania Regulars, and Virginia backwoodsmen drawn up in formidable array. Bouquet bluntly demanded the return of all white prisoners within 13 days, and then ordered his troops to march to Coshocton, well within Indian territory. In due time 206 white captives were freed.

•**PATASKALA**, Village; Licking County; Pop. 2,285; Area Code 614; Zip Code 43062; 20 m. E of Columbus in central Ohio; farming area. Named for the Indian name for Salt Lick.

•**PAULDING**, Village; Seat of Paulding County; Pop. 2,754; Area Code 419; Zip Code 45879; 40 m. NW of Lima in NW Ohio; Named for, one of the three men that captured *Major Andre* during the Revolution, *John Paulding* of Peekskill, NY.

> *Agriculture* -Grain and varied farming
> *Industry/Mfg.* - Clay products, plastics
> *Mayor* - John W. Faust- 399 4011

•**PAULDING COUNTY**, NW Ohio; Area 417 sq. miles; Pop. 21,302; County seat Paulding; Est., February 12, 1820; Named for *John Paulding*, one of the captors of the traitor *John Andre* during the Revolutionary War; Maumee and Auglaize Rivers irrigate this rich corn-producing region.

•**PAYNE**, Village; Paulding County; Pop. 1,399; Area Code 419; Zip Code 45880; NW Ohio; 35 m. E of Fort Wayne, Indiana in a farming region.

•**PEEBLES**, Village; Adams County; Pop. 1,790; Area Code 614; Zip Code 45660; Elev. 813'; Approx. 30 m. NW of Portsmouth in S Ohio.

Set in a hilly agricultural region, it is the site of the Edwin H. Davis State Memorial, 88 acre nature preserve.

•**PEMBERVILLE**, Village; Wood County; Pop. 1,321; Area Code 419; Zip Code 43450; NW Ohio; 10 m. NE of Bowling Green on the Portae River.

•**PENINSULA**, Village; Summit County; Pop. 604; Area Code 216; Zip Code 44264; On the Cuyahoga River in the industrial NE of Ohio, between the metropolises of Cleveland and Akron.

•**PEPPER PIKE,** City; Cuyahoga County; Pop. 6,177; Area Code 216; Zip Code 10 m. E of Cleveland in N Ohio.

Mayor - John T. Avery- 831 8500

•**PERRY,** Village; Lake County; Pop. 961; Area Code 216; Zip Code 44081; NE Ohio; Fruit raising center, just S of Lake Erie shoreline, named for *Oliver H. Perry,* general during the War of 1812.

•**PERRY COUNTY,** SE central Ohio; Area 410 sq. miles; Pop. 31,032; County seat New Lexington; Est., December 26, 1817; Named for *Oliver H. Perry,* Navy commander on Lake Erie during the War of 1812; Clay and coal are the main natural resources here, and recreational centers are in the Wayne National Forest, S county.

•**PERRYSBURG,** City; Wood County; Pop. 10,215; Area Code 419; Zip Code 43551; Elev. 628'; NW Ohio; Overlooks the Maumee River and the city of Maumee; Named for the War of 1812 hero *Com. Oliver Hazard Perry.* The town was laid out in 1817.

In 1816 the site was chosen as the best navigable location at the foot of the Maumee Rapids, and from 1828 to 1840 more shipping took place here than at any other Lake Erie port. The seat of Wood County was here from 1822 to 1866, when it was shifted to Bowling Green.

Agriculture -Grain, truck and varied farming
Industry/Mfg. - Toys, tobacco products
Mayor - Sam uel F. Hunter- 874 7913

•**PERRY'S VICTORY AND INTERNATIONAL PEACE MEMORIAL,** National Monument; Northern Ohio; Authorized 1936; Occupies 21.44 acres; Commemorates Perry's Victory over British Sept. 10, 1813 at Put-in-Bay, Lake Erie, and the years of peace thereafter.

•**PERRYSVILLE,** Village; Ashland County; Pop. 836; Area Code 419; Zip Code 44864; N central Ohio; On the Mohican River, near Pleasant Hill Reservoir, approx. 20 m. SE of Mansfield.

•**PHILLIPSBURG,** Village; Montgomery County; Pop. 705; Area Code 513; Zip Code 45354; SW central Ohio; 20 m. NW of Dayton; Residential.

•PHILO, Village; Muskingum County; Pop. 799; Area Code 614; Zip Code 43771; E central Ohio; Quiet farming community.

•PICKAWAY COUNTY, S central Ohio; area 507 sq. miles; Pop. 43,662; County seat Circleville; Est., January 12, 1810; Named for the Piqua Indians who lived here at one time; Cut through by Darby Creek and part of the Scioto River; Ohio and Erie Canal once passed through this region, an important westward route for pioneers; Plains region, with large cornfields and some woodlands.

•PICKERINGTON, Village; Fairfield & Franklin Counties; Pop. 3,917; Area Code 614; Zip Code 43147; 10 m. NW of Lancaster; Rural residential area near the outskirts of Columbus. Named for the *Abraham Pickerington* who bought land here in 1811 and laid out and named the town Jacksonville. In 1827 the residents changed the name to honor the founder.

•PIKE COUNTY, S Ohio; Area 443 sq. miles; Pop. 22,802; County seat Waverly; Est., January 4, 1815; Named for *Zebulon M. Pike*, (1779-1813) soldier and explorer; Crossed by Scioto River; Mostly rural region supported by corn and other farming and by tourism around the Lake White State Park. Site of several prehistoric earthworks and burial mounds.

•PIKETON, Village; Pike County; Pop. 1,726; Area Code 614; Zip Code 45661; S Ohio; 10 m. S of Waverley in a recreational area along the Scioto River. Named for *General Zebulon Montgomery Pike.*

•PIONEER, Village; Williams County; Pop. 1,133; Area Code 419; Zip Code 43554; NW corner, Ohio; Just S of Michigan state line in a stockraising region along the St. Joseph River.

•PIQUA, City; Miami County; Pop. 20,480; Area Code 513; Zip Code 45358; Elev. 899'; W Ohio; Situated on the Great Miami River.
    The village was settled in 1797, and was called Washington until 1816, when a legislative act gave it the name of a tribe of the Shawnee who established themselves in this region after 1763. The name, Piqua, means "a man risen out of the ashes."

Agriculture - Varied farming
Industry/Mfg. - Clothing, autos, beverages,
   lumber, boxes
Mayor - James E. Henderson 513 773-1284
Daily Newspaper - The Call, 121 E. Ash St.
Chamber of Commerce - 400 N. Wayne, PO Box
   1142
Community Event(s) : Chautauqua Festival;
   Annual, July-August

•**PITSBURG**, Village; Darke County; Pop. 460; Area Code 513; Zip Code 45358; W Ohio; Near Greenville in rolling countryside.

•**PLAIN CITY**, Village; Madison & Union Counties; Pop. 2,102; Area Code 614; Zip Code 43064; Elev. 935'; SW central Ohio.
   Laid out in 1818 by *Issac Bigelow*, it was first called Westminster, then Pleasant Valley; it was finally named Plain City in 1851 because it is situated on Big Darby Plain. In the vicinity of one of Ohio's Amish settlements.

   Mayor - R.H.Lombard 873-5812

•**PLAINFIELD**, Village; Coshocton County; Pop. 221; Area Code 614; Zip Code 43836; E central Ohio; On N tip of Wills Creek Reservoir; Camping, fishing.

•**PLEASANT CITY**, Village; Guernsey County; Pop. 481; Area Code 614; Zip Code 43772; Elev. 800'; E Ohio; Originally called Point Pleasant because of the abrupt slope of Jackson's Hill protruding into the serene valley.
   From 1892, when the Cisco Mine opened, until shortly after the World War, coal mining was the chief industry here and the village thrived. The depletion of the coal deposits caused Pleasant City to decline, some of the residents moving elsewhere. Those who remained have been chiefly engaged in agriculture, although mining is carried on to some extent.

•**PLEASANT HILL**, Village; Miami County; Pop. 1,051; Area Code 513; Zip Code 45359; W central Ohio; Along Stillwater Creek in the agricultural region W of Troy.

•**PLEASANT PLAIN**, Village; Warren County; Pop. 210; Area Code 513; Zip Code 45162; SW Ohio; 30 m. NE of Cincinnati in rolling countryside.

•PLEASANTVILLE, Village; Fairfield County; Pop. 780; Area Code 614; Zip Code 43148; Rural residential town in S central Ohio. 10 m. N of Lancaster.

•PLYMOUTH, Village; Huron and Richland Counties; Pop. 1,939; Area Code 419; Zip Code 44865; N central Ohio; On the W branch of the Huron River, 19 m. NW of Mansfield.

•POLAND, Village; Mahoning County; Pop. 3,084; Area Code 216; Zip Code 44514; Elev. 1,016'; NE Ohio; Originally named Fowlers for *Jonathan Fowler* who came here in 1799; A suburb of Youngstown.

> *Agriculture* - Varied farming
> *Industry/Mfg.* - Auto parts, electronics,
>   cement products
> *Mayor* - Russell L. Blake 216 757-2112
> *Chamber of Commerce* - 308 S Main St.

•POLK, Village; Ashland County; Pop. 351; Area Code 216; Zip Code 44866; N central Ohio; Rural farm center, 10 m. NE of Ashland.

•POMEROY, Village; Seat of Meigs County; Pop. 2,728; Area Code 614; Zip Code 45769; Elev. 590'; SE Ohio, 40 m. SE of Marietta.

Named for *Samuel Pomeroy,* a Boston merchant who in 1804 purchased 262 acres of land on the site of the city. As early as 1770 coal was discovered near by, but it was 1809 before *Nicholas Roosevelt* opened a mine along the river to provide fuel for the steamboats about to appear on the Ohio.

> *Agriculture* - Grain, poultry, truck and
>   varied farming
> *Industry/Mfg.* - Lumber, salt, dairy products,
>   chemicals
> *Mayor* - Clarence Andrews 614 992-2246
> *Daily Newspaper* - The Sentinel, Times
>   Sentinel, 111 Court St.
> *Chamber of Commerce* - 2nd St., Meigs County
>   Courthouse
> *Community Event(s)* : Big Bend Regatta;
>   Annual, June

•PORTAGE, Village; Wood County; Pop. 479; Area Code 419; Zip

Code 43451; Elev. 684'; NW Ohio; Began as a trading post in 1824, and prospered during the oil and gas boom of the 1880's and 1890's.

•PORTAGE COUNTY, NE Ohio; Area 495 sq. miles; Pop. 135,856; County seat Ravenna; Est., February 10, 1807; Named for the old Indian portage or path between the Mahoning and Cuyahoga Rivers, which flow through this county; Several lakes here, formed by dams, such as the Michael J. Kirwan and Milton Lakes.

•PORT CLINTON, City; Seat of Ottawa County; Pop. 7,223; Elev. 580'; N Ohio; 30 m. SE of Toledo.
　　At the mouth of the Portage River, this town was platted in 1828 and got its start when Scotch immigrants, bound for Chicago, were shipwrecked at this point and settled permanently. The town was named in honor of *DeWitt Clinton*, New York governor.

> *Agriculture* - Fruit and truck farming
> *Industry/Mfg.* - Machine shop, boats, plastic, gypsum
> *Mayor* - John F. Fritz 419 734-5522
> *Daily Newspaper* - The News-Herald, 115 West 2nd St., PO Box 550
> *Chamber of Commerce* - 111 W. Perry

•PORT JEFFERSON, Village; Shelby County; Pop. 482; Area Code 513; Zip Code 45360; W Ohio; On the Miami River, just NE of Sidney.

•PORTSMOUTH, City; Seat of Scioto County; Pop. 25,943; Area Code 614; Zip Code 45662; Elev. 527'; S Ohio; Was founded in 1803 by a Virginia land speculator, *Major Henry Massie*.

> *Industry/Mfg.* - Footwear, steel, plastics and boxes
> *Mayor* - Albert White 614 354-8807
> *Daily Newspaper* - The Times, 637 Sixth St.
> *Chamber of Commerce* - PO Box 509, 740 Second St.
> *Community Event(s)* : River Days Festival; Annual, August-September

•PORT WASHINGTON, Village; Tuscarawas County; Pop. 622;

Area Code 614; Zip Code 43837; Elev. 818'; E Ohio; Was once an important shipping center on the Ohio and Erie Canal.

In this vicinity was the short-lived settlement of Salem, established in 1780 to harbor members of the Lichtenau community menaced by Delawares. It is believed that the first white marriage in Ohio territory occured here on July 14, 1780, when the Moravian missionary, *David Zeisberger*, married *Sarah Ohneberg*. Through Salem "of the meek Moravian missions," so legend related, passed the Evangeline of *Longfellows* poem in her search for Gabriel.

•PORT WILLIAM, Village; Clinton County; Pop. 300; Area Code 513; Zip Code 45164; SW Ohio; Rural farm center along the banks of a fork of the Miami River.

•POTSDAM, Village; Miami County; Pop. 289; Area Code 513; Zip Code 45361; W Ohio; Rural farm trading community.

•POWELL, Village; Delaware County; Pop. 387; Area Code 614; Zip Code 43065; Central Ohio; approx. 15 m. N of downtown Columbus, the site of the Columbus Municipal Zoo; Bordered to W by Scioto River.

•POWHATAN POINT, Village; Belmont County; Pop. c2,181; Area Code 614; Zip Code 43942; Elev. 638'; E Ohio; Experienced a coal boom during the 1920's.

•PREBLE COUNTY, SW Ohio; Area 428 sq. miles; Pop. 38,223; County seat Eaton; Est., February 15, 1808; Named for *Edward Preble*, U.S. Navy commander, who led the vessel, *Constitution* to the bombing of Tripoli in 1804; Crossed by Sevenmile and Twin Creeks; Bordered to W by Indiana state line; Tablelands with corn and stockraising farms.

•PROCTORVILLE, Village; Shelby County; Pop. 475; Area Code 419; Zip Code 45360; Elev. 555'; S Ohio; On a high bank overlooking the Ohio River; Home of the Rome Beauty apple, first grown here in 1816.

•PROSPECT, Village; Marion County; Pop. 1,159; Area Code 614; Zip Code 43342; Central Ohio; Along the Scioto River, 12 m. S of Marion in a truck farming area.

•**PUT-IN-BAY**, Village; Ottawa County; Pop. 146; Area Code 419; Zip Code 43456; N Ohio; On S. Bass Island, in Lake Erie, 25 m. NW of Sandusky. Named by *Commodore Perry*. When he was asked what to do with the British Fleet, he replied "Put them in the Bay."

Numerous hotels and summer homes line the lakeshore at this tiny village, and in summer it is crowded with thousands of visitors. (See Bass Island, South).

•**PUTNAM COUNTY**, NW Ohio; Area 486 sq. miles; Pop. 32,991; County seat Ottawa; Est., February 12, 1820; Named for *Isreal Putnam*, Revolutionary War general, commanding at New York and Philadelphia; Blanchard and Ottawa Rivers branch off from AuGlaize River in this county.

•**QUAKER CITY**, Village; Guernsey County; Pop. 698; Area Code 614; Zip Code 43773; E Ohio; 16 m. E of Cambidge in a large coal mining area; Once more populous, with mainly Quaker residents.

In 1850 was known as Millwood. In 1871 the residents picked the name Quaker City.

•**QUNICY**, Village; Logan County; Pop. 633; Area Code 419; Zip Code 43343; W Ohio; On the Miami River in a large farming area W of Bellefontaine. Named in honor of *John Quincy Adams*. *James Baldwin* and *Manlove Chambers* laid out the place in 1830.

•**RACCOON CREEK**, River; S Ohio; Flows S approx. 90 m. from a wetlands area in S Hocking County, through a coal mining region, to its confluence with the Ohio River, S of Gallipolis.

•**RACINE**, Village; Meigs County; Pop. 908; Area Code 614; Zip Code 45771; SE Ohio; On the Ohio River, 25 m. NE of Gallipolis; Near a large lock and dam by the same name.

•**RARDEN**, Village; Scioto County; Pop. 199; Area Code 614; Zip Code 45671; S Ohio; 23 m. NW of Portsmouth in a hilly farmlands region.

•**RAVENNA**, City; Seat of Portage County; Pop. 11,987; Area

Code 216; Zip Code 44266; Elev. 1,138; NE Ohio; Lies between the Cuyahoga and Mahoning Rivers.

It was named for the Italian city after its settlement in 1799 from Ohio.

Agriculture - Grain and varied farming
Industry/Mfg. - Cement products, lumber,
    hardware, furniture, steel
Mayor - Paul H. Jones 296-3864
Daily Newspaper - The Record-Courier, 126 N.
    Chestnut St.
Chamber of Commerce - 216-1/2 W. Main St.

•RAWSON, Village; Hancock County; Pop. 477; Area Code 419; Zip Code 45881; NW Ohio; 10 m. SW of Findley in a quiet area off U.S.Highway 75.

•RAYLAND, Village; Jefferson County; Pop. 566; Area Code 614; Zip Code 43943; E Ohio; On the Ohio River, 13 m. S of Steubenville, in a coal mining and shipping area.

•READING, City; Hamilton County; Pop. 12,879; Area Code 513; Elev. 660'; SW Ohio; 10 m. NE of the city in a residential area.

First named Vorheestown for *Adam Vorhees* who platted it in 1798; Reading was given its present name in honor of *Redingbo, William Penn's* son-in-law. The suburb grew rapidly after World War II, but is now losing population.

•RENDVILLE, Village; Perry County; Pop. 68; Area Code 614; Zip Code 43775; SE central Ohio; Small trading post in the Central Wayne National Forest.

•REPUBLIC, Village; Seneca County; Pop. 656; Area Code 419; Zip Code 44867; N Ohio; 27 m. SW of Sandusky in a farming area.

Agriculture - Grain, cattle and varied
    farming
Mayor - William F. Ernst 733-3725

•REYNOLDSBURG, City; Franklin County; Pop. 20,661; Area Code 614; Zip Code 43068; Central Ohio; 10 m. E of Columbus in a residential area large enough to support its own newspaper. Originally known as Frenchtown in 1831 because of the founder *John French.* The current name is in honor of *John C. Reynolds.*

Mayor - Richard J. Daugherty 866-6391
Community Event(s) : Tomato Festival;
Annual, September

•**RICHFIELD**, Village; Summit County; Pop. 3,437; Area Code 216; Zip Code 44286; Elev. 1,148'; NE Ohio; was the home of *John Brown* during the early 1840's when he made his living here as a sheep raiser and wool broker; Brown (1800-59) was born in Torrington, Connecticut, and came to Hudson, Ohio in 1805.

Mayor - Paul J. Wulff 659-9201

•**RICHLAND COUNTY**, N central Ohio; Area 496 sq. miles; Pop. 131,205; County seat Mansfield; Est., January 30, 1808; Named for the fertile farmlands of the area; Hilly region crossed by several streams, with steel and rubber industries centered around Mansfield.

•**RICHMOND**, Village; Jefferson County; Pop. 624; Area Code 614; Zip Code 43944; E Ohio; In a quiet, creek and lake-strewn farmlands area, 12 m. NW of Steubenville.

•**RICHMOND HEIGHTS**, City; Cuyahoga County; Pop. 10,095; Area Code 216; Zip Code 44143; NE Ohio; 15 m. NE of Cleveland in a residential area just S of Lake Erie.

Mayor - Michael DeSan 486-2474

•**RICHWOOD**, Village; Union County; Pop. 2,181; Area Code 419; Zip Code 43344; 15 m. S of Marion in W central Ohio; Major trading center for farms producing corn, wheat and oats.

Agriculture - Varied farming
Industry/Mfg. - Grain processing, plastics
Chamber of Commerce - 6 S. Franklin St.

•**RIDGEWAY**, Village; Hardin & Logan Counties; Pop. 388; Area Code 419; Zip Code 43345; 11 m. S of Kenton in NW central Ohio; Rural area. Named after the Ridgeway Co. who originally owned this land. *Samuel McCulloch* laid out the town in 1851 and later purchased it from the Ridgeway Co.

•**RIO GRANDE**, Village; Gallia County; Pop. 864; Area Code 614; Zip Code 45674; S Ohio; Elev. 682; 13 m. NW of Gallipolis.

The history of this hamlet is closely linked with that of Rio Grande College, established in 1876 and operated for a number of years under the supervision of the Baptist church. *Nehemiah Atwood*, soldier under *William H. Harrison* during the War of 1812, bought land here in 1818, opened a tavern on the stage route between Gallipolis and Chillicothe, and amasses a great fortune within a few years. He and his wife later endowed $80,000 on the village for a Christian college.

Near the town is the Bob Evans Farm, featuring a museum with old farm implements, a craft barn, and nature trails in a restored nineteenth century setting.

•**RIPLEY**, Village; Brown County; Pop. 2,174; Area Code 513; Zip Code 45167; Elev. 447'; SW Ohio.

In its early days Ripley was a center for steamboat building and piano manufacturing. The place was laid out during the War of 1812 by a native Virginian *Col. James Poage* and called Staunton, a place in VA. The current name is in honor of *Gen. Eleazer Wheelock Ripley*.

Agriculture - Tobacco, grain and varied
    farming
Industry/Mfg. - Beverages, footwear, medical
    supplies
Mayor - Robert L. Rapier 392-4377

•**RISING SUN**, Village; Wood County; Pop. 698; Area Code 419; Zip Code 43457; NW central Ohio; Rural.

•**RITTMAN**, City; Wayne & Medina Counties; Pop. 6,063; Area Code 216; Zip Code 44270; 40 m. S of Cleveland in an area where the once heavily forested flatlands brought about the large paper and wood products industries here.

Agriculture - Fruit, cattle and varied
    farming
Industry/Mfg. - Paper products, salt, dairy
    products, boxes
Mayor - Ashton O. Hall 925-2045
Chamber of Commerce - 91 N. Fifth St.

•**RIVERLEA**, Village; Franklin County; Pop. 528; Area Code 614; central Ohio.

•**RIVERSIDE**, Village; Montgomery County; Pop. 1,475; Area Code 513; SW Ohio.

•**ROAMING SHORES**, Village; Ashtabula County; Pop. 581; Area Code 216; NE Ohio.

•**ROCHESTER**, Village; Lorain County; Pop. 207; Area Code 216; N central Ohio.

•**ROCK CREEK**, Village; Ashtabula County; Pop. 652; Area Code 216; Zip Code 44084; NE Ohio; 16 m. S of Ashtabula in an agricultural area along a creek by the same name, a tributary of the Grand River.

•**ROCKFORD**, Village; Mercer County; Pop. 1,245; Area Code 419; Zip Code 45882; Elev. 807'; W Ohio; On the site of an Indian trading post run by *Anthony Shane*, a half-breed, before the War of 1812.

   When the government gave land grants to the Indians, Shane's Crossing, as Rockford was first called, became a trading center for Shawnee farmers. White settlers pressed into the region after the Treaty of 1818, and the Indians began moving farther west.

> *Agriculture* - Varied farming
> *Industry/Mfg.* - Food packing, oil, quarrying
> *Chamber of Commerce* - Main St.

•**ROCKY RIDGE**, Village; Ottawa County; Pop. 457; Area Code 419; Zip Code 43458; N Ohio; 22 m. SE of Toledo in the rocky lands between the Portage and Toussaint rivers.

•**ROCKY RIVER**, City; Cuyahoga County; Pop. 21,084; Area Code 216; Zip Code 44116; NE Ohio; At the mouth of the Rocky River on Lake Erie, 10 m. W of Cleveland city center.

> *Mayor* - Earl Martin 331-0600

193

•**ROGERS**, Village; Columbiana County; Pop. 298; Area Code 216; Zip Code 44455; E Ohio; Rural.

•**ROME**, Village; Adams County; Pop. 135; Area Code 614; Zip Code 44085; S Ohio; In a sparsely populated region.

•**ROSSBURG**, Village; Darke County; Pop. 260; Area Code 513; Zip Code 45362; W Ohio; 12 m. N of Greenville in a rural area.

•**ROSS COUNTY**, S Ohio; Area 687 sq. miles; Pop. 65,004; County seat Chillicothe; Est., August 20, 1798; Named for *James Ross*, Pennsylvania senator and political leader in the late 1790s; Traversed by Scioto River, along which are several important prehistoric Indian earthworks; Farmlands; One of the first populated areas of Ohio territory after the Indians were driven out.

•**ROSSFORD**, City; Wood County; Pop. 5,978; Area Code 419; Zip Code 43460; Elev. 630'; NW Ohio; Got its start in 1896 when *Edward Ford* resigned as head of the Pittsburgh Plate Glass Company and came here to establish a plant of his own.

The Ford plant merged with the Libbey-Owens Corporation in 1930, the present Libbey-Owens-Ford Company Plant.

Mayor - Louis Bauer Jr. 666-0210

•**ROSWELL**, Village; Tuscarawas County; Pop. 264; Area Code 614; E Ohio.

•**RUSHSYLVANIA**, Village; Logan County; Pop. 610; Area Code 513; Zip Code 43347; W Ohio; In a highlands area 10 m. NE of Bellefontaine; Named for the Rush River, which passes through town.

•**RUSHVILLE**, Village; Fairfield County; Pop. 299; Area Code 614; Zip Code 43150: Elev. 1,053'; S central Ohio; NE of Lancaster. Named for Rush Creek.

This town was the birthplace of *Benjamin Russell Hanby*, schoolteacher and composer of the song, "Darling Nellie Gray" in the nineteenth century. The story was inspired by the tale of a runaway slave's love for a young girl he left behind on the plantation. In 1802, *Moses Plummer* built a mill here.

•**RUSSELLS POINT**, Village; Logan County; Pop. 1,156; Area Code 513; Zip Code 43348; W Ohio; On S Indian Lake, 13 m. NW of Bellefontaine; the amusement center for visitors and vacationists at Indian Lake.

•**RUSSELLVILLE**, Village; Brown County; Pop. 445; Area Code 513; Zip Code 45168; SW Ohio; 26 m. S of Hillsboro in a rural area.

•**RUSSIA**, Village; Shelby County; Pop. 438; Area Code 419; Zip Code 45363; W Ohio; 15 m. SW of Sidney in a corn farming area.

•**RUTLAND**, Village; Meigs County; Pop. 635; Area Code 614; Zip Code 45775; SE Ohio; 6 m. W of Pomeroy and the Ohio River in a hilly area.

•**SABINA**, Village; Clinton County; Pop. 2,799; Area Code 513; Zip Code 45169; Elev. 1,051; SW Ohio; 11 m. NE of Wilmington.
This trading center is set in a rich farming region, and is the site of a Methodist summer camp and conference center built in 1892.

•**SAINT BERNARD**, City; Hamilton County; Pop. 5,396; Area Code 513; Zip Code 452–; SW Ohio; 7 m. N of Cincinnati, along Mill Creek in an industrial-residential area above the city center.

Mayor - Jack Hausfeld 242-7770
Chamber of Commerce - 4729 Vine St.

•**ST.CLAIRSVILLE**, City; Seat of Belmont County; Pop. 5,452; Area Code 614; Zip Code 43950; Elev. 1,260'; E Ohio; Named for *Arthur St.Clair*, first governor of the Northwest Territory. In 1801 *David Newell* platted the town and called it Newellston originally.

Mayor - Edgar White 695-1324
Chamber of Commerce - PO Box 368

•**SAINT HENRY**, Village; Mercer County; Pop. 1,596; Area Code 419; Zip Code 45883; W Ohio; In a rural area near the Indiana state line.

•**ST.JOSEPH RIVER**, River; NW Ohio; is over 100 miles in

195

length. The river rises in S Michigan then flows SW in NW Ohio and at Fort Wayne, Indiana forms the Maumee River with St.Marys River.

•ST.LOUISVILLE, Village; Licking County; Pop. 375; Area Code 614; Zip Code 43071; E central Ohio; On the Licking River, 11 m. N of Newark.

•SAINT MARTIN, Village; Brown County; Pop. 126; Area Code 513; Zip Code 45170; SW Ohio; On the Miami River, 37 m. NE of Cincinnati; Rural.

• ST. MARYS, City; Auglaize County; Pop. 8,414; Area Code 419; Zip Code 45885; Elev. 926'; 80 m. NW of Columbus in W Ohio; Incorporated a village 1820, city 1903.

Girty's Town, as St. Marys was once called, was a headquarters and supply depot for *Generals Harmer, Wayne and Harrison* during the Indian campaigns. Strategically located on the Great Lakes-Ohio River rwatershed at the north end of Pioneer Portage, the fort was important as a trading center.

During the 1790's, known as Ft. St.Marys, it was a supply depot. Later was the site Ft.Barbee during the War of 1812.

Agriculture - Grain, poultry and varied farming
Industry/Mfg. - Cotton and rubber products
Mayor - Kay E. Albert 394-3303
Daily Newspaper - The Leader, 102 E Spring St.
Chamber of Commerce - 205 W. Spring St.

•ST.MARY RIVER, River; NW Ohio; starts in Auglaize County and runs for 110 miles and forms the Maumee River with the St.Joseph River in Fort Wayne, Indiana.

•SAINT PARIS, Village; Champaign County; Pop. 1,742; Area Code 513; Zip Code 43072; Elev. 1,058'; was settled in 1813 by *David Huffman*, and has the two-story frame KISER HOUSE (L) on US 36 near the center of the village. Built in the early years of the last century under Jeffersonian influence, it has fluted Ionic pillars on its high portico; and several balconies now break its chaste lines. The builder is said to have made a fortune by manufacturing horseshoes for the army of the Czar of Russia.

Agriculture - Grain and truck farming
Industry/Mfg. - Dairy products

•SALEM, City; Columbia County; Pop. 12,869; Area Code 216; Zip Code 44460; Elev. 1,230'; 20 m. SW of Youngstown in E Ohio; a town of varied industrial occupations, is a Quaker center which calls itself "Ohio's city of Friends." The Quakers came here from Salem, New Jersey, in 1801, and were joined by groups from Pennsylvania and Virginia. The town was an important station on the Underground Railroad and the headquarters for the Anti-Slavery Bugle. Its manufactures include china, lumber, furnaces, machinery, metal products, flour, and dairy products.

Agriculture - Grain. fruit and varied farming
Industry/Mfg. - Dairy products, coal, household appliances, plastics
Mayor - Frank D. Aauria 332-4241
Daily Newspaper - The News, 161 N. Lincoln Ave.
Chamber of Commerce - 417 E. State St.

•SALESVILLE, Village; Guernsey County; Pop. 139; Area Code 216; Zip Code 43945; Elev. 860'; E central Ohio near Leatherwood Creek in a farming area.

Here in 1828, *Joseph Dylkes* stood up in church one morning and announced that he was God. Some believed him and in no time at all a new religious sect was under way. However, when Dylkes failed to perform a well-publicized miracle, he and some of his disciples were forced to leave and found "new Jerusalem" somewhere else. *William Dean Howells* told the much-embellished story in his novel, *The Leatherwood God.*

•SALINEVILLE, Village; Columbia County; Pop. 1,629; Area Code 216; Zip Code 43945; Elev. 950'; 18 m. W of East Liverpool in E Ohio; Named for the salt springs in the area.

A salt well was sunk here in 1809. Twenty wells were operating along the Little Yellow Creek in 1835, and the salt was hauled over the Alleghenies and profitably sold at $5 a bushel. The last well closed in 1880, but in the meantime, coal mining took over as the much more profitable business in Salineville.

•SANDUSKY, City; Seat of Erie County; Pop. 31,360; Area Code

216; Zip Code 44870; Elev. 600'; N Ohio; On Sandusky Bay juncture at Lake Erie.

The name Sandusky means "cold water" from the Iroquoian word "Sandoos-tie". Ft. Sandusky (est. 1761) was destroyed by fire in 1763. During the War of 1812 it was a well known supply post. It had earlier been called Ogontz Place (Ottawa Chieftan). Later it was occupied by *Zalmon Wildman* of Danburg, Connecticut as an American Revolution land grant (1816).

A well known resort site is Cedar Point, opened nearby in 1822. Also home of Cedar Point Amusement Park that attracts people from all over the country during the summer months.

Long before any Americans came here, the French had explored the region. When LaSalle sailed across Lake Erie in 1679, his annalist, *Father Louis Hennepin*, wrote of the Bass Islands northwest of the site of the city. A map published in Amsterdam in 1720 showed a body of water called Lac Sandouske, the present Sandusky Bay. For many decades the tribes of the Iroquois Confederacy dominated this entire region, and the lake and the lands along its south shore were vast fishing and hunting preserves. In 1760, when *George Croghan*, an English trader, landed at Cedar Point, he found Ottawas and Wyandottes camping there. His party sailed across the bay the next day and found "the bay was so foggy that the Drum was obliged to beat all day to keep the Boats together."

It was 1816 before permanent settlers came. In the following year *Zalmon Wildman*, of Danbury, Connecticut, laid out the tract bounded by Hancock, Jefferson, and Decatur Streets, and called it Portland. Another New Englander, *Issac Mills*, claimed a portion of the site; a settlement was effected, and in 1818 a larger plat was surveyed which was named Sandusky City. The "City" was dropped in 1844.

The town quickly achieved prominence as a port of entry and a shipping center. For many years it was a stopping place for all vessels that regularly sailed the Great Lakes. Passenger boats from Buffalo landed thousands of immigrants who then went off into the interior to make new homes. In 1822 there were 178 lake arrivals; in 1826, 355; most of them from Detroit or Buffalo. Through the 1820's, 1830's, and 1840's, long caravans of wagons bulging with corn and wheat rumbled into the town from all parts of northern Ohio. In October 1828, on a single day 285

198

grain wagons arrived. Boats carried the produce to Canada and the East, and in time the town became one of the largest grain markets in the Nation. In 1851, the local Clarion reported, 500,000 bushels of corn and 2,000,000 bushels of wheat were shipped from this point.

An English clergyman visiting the place in 1834 was unfavorably impressed: "...the state of religious and moral feeling is evidently very low here and I heard more swearing and more Sabbath breaking than I had before witnessed...There were many groceries, as they called themselves here, groggeries, as their enemies called them, and they were all full."

In 1835, after Sandusky had lost out to Cleveland as the terminus for the Ohio and Erie Canal ground was broken for the constructin of the Mad River Railroad. The second railroad in Ohio, it reached Bellevue in 1839, Dayton in 1851. It was this line that brought *Charles Dickens* to Sandusky in 1842. He spent the night at Colt's Exchange Hotel, still standing at the southeast corner of Wayne and Water Streets, and recorded his impressions of the proprietor in his American Notes. "When I say that he constantly walked in and out of the room with his hat on; and stopped to converse in the same free-and-easy state; and lay down on our sofa, and pulled his newspaper out of his pocket; and read it at his ease; I merely mention these traits as characteristic of the country..."

Sandusky grew rapidly. Made the seat of Erie County in 1838, it had about 1,500 residents two years later, and 4,000 at the end of the 1840's. Large numbers of the Irish came to this dominantly Yankee community, and the Germans came in even greater numbers. Sandusky was on its way to becoming a large city when, on June 25, 1849, cholera struck, with dreadful results. Since 1832 there had been half a dozen minor outbreaks of cholera. The epidemic of 1849 was the greatest and the most tragic. Business came to a standstill. Half the people fled the city, many of them never to return. An observer reported: "So malignant was the epidemic that it was no unusual thing for business men to be attacked in their shops and stores, go to the cabinet warehouse and engage their coffins, and then go home, lie down and die before their coffins could get there." Nearly 400 people died in little more than two months, and Sandusky became a city of the dead.

Slowly the plague ebbed away. Unnoticed was the autumn 1850 arrival, *via Uncle Tom's Cabin,* of *George, Eliza, and Harry*

Harris. (Sandusky was an important station on the Underground Railroad.) Former residents returned and new additions of German immigrants again swelled the city's population. By 1855 there were nearly as many Germans here as Americans. They built churches, founded newspapers and theaters, started new enterprises, and gradually took over the city. The breweries, wineries, and fish houses for which Sandusky has been widely known were begun by the Germans during the 1850's and 1860's.

Through the remaining part of the century, and until Prohibition came, scores of big-cruppered draft horses clanged along the streets, hauling thousands of barrels of beer to the railroad depots and to outlying towns. From the deep, dank wine cellars on Water Street went millions of bottles of sweet, dry, and sparkling wines to all parts of the country, and Sandusky wines won medals of honor in Rome, Paris, and other European centers. So large were the fish hauls in the spawning grounds near the Bass Islands that for decades the city was known as the largest fresh-water fish market in the world. There were years when the numerous fish houses along the water front shipped as many as 10,000,000 pounds of fish - pickerel, whitefish, herring, perch, sturgeon, catfish, and other kinds - to the East and the Middle West. People called the place "Fishtown," and held their noses when they walked along Railroad Street.

As the nineteenth century neared its end, other enterprises arose to add their fillip to this full-flavored community. Cedar Point opened as a resort in 1882, and inaugurated Sandusky's long career as a tourist center. Because the bay is the only point between Buffalo and Monroe, Michigan, where ice is sure to form, ice harvesting was a colorful minor industry from the 1880's to 1918, and long lines of railroad cars annually hauled several hundred thousand tons of cut ice from Sandusky to the junction towns and large cities in Ohio. For many years building sand dredged from the lake was an important export, and after 1906 the transshipping of coal across the upper Great Lakes rose steadily in volume.

Industry/Mfg. - Varied manufacturing, trade
   and services
Mayor - John R. Mears 625-6120
Daily Newspaper - The Register, 314 W. Market
   Street
Chamber of Commerce - PO Box 2341

•SANDUSKY BAY, Bay; N Ohio; Inlet of Lake Erie, extending approx. 20 m. W from entrance at city of Sandusky; Crossed by an automobile bridge between Bay View and Danbury.

French *Father Louis Hennepin* showed "Lac Sandouske", the present Sandusky Bay in his 1720 map of the area. The name was adapted from the word "San-doos-tee", which was an Indian word for "cold water". The bay provides a portage today at the city of Sandusky, and fruit is raised along the inner bayshore.

•SANDUSKY COUNTY, N Ohio; Area 409 sq. miles; Pop. 63,267; County seat Fremont; Est., February 12, 1820; Name is derived from an Indian word meaning "cold water"; Bordered to NE by the "cold water" of Lake Erie and Sandusky Bay; Sandusky River flows through central county along which, Wyandot Indians once lived; Rye, barley, and cabbage farms and peach and cherry orchards cover the acres in this region; The highway through this region was known as the Western and Maumee Pike, an Indian path-turned stagecoach line-turned state highway.

•SANDUSKY RIVER, River; N Ohio; Flows approx. 150 m. W from a lakes region in Richland County, and then N to mouth at Sandusky Bay; Irrigates a large, flat farmlands region.

•SARAHSVILLE, Village; Nobel County; Pop. 226; Area Code 614; Zip Code 43779; SE Ohio; 30 m. S of Cambridge in a large coal mining area.

•SARDINIA, Village; Brown County; Pop. 826; Area Code 513; Zip Code 45171; SW Ohio; 22 m. S of Hillsboro in a quiet farming area.

•SAVANNAH, Village; Ashland County; Pop. 351; Area Code 419; Zip Code 44874; N central Ohio; On the Vermillion River, 12 m. N of the city of Ashland.

•SCIO, Village; Harrison County; Pop. 1,003; 5614; Zip Code 43988; E Ohio; One of the larger farm communities in an area where *General Custer* once lived. Named by *Wm. Anway* for his home town in N.Y.

•SCIOTO COUNTY, S Ohio; Area 608 sq. miles; Pop. 84,545; County seat Portsmouth; Est., March 24, 1803; Named for a

Wyandot Indian word meaning "deer", which also gave its name to the large river flowing through this area; Bordered to S by Ohio River; Steel industry along the rivers, and in N county, corn farms and hills mark the landscape.

•SCIOTO RIVER, River; Central to S Ohio; Flows approx. 237 miles E and S from Auglaize County, through the city of Columbus, to confluence with the Ohio River at the city of Portsmouth; Site of several prehistoric Indian villages, as evidenced by many earthworks along the waterway; Recreational facilities.

•SCOTT, Village; Paulding and Van Wert Counties; Pop. 340; Area Code 419; Zip Code 45886; NW central Ohio; 13 m. N of city of Van Wert.

•SEAMAN, Village; Adams County; Pop. 1,039; Area Code 614; Zip Code 45679; S Ohio; 60 m. E of Cincinnati in a hilly farming area.

•SEBRING, Village; Mahoning County; Pop. 5,078; Area Code 216; Zip Code 44672; NE Ohio; 5 m. E of Alliance in a small town and suburban setting. Named for *George Sebring* the founder.

•SENECA COUNTY, N Ohio; Area 551 square miles; Pop. 61,901; County seat Tiffin; Est., February 12, 1820; Named for county in New York, which in turn was named for a local Indian tribe; Flat lands traversed by the Sandusky River.

•SENECAVILLE LAKE, Lake; E Ohio; Approx. 8 m. long; Formed by a damming of Wills Creek, in a hilly coal mining and farmland region; Water reclamation.

•SEVEN MILE, Village; Butler County; Pop. 841; Area Code 513; Zip Code 45062; SW Ohio; 8 m. N of Hamilton along Sevenmile Creek, for which the village was named; Residential.

Mayor - John F. Kelley 524-4421
Chamber of Commerce - 5733 Skyline Ln.
Community Event(s) : Seven Hills Home Day;
    Annual, July

•SEVILLE, Village; Medina County; Pop. 1,568; Area Code 216;

Zip Code 44237; 18 m. W of Akron on the Chippewa River.

Henry Hosmer settled here in 1816 and was known as Burgh until 1828 when the town was platted and renamed for the place in Spain of the same name.

Agriculture - Grain and varied farming
Industry/Mfg. - Cement products, food packing
Chamber of Commerce - 29 W. Main St.

•**SHADYSIDE**, Village; Belmont County; Pop. 4,315; Area Code 614; Zip Code 43947; Elev. 700'; E Ohio; Has grown into a comparatively tidy residential town since its platting in 1901.

Mayor - Charles F. Morgan 676-5972
Chamber of Commerce - 541 W. 39th

•**SHAKER HEIGHTS**, City; Cuyahoga County; Pop. 32,487; Area Code 216; Zip Code 441 + zone; Elev. 860'; NE Ohio; NE of Cleveland; Takes its name from the Shakers who founded a religious community here in the early years of the nineteenth century.

Its later development resulted from the efforts of *O.P. and M.J. Van Sweringen*, railroad tycoons, who acquired the site in 1905, connected it with downtown Cleveland by a rapid transit line, and laid out the pretentious circular common with its fancy stores and Colonial Inn. Today, Shaker Heights is a restricted community of expensive homes and estates, of landscaped lawns, lakes, and parks.

Mayor - Walter C. Kelley 752-5000

•**SHARONVILLE**, City; Hamilton County; Pop. 10,108; Area Code 513; Zip Code 45241; SW Ohio; Elev. 598; 13 m. NE of Cincinnati in a hilly residential area.

Simon Hegerman surveyed this town in 1796, and today it is an important transportation center because of the large freight yards and shops maintained by major railroad lines.

Mayor - John S. Dowlin 563-1144

•**SHAWNEE**, Village; Perry County; Pop. 924; Area Code 614;

203

Zip Code 43782; SE central Ohio; In the Central Wayne National Forest; One of the larger trading centers in the large recreational area here.

•SHAWNEE HILLS, Village; Delaware County; Pop. 430; Area Code 614; Zip Code 43065; Central Ohio; Along the Scioto river, 11 m. N of Columbus; Residential area.

•SHEFFIELD, Village; Lorain County; Pop. 1,886; Area Code 216; Zip Code 44054; N Ohio; 6 m. E of Lorain and just S of Lake Erie in a residential area.

•SHEFFIELD LAKE, City; Lorain County; Pop. 10,484; Area Code 419; Zip Code 44875; N Ohio; 5 m. NE of Lorain city, on Lake Erie's shoreline; Residential and resort town.

> *Mayor* - Donald L. Smith 949-7141

•SHELBY, City; Richland County; Pop. 9,645; Area Code 419; Zip Code 44875; 12 m. NW of Mansfield.

> *Agriculture* - Grain and varied farming
>   poultry
> *Industry/Mfg.* - Recreational equipment, auto
>   parts
> *Mayor* - Henry R. Cline 347-5131
> *Daily Newspaper* - The Globe, 37 W. Main
> *Chamber of Commerce* - 23 W. Main

•SHELBY COUNTY, W Ohio; Area 408 sq. miles; Pop. 43,089; County seat Sidney; Est., January 7, 1819; Named for county in Kentucky; Crossed by Miami and Lorami Rivers; Former Indian lands, with headquarters of the Miami Tribes located at Pickawillany Village, near Piqua.

•SHERRODSVILLE, Village; Carroll County; Pop. 396; Area Code 216; Zip Code 44675; NE Ohio; On One Leg Creek, just S of Atwood Lake.

•SHERWOOD, Village; Defiance County; Pop. 915; Area Code 419; Zip Code 43556; NW Ohio; 9 m. W of city of Defiance.

•SHILOH, Village; Richland County; Pop. 857; Area Code 419;

Zip Code 44878; N central Ohio; Small farming center, 17 m. N of Mansfield.

•SHREVE, Village; Wayne County; Pop. 1,608; Area Code 216; Zip Code 44676; NE central Ohio; 11 m. SW of Wooster.

•SIDNEY, City; Seat of Shelby County; Pop. 17,657; Area Code 419; Zip Code 45365; Elev. 1,002'; W Ohio; Named for *Sir Philip Sidney*, the English poet.

When platted in 1820 Sidney was surrounded by great stretches of hardwood forests. Growth was slow until the Miami and Erie Canal was completed in 1845 and a railroad came in 1853. Sawmills and woodworking mills then arose and turned out large numbers of wagons, carriages, and school desks.

> *Agriculture* - Grain, cattle and varied
> farming
> *Industry/Mfg.* - Household appliances, dairy
> products, grain, machinery
> *Mayor* - Gary Van Fossen 498-2335
> *Daily Newspaper* - The News, 911 Vandemark Rd
> *Chamber of Commerce* - 133 S. Ohio Ave., PO
> Box 298

•SILVER LAKE, Village; Summit County; Pop. 2,915; Area Code 216; NE Ohio.

> *Mayor* - Clyde L. Conn 923-5233

•SILVERTON, City; Hamilton County; Pop. 6,172; Area Code 513; Elev. 812'; SW corner of Ohio; is a strictly residential community of homes lying on the outskirts of Cincinnati.

> *Mayor* - Richard W. Benken 793-7980

•SINKING SPRING, Village; Highland County; Pop. 239; Area Code 614; Zip Code 45172; S central Ohio; 17 m. SE of Hillsboro in a hilly, creek-fed region where prehisstoric Indians have left their mark on the earth.

•SMITHFIELD, Jefferson County; Pop. 1,308; Area Code 614; Zip Code 43948; E Ohio; 15 m. SW of Steubenville in a coal mining area.

•SMITHVILLE, Village; Wayne County; Pop. 1,467; Area Code 216; Zip Code 44677; NE central Ohio; 6 m. NE of Wooster in a quiet residential-rural area.

•SOLON, City; Cuyahoga County; Pop. 14,341; Area Code 216; Zip Code 44139; NE Ohio; 15 m. SE of downtown Cleveland in the residential outskirts of Cleveland.

Mayor - Charles J. Smercina 248-1155
Chamber of Commerce - 30675 Solon Rd.

•SOMERSET, Village; Perry County; Pop. 1,432; Area Code 614; Zip Code 43783; Elev. 1,010'; S central Ohio; Laid out in 1810 by *John Fink* and *Jacob Miller.*

Between 1829 and 1857 Somerset was the County seat; the old square courthouse still stands, marking the highest elevation in the county. St. Mary's Academy was established here in 1830, and later was removed to Columbus where it is known as St. Marys of the Springs. Somerset's great pride, lies in memories of *Philip Henry Sheridan,* who spent his boyhood here.

An equestrian Statue of *Phil Sheridan,* on the public square, honors the Civil War general, who was born in Albany, N.Y. in 1931. Sheridan came here with his parents at the age of one year. He was graduated from West Point in 1853, engaged in Indian warfare, and was a captain at the beginning of the Civil War. His brilliant tactics against *General Rosecrans* and a daring charge at Missionary Ridge attracted the attention of *General Grant* who placed him in command of his cavalry. Continued successes gave him leadership of the Army of the Shenandoah, in the latter's surrender at Appomatox. After the Civil War Sheridan was sent to Mexico. In 1883 he was given chief command of the Army, and was raised to the rank of general shortly before his death at Nonquit, Massachusetts in 1888.

•SOMERVILLE, Village; Butler County; Pop. 357; Area Code 513; Zip Code 45064; SW Ohio.

•SOUTH AMHERST, Village; Lorain County; Pop. 1,848; Area Code 216; N central Ohio; a quarrying center. At one time the village was named Podunk; later, because of the political sentiments of its residents, it was nicknamed the Little Whighole.

Mayor - Kenneth R. Jones 986-5901

•SOUTH BLOOMFIELD, Village; Pickaway County; Pop. 934; Area Code 614; Zip Code 43152; S central Ohio.

•SOUTH CHARLESTON, Village; Clark County; Pop. 1,682; Area Code 513; Zip Code 45368; W central Ohio; 12 m. SE of Springfield in a residential area.

Agriculture - Varied farming
Industry/Mfg. - Wood products
Mayor - Robin G. Rea 462-8888

•SOUTH EUCLID, City; Cuyahoga County; Pop. 25,713; Area Code 216; Zip Code 44121; NE Ohio; Just S of Euclid in the Cleveland metropolitan area; Residential and commercial.

Mayor - Arnold D'Amico 381-0400
Chamber of Commerce - 4461 Mayfield

•SOUTH LEBANON, Village; Warren County; Pop. 2,700; Area Code 513; Zip Code 45065; SW Ohio; 5 m. S of Lebanon along the Little Miami River; Residential

•SOUTH POINT, Village; Lawrence County; Pop. 3,918; Area Code 614; Zip Code 45680; Elev. 560'; S Ohio; So named because it is the most southerly point in Ohio, is a typical river farming community.

•SOUTH RUSSELL, Village; Geauga County; Pop. 2,784; Area Code 216; NE Ohio.

Mayor - D.E.Barribal 338-784

•SOUTH SALEM, Village; Ross County; Pop. 252; Area Code 614; Zip Code 45681; S Ohio; Near Chillicothe in a rural area.

•SOUTH SOLON, Village; Madison County; Pop. 416; Area Code

614; Zip Code 43153; SW central Ohio; 20 m. S of Springfield in a rural area.

•**SOUTH VIENNA**, Village; Clark County; Pop. 464; Area Code 513; Zip Code 45369; 11 m. E of Springfield in a large farming area in W Ohio.

•**SOUTH WEBSTER**, Village; Scioto County; Pop. 886; Area Code 614; Zip Code 45682; S Ohio; 20 m. NE of Portsmouth in the S Wayne National Forest; Rural trading center.

•**SOUTH ZANESVILLE**, Village; Muskingum County; Pop. 1,739; Area Code 614; Zip Code 43701; E central Ohio; Just S of Zanesville in a residential area.

•**SPARTA**, Village; Morrow County; Pop. 219; Area Code 614; Zip Code 43350; Central Ohio; 35 m. NE of Columbus.

•**SPENCER**, Village; Medina County; Pop. 764; Area Code 216; Zip Code 44275; 33 m. W of Akron near the Black River in N Ohio. Named after the township in 1832.

•**SPENCERVILLE**, Village; Allen County; Pop. 2,184; Area Code 419; Zip Code 45887; NW Ohio; 15 m. SW of Lima in a farming region; Serves as a produce trading center.

•**SPRINGBORO**, Village; Warren County; Pop. 4,962; Area Code 513; Zip Code 45066; SW Ohio; 14 m. S of Dayton in a residential and light industrial area.

Mayor - Robert K. South 748-1041

•**SPRINGDALE**, City; Hamilton County; Pop. 10,111; Area Code 513

Mayor - Raymond R. Johnson 671-0885

•**SPRINGFIELD**, City; Seat of Clark County; Pop. 72,563; Area Code 513; Zip Code 455 + zone; Elev. 980'; Central Ohio; 80 m. N of Cincinnati on Buck Creek; Incorporated, town in 1801; city in 1850.

Two years after Kentuckian *James Demint* built a log cabin along the north bank of Buck Creek in 1799, a settlement was platted along the river bottomlands across from Demint's home. Demint was the area's first permanent non-Indian resident, but by 1802 the small settlement included eight cabins. One of the early residents christened the town Springfield because of the spring water flowing down the hills that bordered the valley of Buck Creek. For several years the city grew; good harvests brought industry, industry brought people. Although Springfield was named the county seat in 1818, the lack of a good transportation system from Springfield to other cities kept the city from prospering as well as its early citizens hoped. With the completion of the national road into Springfield in 1838, the city's economy prospered. Since the turn of the century, industry has become the city's main economic source.

Wittenberg University was established here by the Lutheran Church in 1845.

> *Industry/Mfg.* - Electronics, dairy products,
> trucks, heavy equipment
> *Higher Education* - Wittenbert University
> *Mayor* - Roger Baker 324-7700
> *Daily Newspaper* - The News, 202 N. Limestone
> Street
> *Chamber of Commerce* - 102 W. Main St.

•**SPRING VALLEY**, Village; Greene County; Pop. 541; Area Code 513; Zip Code 45370; SW central Ohio; 8 m. S of Xenis, along the wooded banks of the Little Miami River. Named for the township when it was platted in 1842.

Mineral water is bottled and shipped from the nearby springs. At the S edge of Spring Valley, U.S. 42 crosses the river, and in the Autumn this section of country offers gorgeous views of the wooded valley and slow-winding river.

•**STAFFORD**, Village; Monroe County; Pop. 98; Area Code 614; Zip Code 43786; 30 m. NE of Marietta in SE Ohio; Rural section of the E Wayne National Forest.

•**STARK COUNTY**, NE Ohio; Area 576 sq. miles; Pop. 378,823; County seat Canton; Est., February 13, 1808; Named for *John Stark*, Revolutionary War brigadier-general; Fed by the Tuscarawas River. (See Canton, Massillon).

•**STEUBENVILLE**, City; Seat of Jefferson County; Pop. 26,400; Area Code 614; Zip Code 43952; Elev. 830'; 90 m. E of Cleveland on the Ohio River near the West Virginia border. It is now part of the metropolis of Weirtown W.V., 42 m. W of Pittsburgh, PA; Inc.; village in 1805; city in 1851.

The town was named after Fort Steuben, which was named after *Baron von Steuben*, a Prussian drillmaster and U.S. Revolutionary War supporter.

Fort Steuben was built in 1787 to protect a section of government land known as the "Seven Ranges". In 1790 the Fort was leveled by a fire.

Jacob Walker arrived in 1765 and bought 400 acres of land at .16 an acre. In 1797 *Bezaled Wells* and *James Ross* platted the town.

The city covers an elevated plain that old steamboat men proclaimed "the best town site on the Ohio". The city's basic nationalities are Irish, Welsh, English, German, Slavs and Latins. During the 1800's Steubenville became an important port as the traffic on the Ohio river increased.

The city has prospered as an industrial center and a major steel producer.

> *Industry/Mfg.* - Metal containers, coal, gas, steel
> *Higher Education* - College of Steubenville
> *Mayor* - William Crabbe 282-4561
> *Daily Newspaper* - The Herald-Star, 401 Herald Square
> *Chamber of Commerce* - 162 N. Fourth St., PO Box 278

•**STOCKPORT**, Village; Morgan County; Pop. 558; Area Code 614; Zip Code 43840; SE Ohio; Along the navigable portion of the Muskingum River, 30 m. NW of Marietta; Scenic stock-raising farms surround this village.

•**STONE CREEK**, Village; Tuscarawas County; Pop. 150; Area Code 614; Zip Code 43154; Elev. 924'; E Ohio; Was formerly called Phillipsburg for *Phillip Leonard*, who laid out the village along the narrow bed of Stone Creek in 1854.

•**STOUTSVILLE**, Village; Fairfield County; Pop. 537; Area Code

614; Zip Code 43154; 15 m. SW of Lancaster in S central Ohio; Rural farming region. Named after native New Englander *Benjamin Stout* who laid out the town in 1854.

•**STOW**, City; Summit County; Pop. 25,303; Area Code 216; Zip Code 44244; NE central Ohio; 10 m. NE of Akron in a residential area. Named after *Judge Joshua Stow*, a native of Middletown, Connecticut.

Mayor - C.Paul Hutchinson 688-8206
Chamber of Commerce - 137 S. Main St.

•**STRASBURG**, Village; Tuscarawas County; Pop. 2,091; Area Code 614; Zip Code 44680; Elev. 914'; E Ohio; Named after the earlier settlers (1828) hometown in Germany.

Strasburg is notable chiefly as the location of the Garver Brothers Store, N. Wooster Ave., where it is possible to buy a needle or a reaping machine, a pair of overalls or a fur coat. This extraordinary small-town department store occupied 90,000 square feet of floor space and grossed more than $500,000 annually during the leanest years of the early 1930's; the American Magazine called it "the largest country store in America". The store founder was *Phillip Garver* in 1866.

•**STRATTON**, Village; Jefferson County; Pop. 356; Area Code 614; Zip Code 43961; E Ohio; On the Ohio River, 13 m. N of Steubenville in a coal and clay mining area.

•**STREETSBORO**, City; Portage County; Pop. 9,055; Area Code 216; Zip Code 44240; Elev. 1,136'; NE Ohio; Named for Titus Street, original owner of the township, at the time of its settlement in 1822.

Mayor - Victor J. Pavlick 626-4942
Chamber of Commerce - Box 7 Streetsboro Plaza

•**STRONGVILLE**, City; Cuyahoga County; Pop. 28,577; Area Code 216; Zip Code 44136; NE Ohio; 30 m. SW of Cleveland in the dairy farming region which rims the metropolitan area. Named after *Gov. Caleb Strong* of Massachusetts who owned the land in the area.

211

Agriculture - Varied farming
Industry/Mfg. - Dairy products
Mayor - Walter F. Ehrnfelt 238-5720
Chamber of Commerce - 18829 Royalton Rd.

•STRUTHERS, City; Mahoning County; Pop. 13,624; Area Code 216; Zip Code 44471; NE Ohio; 5 m. SE of Youngstown in the suburban section of this vast steel milling region. In 1799 pioneer *John Struthers* bought 400 acres along the banks of Yellow Creek. His son Thomas founded the place in 1866.

Mayor - Daniel J. Hurite 755-2181

•STRYKER, Village; Williams County; Pop. 1,423; Area Code 419; Zip Code 43557; NW Ohio; On Tiffin Creek, about 17 m. N of Defiance in a corn-farming region.

•SUGAR BUSH KNOLLS, Village; Portage County; Pop. 201; Area Code 216; NE Ohio.

•SUGARCREEK, Village; Tuscarawas County; Pop. 1,966; Area Code 614; Zip Code 44681; 8 m. W of Dover in E Ohio; Along a branch of the Sugar Creek; Farm trading center. Named in 1818 after the township.

Agriculture - Grain and varied farming
Industry/Mfg. - Clay, dairy products, coal
Community Event(s) : Ohio Swiss Festival;
Annual, September-October

•SUGAR GROVE, Village; Fairfield County; Pop. 407; Area Code 614; Zip Code 43155; S central Ohio; Along the Hocking River, 6 m. S of Lancaster. Named for the descriptive flora found in the fertile land at the confluence of Rush Creek and the Hocking River.

•SUMMERFIELD, Village; Noble County; Pop. 299; Area Code 614; Zip Code 43788; SE Ohio; 40 m. NE of Marietta in a rural area near the borders of the Wayne National Forest.

•SUMMIT COUNTY, NE Ohio; Area 410 sq. miles; Pop. 524,472; County seat Akron; Est., March 3, 1840; Named for the highlands here, and because this area was the highest alomg the Erie Canal; Cut through by Cuyahoga River; Economy focused around Akron's rubber industries, and most of the county is part of that city's metropolitan area.

•SUMMITVILLE, Village; Columbiana County; Pop. 146; Area Code 216; Zip Code 43962; E Ohio; In a hilly coal mining area.

•SUNBURY, Village; Delaware County; Pop. 1,911; Area Code 614; Zip Code 43074; Elev. 965; Central Ohio; 12 m. SE of Delaware city in a dairy and grain farming region.

> *Agriculture* - Grain and varied farming
> *Industry/Mfg.* - Grain milling, dairy products
> *Mayor* - Harold Kintner 965-3946

•SWANTON, Village; Fulton County; Pop. 3,424; Area Code 419; Zip Code 43558; NW Ohio; 20 m. W of Toledo in a nursery and farming district.

> *Agriculture* - Varied farming
> *Industry/Mfg.* - Wood products, plastics,
> boxes
> *Mayor* - Louis A. Carson 826-2816

•SYCAMORE, Village; Wyandot County; Pop. 1,059; Area Code 419; Zip Code 44882; 14 m. S of Tiffin in NW central Ohio. Named for the creek that runs through the place.

> *Agriculture* - Grain. cattle and varied
> farming, poultry

•SYLVANIA, City; Lucas County; Pop. 15,527; Area Code 419; Zip Code 43560; NW Ohio; 11 m. NW of Toledo, just S of the Michigan state line.

> *Agriculture* - Truck, grain and varied
> farming
> *Industry/Mfg.* - Quarrying, concrete products
> *Mayor* - James E. Seney 882-7102
> *Chamber of Commerce* - PO Box 242
> *Community Event(s)* : Outdoor Art Festival;
> Annual, September

•SYRACUSE, Village; Meigs County; Pop. 946; Area Code 614; Zip Code 45779; SE Ohio; On the Ohio River, 6 m. s of Pomeroy, with a small port.

•TALLMADGE, City; Summit County; Pop. 15,269; Area Code 216; Zip Code 44278; NE central Ohio; Just E of Akron; Residential.

Mayor - John r. Doepker 633-5095
Chamber of Commerce - 427 Commerce St.

•TARLTON, Village; Pickaway County; Pop. 394; Area Code 614; Zip Code 43156; S central Ohio; 12 m. SE of Circleville in a rural area.

•TERRACE PARK, Village; Hamilton County; Pop. 2,044; Area Code 513; Zip Code 45174; Elev. 533'; 20 m. E of Cincinnati in SW Ohio; Along the Little Miami River.
    In this suburban community stands the John Robinson House. The circus king lived in this two-story white structure in the early 1900's, he also built an "Elephant House" adjoining it, surmounted by an imposing likeness of an elephant.

•THE VILLAGE OF INDIAN HILL, City; Hamilton County; Pop. 5,521; Area Code 513.

•THORNVILLE, Village; Perry County; Pop. 838; Area Code 614; Zip Code 43076; S central Ohio; 13 m. S of Newark in a rural-vacation spot.

•THURSTON, Village; Fairfield County; Pop. 527; Area Code 614; Zip Code 43157; S central Ohio; 12 m. NE of Lancaster in a rural area.

•TIFFIN, City; Seat of Seneca County; Pop. 19,549; Zip Code 44883; Elev. 761'; N Ohio; On the Sandusky River as it winds northward toward Sandusky Bay.
    Erastus Bowe saw the site during an expedition in the War of 1812, and returned in 1817 to build Pan Yan Tavern, which later became a stagecoach stop. Around the Pan Yan a settlement called Oakley sprang up. In 1820, Josiah Hedges purchased a section of land on the south side of the river opposite Oakley, and

established a new settlement, calling it Tiffin, after *Edward Tiffin*, first governor of Ohio. Until 1850, when the two villages were united, there was much rivalry between them.

One of Ohio's best-known eccentrics, *J.N.Free*, (1828-1906), better known as "the immortal J.N.," was a frequent visitor in Tiffin during the later part of the nineteenth century.

Agriculture - Cattle grain and varied
    farming
Industry/Mfg. - Clay, glass and dairy
    products, tools and dies, doors
Higher Education - Heidelberg College, Tiffin
    University
Mayor - Thomas L. Yager 447-3440
Daily Newspaper - The Advertiser-Tribune,
    PO Box 218, 320 Nelson St.
Chamber of Commerce - 70 E. Terry St.

•TILTONSVILLE, Village; Jefferson County; Pop. 1,750; Area Code 614; Zip Code 43963; E Ohio; On the Ohio River, about 20 m. S of Steubenville in a coal mining and shipping area. Named after *John Tilton* who platted out the town in 1806.

•TIMBERLAKE, Village; Lake County; Pop. 885; Area Code 216; NE Ohio.

•TIPP CITY, City; Miami County; Pop. 5,595; Area Code 513; Zip Code 45371; W central Ohio; Along the Miami River about 7 m. S of Troy.

Agriculture - Varied farming
Industry/Mfg. - Food packing, dairy products
    toys, paper
Mayor - David R. Cook 667-8424
Chamber of Commerce - PO Box 134
Community Event(s) : Mum Festival; Annual,
    October

•TIRO, Village; Crawford County; Pop. 279; Area Code 419; Zip Code 44887; N central Ohio; 13 m. NE of Bucyrus in a rural area.

•TOLEDO, City; Seat of Lucas County; Pop. 354,635; Area Code 419; Zip Code 436 + zone; Elev. 587'; On Maumee River at SW corner of Lake Erie in NW Ohio; Stretches for 15 m. along both sides of the Maumee River a short distance SW of Maumee Bay, the westernmost tip of Lake Erie.

Toledo was not incorporated until 1837, but the site was visited by a white man as early as 1615 when *Etienne Brule*, a French-Canadian guide for *Samuel de Champlain*, found the Erie Indians living among the swamps and dense forests at the mouth of the Maumee. Not until after the Battle of Fallen Timers in 1794, fought a few miles southwest of present Toledo, did settlers begin to move northward from the Ohio River and westward from the Allegheny Mountain passes. Under orders from *Anthony Wayne*, a stockade that was given the name Fort Industry was erected on the present site of Toledo. But the few who came to this region fled with the outbreak of the War of 1812; not until the end of that war was the area opened for permanent settlement.

In 1817 a treaty conveyed to the Government practically all the Indian land remaining in the vicinity, and that same year a Cincinnati syndicate purchased a 974-acre tract at the mouth of Swan Creek and named the first permanent settlement Port Lawrence. The syndicate failed in 1820, but was revived in 1832. A year later Port Lawrence voted to consolidate with Vistula, a river settlement to the north.

The inhabitants chose the name Toledo, but the reason for this choice is buried in a welter of legends. One recounts that *Washington Irving*, who was traveling in Spain at the time, suggested the name to his brother, a local resident; This explanation ignores the fact that Irving returned to the United States in 1832. Others award the honor to *Two Stickney*, son of the major who quaintly numbered his sons and named his daughters after States. The most popular version attributes the naming to *Willard J. Daniels*, a merchant, who reputedly suggested Toledo because it "is easy to pronounce, is pleasant in sound, and there is no other city of that name on the American continent."

Whatever the origin, it eventually resulted in a peculiar rapprochement with the Spanish city of the same name. The city's oldest newspaper is named the Toledo Blade and was awarded the royal coat of arms by the Spanish Government. In 1931 the University of the City of Toledo was granted permission to use the arms of Ferdinand and Isabella as its motif, and three years later a goodwill delegation of local citizens returned from the Spanish city burdened with gifts for the museum of art and the new cathedral.

216

What is now Toledo was in the 1830's a plexus of little communities. On the west bank were Manhattan, Marengo, and Miami; on the east lay Lucas City, Mendota, Oregon, and Orleans. Perrysburg, far up the river, was soon the leading community, a commentary on the short-sightedness of the early settlers who failed to visualize the shipping possibiliies of the region nearer the bay.

The early years were hard. An epidemic of Asiatic cholera, intensified by the swampy nature of the region, ravaged the countryside in 1832 and 1833. In 1838 a drought destroyed crops, dried up streams and swamps, and even killed forest trees. And following hard upon the financial panic of 1837 came two years of "uncommonly sickly" business.

Into these unsettled times was injected the "Toledo War" of 1835-6, a protracted dispute between Ohio and Michigan over the location of their common boundary.

Early maps of the Northwest Territory had placed the tip of Lake Erie too far south, and Lake Michigan too far north. The Ohio constitution, accepted by Congress, specified that the line drawn east and west should in no event strike Lake Erie below the northern cape of the Maumee River. Michigan contested this alignment and claimed the site of the city and its harbor. When Toledoans attempted to take public office under Ohio laws, Michigan's legislature passed a Pains and Penalties Act (1835), providing heavy fines and imprisonment for anyone attempting to establish unauthorized jurisdiction in the area. Michigan's 21-year-old acting governor, *Stevens T. Mason,* called out the militia to enforce the Act, and in reply, *Governor Robert Lucas* of Ohio, accompanied by 1,000 soldiers, arrived in Perrysburg in March 1835, determined to chase the Michigan troops out of Toledo.

Governor Lucas ordered his men to march on Toledo; Governor Mason ordered his militia to drive Lucas out of Perrysburg. Before actual fighting began, however, emissaries from *President Jackson* arrived and persuaded the governors to subscribe to a temporary truce. Minor raids continued despite the action, and a force of 200 Michigan men entered Toledo on April 11, 1835, pulled down Ohio's flag, and dragged it through the streets. On April 26, another Michigan band fell upon the Ohio boundary commissioners and their staff, arrested nine, and marched them into Michigan.

Governor Lucas then made a shrewd move by calling a special session of the legislature on June 8, which immediately created Lucas County out of that part of Wood County involved in the dispute. The new county was directed to hold court in Toledo on the first Monday in September. To enforce its edict the legislature voted an appropriation for an army. The climax came with the first session of this court in Toledo. On September 6, the Detroit militia assembled at Monroe, just north of the city, ready to march into Toledo the follwoing day when the court was to sit. But the three Ohio judges, escorted by 30 mounted men, rode into the city at one o'clock in the morning of September 7, and by the light of a tallow candle held a brief session of court in a frame schoolhouse on Erie Street. They quickly appointed commissioners for Lucas County, and then, fearing the Michigan militia, rode off in such haste that *Judge Conant's* beaver hat, in which the minutes were hidden, was brushed off by the branch of a tree. It was bravely retrieved by *Colonel Van Fleet,* and later in the day Ohio was able to show documentary proof that on September 7, 1835, it had "exercised jurisdiction over the disputed territory by holding a Court of Common Pleas in due form of law."

President Jackson, who favored the Ohio claim, tried to solve the problem by removing Acting-*Governor Mason* from office and appointing *John S. Horner* to the post. Met with jeers and burned in effigy, Horner resigned in less than a month, and at the October election Michigan adopted a constitution and elected Mason to the governorship. Congress proposed, as a condition of Michigan's entrance into the Union as a State, that Ohio be given the disputed territory, and in exchange offered Michigan the Upper Peninsula. Michigan accepted under protest, not knowing of the immense ore wealth of the peninsula, and was admitted to the Union June 1836. Toledo became an acknowledged part of Ohio.

Celebrating the end of the "war", Toledo fired guns, rang bells, and paraded around the schoolhouse where the candlelight session of court had been held. Seven months later, on January 7, 1837, Ohio's legislature incorporated the city of Toledo.

Spurred by the opening of the Erie Canal in New York, Ohio lake cities clamored in the 1830's for canals to the Ohio River. Already the Ohio and Erie Canal had made Cleveland, as its northern terminus, a boom town. Toledo, Sandusky, and Charleston (Lorain) strove to acquire the lake end of another canal farther west. But the city at the mouth of the broad Maumee was the inevitable choice as the lake terminus for canals that tapped the resources of western Ohio and eastern Indiana. The first canal barge arrived over the Wabash and Erie Canal in 1843 from Lafayette, Indiana. Two years later the Miami and Erie Canal was opened to the Lake. The two canals, joining at Defiance, extended to the lake along the Maumee River, with outlets at Maumee, Toledo, and Manhattan (now a part of the city of Toledo). Business flourished. From the beginning most of the canal boats used Toledo's outlet at Swan Creek. Grain elevators and warehouses were built along the stream. Across from the old packet docks, between Perry and Lafayette Streets, a solid line of stores prospered on the canal trade.

Toledo expanded along the river bank for more than a mile. Mills, foundries, and factories, attracted by the superior shipping facilities, came to the city, and the population leaped from 3,829 in 1850 to 13,000 in the following decade. Three million bushels of foodstuffs passed through the port in 1846, the first year of the joint operation of the canals. In 1836, the same year the Wabash and Erie Canal was begun, The Erie and Kalamazoo Railroad (the first in Ohio) was completed, with Toledo its southern terminus. Its iron-topped wooden rails extended to Adrian, Michigan. The cars were at first horse-drawn, but in the secnd year two small locomotives replaced old Dobbin. An early engraving depicts a small engine, labeled Adrian No.I, pulling a car that resembles a modern auto-trailer. From this simple beginning Toledo's great rail system developed.

Toledo, typically Ohioan, played an active role in the abolitionist movement and the Civil War. Fifth in importance among the Underground Railroad stations along Lake Erie, it ranked below Sandusky, Cleveland, Ashtabula, and Conneaut. But, as *W.H.Siebert* observes in The Undergound Railroad from Slavery to Freedom, "the remote position and sparse settlement of the northwestern section of the State probably explains the failure to find many traces of routes in that region." A prominent group of Underground Railroad conductors, including congressmen, a Quaker, an Irishman, a Negro, and some New Englanders, was active at Toledo, and a small boat, The Phoebus, carried the slaves to Detroit. During the war Toledo sent a full quota of soldiers into the field and furnished a large and prominent list of officers, including *General James B. Steedman, General John W. Fuller, and Brigadier General Issac R. Sherwood.*

The Civil War decade was a period of sustained growth.

Toledo began to emerge as a railroad terminus with the iron horse bringing increasing cargoes for lake shipment. Major triumphs, too, were the first scheduled streetcar service, a horse-car line on Summit Street, in 1862, and the building of the first bridge over the Maumee at Cherry Street three years later, joining for the first time the west community with the east. In 1869 new lines of rails came into town from several directions with the completion of the Wheeling & Lake Erie and the Toledo, Ann Arbor & Northern Railroads.

The material expansion of the war decade was followed by cultural and institutional growth. The first unit of Toledo's extensive park system was established in 1871. *Jessup W. Scott* endowed in 1872 the Toledo University of Arts and Trades, progenitor of the present University of the City of Toledo, and in the same year the first public library was opened at Summit and Madison Streets.

The net of railroads spread with the completion of the Toledo & Woodville Railroad in 1873; three years later the Toledo, Columbus & Hocking Valley Railroad tapped southern Ohio's coal fields and started an increasing stream of coal, the origin of which finally reached into West Virginia and Kentucky. By 1880 Toledo's population had reached 50,000 , and the railroad era that was to make the city the Nation's thrid-largest rail center had not yet reached its peak.

The 1880's brought a new industrial epoch to Toledo, with glass the measure of the city's new importance. The recently discovered Maumee Valley gas field, an apparently inexhaustibel producing area, lured the new industry with cheap fuel. In 1888, *Edward Libbey* closed his East Cambridge, Massachusetts, glass factory and, bringing 100 glass craftsmen with him, founded the Libbey Glass Company of Toledo. For a while he manufactured high-grade crystal ware and lamp globes. Then, at Wheeling, West Virginia, he hired *Michael Owens*, glass blower extraordinary, as superintendent of his Toledo plant; together they revolutionized the glass business. Owens first invented an automatic foot pedal to open molds, thereby eliminating much of the child labor from the industry, and a short time later developed a semi-automatic machine to make drinking glasses. The third of Toledo's noted glassmakers, *Edward Ford*, son of America's pioneer plate-glass manufacturer, came to Toledo in 1896 to establish a plate-glass plant. He built his plant below Toledo on the east side of the Maumee, founding there the model industrial town of Rossford and one of the largest plate-glass factories in the world.

By 1890 Toledo's docks totaled 18 miles and were receiving 2,500,000 tons of coal and 250,000 tons of iron ore annually. There was an increasing rail importance, too, with 184 passenger trains daily, and a vast volume of freight handled in the local yards. To its already important lumber, furniture, and allied industries Toledo added iron and steel and assorted producst; in all there were 750 manufacturing establishments.

But the "gay nineties" brought other more immediate excitement. The Wheeler Opera House burned to the ground in 1893, and two years later the "new magnificent" Valentine Theater opened with Rip Van Winkle. But the biggest flurry of the year came when, after the search for oil had moved northward from the great Lima field, the Klondike oil well geysered up in a marshy field on Millard Avenue in East Toledo. Wells went down all over the East Side, particularly in the Ironville district. The Klondike and the Lima field in time became dwindling producers, but they were influential in establishing Toledo as the largest refining center between Chicago and the Atlantic seaboard. Thousand-mile pipe lines now bring oil all the way from the great mid-continental oil fields to Toledo for refining.

The era that elsewhere inspired *Lincoln Steffens'* Shame of the Cities saw the rise of two famous reform leaders in Toledo. *Samuel M. Jones* became mayor in 1897, and began to apply to the city government the same "Golden Rule" policy with which he had managed his oil-well supplies factory. As "Golden Rule" Jones he became a national celebrity; until his death in 1904, he warred against misuse of public funds, favoritism, and bossism, and repeatedly defeated both major parties with his nonpartisan ticket. He established in Toledo one of the first municipal utilities, the Toledo Municipal Gas Company, the city's first free kindergardens, public playgrounds, band concerts, and the eight-hour day for city employees. *Brad Whitlock*, his successor as mayor from 1905 to 1913, four times elected, carried on the independent movement. He was instrumental in securing the passage of a State law providing for the election of all judges on a nonpartisan balot, and was prominently identified with the campaign leading to the adoption of Ohio's initiative and referendum law in 1912.

There were significant cultural advances also toward the end of the century. In 1898 St. John's College was founded by the Jesuit Fathers. And in 1899 the later extensive Toledo Zoo was started with an initial menagerie of a woodchuck, two badgers, and a golden eagle. The following year the Toledo Museum of Art was founded with its first exhibition held in a downtown storeroom.

The 30-year span from 1870 to 1900, with its innovations of rail, oil, and glass, lifted Toledo's population from 31,000 to 131,000. In the first decade of the new century, Toledo found new sources of growth. In 1903 *Michael Owens* invented a machine that drank in molten glass and turned out bottles by the tens of thousands. To meet demands that poured in from all parts of the world for these low-priced bottles, the Owens Bottle Machine Company and the Owens European Bottle Machine Company were formed in 1905, with Libey as president and Owens as general manager. Several new railroads entered the city in this period, which was the beginning of the heyday of the electric lines. But the most significant development concerned the new "gasoline buggy." In 1908 *John Willys* came to Toledo and bought the Toledo-Pope plant, where one of the earliest automobiles had been built, and moved his recently acquired Overland automobile factory here from Indianapolis. As the firm expanded, Toledo's growth became increasingly geared with that of the automobile industry. The glass industry still boomed; in 1912, Libbey, on Owen's advice, purchased a patent for unperfected flatglass machinery, and in a few years Owens had adapted it to a practical process. The first unit of the present Toledo Museum of Art was opened in 1912, with Libbey's contribution of $50,000 and the site constituting the largest gifts toward its erection.

The streetcar war that was waged in the following year, and the opening of the new Cherry Street Bridge in 1914 were of little moment beside the growth of the automobile industry that brought the city its greatest boom years. Willys-Overland each year was turning out successive "improved models" in greater and greater numbers. Automotive-parts manufacture was also flourishing. Champion Spark Plug established its plant in 1914, and the Warner Manufacturing Company, predecessor of Toledo's Chevrolet plant, was turning out automobile gears. In the war years many of Toledo's plants devoted part of their facilities to war supplies. There was fitting climax, also, to these hectic years, on July 4, 1919, when "the battle of the century" between *Jack Dempsey* and *Jess Willard* was fought at Bay View Park, with Dempsey making a tigerish conquest of the world's heavyweight title. The boom decade saw Toledo's population increase by 75,000

A city of nearly 250,000 in 1921, Toledo entered in that year the annals of sensational crime with a million-dollar post-office robbery. It was a decade of fabulous figures. Willys-Overland production soared, until at its peak 25,000 workers were turning out an automobile very half-minute. The money that swamped the town overflowd into cultural improvements: An impressive addition to the museum of art was completed in 1926, and two years later citizens voted a $2,850,000 bond issue for an extensive building program for the University of the City of Toledo. In the same yer Transcontinental Airport was dedicated. Presque Isle's $20,000,000 coal and iron-ore docks, an ultra-modern symbol of Toledo's importane as a lake and rail port, were opened in 1930. In the same year the local glass manufacturing names were merged into the Libbey-Owens-Ford Glass Company.

Although World War II years meant a resurgence of prosperity especially for the new "Jeep" manufacturers, the late 1960's and 1970's saw a slow decline in the nation's demand for many of Toledo's traditional manufactures. However, the city's port remains the largest mover of soft coal in the world, and the glass companies are manufacturing plastic containers and other packaging along with their older products. As 1980 began, about $200 million in downtown construction was planned or being built.

POINTS OF INTEREST

TOLEDO MUSEUM OF ART - White Vermont marble
structure with an Ionic facade; founded
(1901) by *Edward Drummond Libbey* ; ranks
in top ten among U.S. art museums in attendance.
TOLEDO ZOOLOGICAL PARK - Occupies 23 acres;
contains an aquarium, seal pool, barless
bear pits, monkey mountain, a conservatory,
bandshell and open air amphitheater.

Higher Education - University of Toledo
Mayor - Doug DeGood 247-6332
Daily Newspaper - The Balde, 541 Superior St.

223

Chamber of Commerce - 218 Huron St.
Community Event(s) : City Recreation
    Festival; Annual, August, Greek-American
    Family Festival; Annual, September, Hun-
    garian Wine Festival; Annual, September
    Independence Day of Mexico; Annual, Sept.
    International Festival; Annual, May, Out-
    door Jubilee; Annual, August, Syrian-
    Lebanese-American Family Festival; Annual,
    September, Toledo Area Artist's Exhibition;
    Annual, May-June, Toledo Festival of the
    Arts; Annual, June

•**TONTOGANY**, Village; Wood County; Pop. 367; Area Code 419; Zip Code 43565; NW Ohio; 7 m. NW of Bowling Green in a grain farming area.

•**TORONTO**, City; Jefferson County; Pop. 6,934; Area Code 614; Zip Code 43964; Elev. 695'; E Ohio; an important clay-products center.

Toronto was laid out in 1818 by *John Depuy* and called Newburg for a while, then Sloan's Station. In 1881 it was given its present name because a prominent citizen originally came from the Canadian city.

Part of the site was deeded by the Government to "Auver" *Mike Myers,* Indian fighter and scout, as payment for his services in opening the Ohio country to settlement.

Agriculture - Varied farming
Industry/Mfg. - Cement products, coal, steel,
    paper
Mayor - George V. Cattrell 537-2750
Chamber of Commerce - PO Box 250

•**TREMONT CITY**, Village; Clark County; Pop. 374; Area Code 513; Zip Code 45372; 8 m. NW of Springfield in W central Ohio.

•**TRENTON**, City; Butler County; Pop. 6,401; Area Code 513; Zip Code 45067; 35 m. N of Cincinnati in SW Ohio; suburban-commercial area.

Mayor - John Madoffori 988-6304

•**TRIMBLE**, Village; Athens County; Pop. 579; Area Code 614; Zip Code 45782; SE Ohio; 50 m. S of Zanesville in the central

Wayne National Forest; Rural trading post.

•**TROTWOOD**, City; Montgomery County; Pop. 7,802; Area Code 513; Zip Code 454–; SW Ohio; 10m. NW of Dayton.

> *Agriculture* - Grain, cattle and varied
>   farming, tobacco
> *Industry/Mfg.* - Campers and truck bodies
> *Mayor* - Richard J. Haas 837-7771

•**TROY**, City; Seat of Miami County; Pop. 19,086; Area Code 513; Zip Code 45373; Elev. 840'; W central Ohio.
    Troy is situated on a rich agricultural plain. *Michael Garver* purchased 320 acres of land here in 1798, erected a log cabin, cleared a small field, and urged immigrants to become his neighbors.

> *Agriculture* - Tobacco, grain and varied
>   farming
> *Industry/Mfg.* - Food packing, boxes, elec-
>   tronics, plastics
> *Mayor* - Robert A. Fletcher 335-1725
> *Daily Newspaper* - The News, 224 S. Market St.
> *Chamber of Commerce* - 25 S. Plum St., PO
>   Box 56

•**TRUMBULL COUNTY**, NE Ohio; Area 615 sq. miles; Pop. 241,863; County seat Warren; Est., July 10, 1800; Named for *Jonathan Trumbull*, secretary and aide-de-camp to *George Washington* during the Revolutionary War, as well as Connecticut statesman.

•**TURKEYFOOT ROCK PARK**, State park; NW Ohio; S of Toledo near Fallen Timbers; Surrounding a three-ton limestone boulder with petroglyphs resembling turkey feet.
    It is assumed that the carvings here were made by an aboriginal artist. Opposite Turkeyfoot and in the stretch of river below are some of the favored spots of local fishermen. The stream here is shallow enough for wading, but nonswimmers must watch for occasional deep holes. When conditions are right, bass, pike, and pickerel will rise to either fly or bait. The dignified, if somewhat absurd, great blue heron may be standing at the margin of the stream, his swordlike beak poised to snatch

the first unwary sprat he sees.

At this point the highway rises from the level of the river to the bluffs some 60 feet above, passing black loamy fields fat with corn and wheat. When *General Wayne* saw the green waves of Indian cornfields during his approach to Fallen Timbers, he said the land was the richest he had ever seen.

•TUSCARAWAS, Village; Tuscarawas County; Pop. 917; Area Code 216; Zip Code 44682; E central Ohio; 10 m. S of New Philadelphia: Named for the river which flows nearby.

•TUSCARAWAS COUNTY, E Ohio; Area 569 sq. miles; Pop. 84,614; County seat New Philadelphia; Est., February 13, 1808; Name is derived from the Indian word meaning "open mouth"; River by the same name flows through this region; Site of the first town in Ohio, Schoenbrunn, which is now a state park; Deposits of iron ore, coal and fire clay attracted German immigrants, as well as the builders of the Erie canal in the early 1800s.

•TWINSBURG, City; Summit County; Pop. 7,632; Area Code 216; Zip Code 44087; Elev. 985'; NE Ohio; Clusters about its six-acre village square, a gift of the Wilcox twins, *Moses and Aaron,* for whom the town was named.

Mayor - Anthony A. Perici 425-7161
Chamber of Commerce - Bank Annex Bldg.

•UHRICHSVILLE, City; Tuscarawas County; Pop. 6,130; Area Code 614; Zip Code 44683; Elev. 856'; E Ohio; Settled in 1804 by *Michael Uhrich* of Pennsylvania; Originally named the place Waterford.

Uhrich built a flour mill two years later, but the platting of the town was delayed until 1833.

Completion of the Ohio and Erie Canal brought a phenomenal development between 1830 and 1850. In the later years the arrival of the Steubenville & Indiana Railroad provided the community with additional trading and shipping facilities.

Agriculture - Varied farming
Industry/Mfg. - Clay, tobaco and dairy
products, coal

226

Mayor - Burton E. Peck 922-1243
Daily Newspaper - The Chronicle, 109 N.
   Water Street
Chamber of Commerce - PO Box 49
Community Event(s) : National Clay Week
   Festival; Annual, June

•UNION, Village; Montgomery County; Pop. 5,219; Area Code 513; Zip Code 45322; SW central Ohio; In the rural countryside outside of the Dayton metropolitan area.

Mayor - William R. Cooper 836-8624
Chamber of Commerce - 225 W. Oak St.

•UNION CITY, Village; Darke County; Pop. 1,716; Area Code 513; Zip Code (rural); Elev. 1,108; W Ohio; On the Indiana state line.

•UNION COUNTY, W central Ohio; Area 434 sq. miles; Pop. 29,536; County seat Marysville; Est., January 10, 1820; Named because it was formed from the union of four other counties; Rolling farmlands, with orchards, flocks, green and yellow grain fields and large oaks create a mosaic picture of this rural area; Traversed by several small streams.

•UNIONVILLE CENTER, Village; Union County; Pop. 272; Area Code 419; Zip Code 43077; W central Ohio; Rural trading post near Marysville.

•UNIOPOLIS, Village; Auglaize County; Pop. 259; Area Code 419; Zip Code 45888; W central Ohio; 10 m. S of Lima in a farming area.

•UNIVERSITY HEIGHTS, City; Cuyahoga County; Pop. 15,401; Area Code 216; Zip Code 44118; Elev. 600'; 10 m. W of Cleveland in NE Ohio; a restricted residential community.

   This city is the site of John Carroll University, founded by the Jesuit priests in 1886. Its campus comprises seven Gothic buildings set in the midst of a 50 acre campus. The school was incorporated as St. Ignatius College in 1890, and as John Carroll University in 1923. The curriculum is liberal arts-oriented.

Mayor - Beryl E. Rothschild 932-7800

•**UPPER ARLINGTON**, City; Franklin County; Pop. 35,648; Area Code 614; Zip Code 43221; Central Ohio; Just NW of Columbus; On the Scioto and Olentangy Rivers in a residential section of the city.

This town is the site of the Ohio State University, founded as a state agricultural and technical college in 1873 with 17 students enrolled. Upper Arlington is a wealthy suburb, covered to the northwest by the Scioto Country Club.

Mayor - Richard H. Moore 457-5080

•**UPPER SANDUSKY**, City; Seat of Wyandot County; Pop. 5,967; Area Code 419; Zip Code 43351; Elev. 880'; 18 m. NW of Marion in NW central Ohio; on a plateau overlooking the Sandusky River; Established in 1843.

During the eighteenth century, a Wyandot Indian town was located here. Along the sides of the Sandusky River, the Indians planted corn, while four miles to the north at Tarhe's Town their councils of war met. After a few battles with United States troops, the Wyandot's signed a treaty which allowed them to retain this site and most of Wyandot county as a reservation. After being relocated a couple times, the Indians were moved west of the Mississippi, leaving Ohio permanently to settlers. There are two monuments, a museum and a cemetery in the Upper Sandusky area which pay tribute to the original inhabitants of the town. In 1842, while visiting America, the English novelist *Charles Dickens* visited Upper Sandusky. In *American Notes* he wrote about the log inn where he stayed.

Agriculture - Grain, cattle and varied
farming
Industry/Mfg. - Cement and dairy products,
tools, quarrying, lumber
Mayor - Kenneth Richardson 294-3862
Daily Newspaper - The Chief-Union, PO Box
180, 111 W.
Chamber of Commerce - R.R.#4

•**URBANA**, City; Seat of Champaign County; Pop. 10,762; Area Code 513; Zip Code 43078; Elev. 1,031'; W central Ohio.

228

A few families were living here in 1805 when the town site was laid out by *Col. Wm. Ward*, but the establishment of a training camp on the square in 1812 by *General Hull* caused various public buildings and mercantile establishments to rise. Expansion followed the coming of the Pennsylvania, New York Central, and Erie Railroads between 1848 and 1901.

Urbana College (1850) is located here.

Agriculture - Grain and cattle farming
Industry/Mfg. - Electronics, tool and dies, auto parts, plastics
Higher Education - Urbana College
Mayor - David S. Cameron 653-3812
Daily Newspaper - The Citizen, 220 E. Court St., PO Box 191
Chamber of Commerce - 300 N. Main St.
Community Event(s) : Pioneer Days and Steam Threshers Festival; Annual, July

•**URBANCREST**, Village; Franklin County; Pop. 880; Area Code 614; Central Ohio.

•**UTICA**, Village; Knox and Licking Counties; Pop. 2,238; Area Code 614; Zip Code 43080; Elev. 961'; Central Ohio; On the Licking River, 14 m. N of Newark. In 1815 first known as Wilmington the name was changed to Utica for the city in New York.

This village serves as a trading place for a wide rural area. Its business structures crowd close to each other, with several balconies suspended over the sidewalks.

Agriculture - Grain, cattle and varied farming
Industry/Mfg. - Animal feed
Chamber of Commerce - PO Box 214
Community Event(s) : Old Fashioned Ice Cream Festival; Annual, May

•**UTOPIA**, Village; Clermont County; Pop. (Rural); Area Code 614; S Ohio; On the Ohio River.

This handful of houses strung along the highway is interesting because of its ghostly past. In 1844 *Judge Wade Loofborough* acquired land here and established a communistic village of 12 families. The enterprise lasted two years before internal troubles over the question of individual liberty and personal initiative broke it up. It was then sold to a spiritualistic

229

community of 100 souls headed by *John Wattles*. They made the tragic error of building their living quarters below the high-water level of the river. In December 1847 the rains came, the flood struck an occupied dormitory, the walls collapsed, and 17 people were drowned. The experiment was abandoned and the group scattered.

Most of the houses are now on the higher ground. The low-lying houses were destroyed or buried in mud in 1937.

•**VALLEY HI**, Village; Logan County; Pop. 60; Area Code 419; W Ohio.

•**VALLEY VIEW**, Village; Cuyahoga County; Pop. 1,576; Area Code 216; Zip Code (with Cleveland); NE Ohio; Approx. 12 m. S of Cleveland on the Cuyahoga River; Residential.

•**VAN BUREN**, Village; Hancock County; Pop. 342; Area Code 419; Zip Code 45889; NW Ohio; Elev. 737'; 6 m. N of Findlay. Named for *President Martin Van Buren* ; One of the few dry spots in the pioneer days when this region was covered in swampland.

•**VANDALIA**, City; Montgomery County; Pop. 13,161; Area Code 513; Zip Code 45377; Elev. 994'; SW Ohio; Settled in 1838, and when it apeared that the National Road would end here instead of at Vandalia, Illinois, the community took the name of the Illinois town.

> *Industry/Mfg.* - Auto parts, dairy products
> *Mayor* - William Harrah 898-5891
> *Chamber of Commerce* - PO Box 224

•**VANLUE**, Village; Hancock County; Pop. 390; Area Code 419; Zip Code 45890; NW Ohio; 11 m. SE of Findlay in a large farming area. Named for either or both *William Vanlue* who platted the town in 1847 or an earlier settler *Regin Vanlue* (1834) who was the justice of the peace here for 15 years.

•**VAN WERT**, City; Seat of Van Wert County; Pop. 11,035; Area Code 419; Zip Code 45891; NW Ohio; 70 m. SW of Toledo. Established by *Capt. James Watson Riley* in 1835. Named for *Issac Van Wart*, Revolutionary war hero. Spelling of name was modified later. Marsh Foundation School (1923) by *George H. Marsh.* Incorporated village in 1848, city in 1891.

Agriculture - Grain, cattle and varied
    farming
Industry/Mfg. - Dairy products, quarrying,
    boxes
Mayor - H.L.Murphy 238-0308
Daily Newspaper - The Times-Builletin, Box
    271, 700 Fox Rd.

•VAN WERT COUNTY, NW Ohio; Area 409 sq. miles; Pop. 30,458; County seat Van Wert; Est., February 12, 1820; Named for *Issac Van Wert,* one of the captors of the traitor *John Andre* during the Revolutionary War; Prairielands, with vegetable farming and nurseries important; Bordered to W by Indiana state line.

•VENEDOCIA, Village; Van Wert County; Pop. 161; Area Code 419; Zip Code 45894; 14 m. SE of the city of Van Wert in NW Ohio.

•VENICE, Village; Sandusky County; Pop. (Rural); Area Code 216; Zip Code 44870; Elev. 586'; N Ohio; Clusters around Cold Creek at the point where it empties into Sandusky Bay. The village grew out of a trading post built before 1812.

The Gallagher Mill, overlooking Cold Creek, was completed in 1833.

•VERMILLION, City; Erie and Lorain Counties; Pop. 11,012; Area Code 216; Zip Code 44089; Elev. 664'; on Lake Erie in N Ohio just E of Sandusky; settled in 1808, lies along the winding Vermilion River. The Ottawa Indians came to the region because the local clay made excellent red paint. Like many other towns along Lake Erie, Vermillion is both a fishing center and a tourist resort. Somnolent in winter, the town comes to life with the first touch of spring; all manner of boats come out of hiding, and the fields are webbed with great stretches of nets drying and undergoing repairs. By the time the fishing boats have started on their seasonal activities, tourists are passing through the town in large numbers, disturbing its quiet preoccupaton. An annual regatta is held here in August which attracts boating enthusiasts from the various lake ports.

231

Agriculture - Varied farming
Industry/Mfg. - Soft drinks, auto. Resort area
Mayor - Jim L. Okom 335-1521
Chamber of Commerce - 5488 Liberty Ave.
Community Event(s) : Festival of the Fish;
    Annual, June

•VERONA, Village; Preble County; Pop. 571; Area Code 513; Zip Code 45378; SW Ohio; 25 m. NW of Dayton; Rural.

•VERSILLES, Village; Darke County; Pop. 2,384; Area Code 513; Zip Code 45380; W Ohio; 40 m. NW of Dayton.

Agriculture - Grain, tobacco, fruit and
    varied farming
Industry/Mfg. - Clothing, campers, dairy
    farming

•VINTON, Village; Gallia County; Pop. 375; Area Code 614; Zip Code 45686; S Ohio; 18 m. N of Gallipolis on Raccoon Creek; Rural.

•VINTON COUNTY; S Ohio; Area 411 sq. miles; Pop. 11,584; County seat McArthur; Est., March 23, 1850; Named for *Samuel F. Vinton*, politician and railroad president in Ohio; Raccoon Creek flows through this region, which has been called the "Wonderland of Ohio" because of its once-untouched hilly countryside; Coal mining has scarred this otherwise rural region.

•WADSWORTH, City; Medina County; Pop. 15,166; Area Code 216; Zip Code 44281; Elev. 1,173; NE central Ohio; 35 m. S of Cleveland. Named after the township which was named for *Gen. Elijah Wadsworth* who was the largest landowner in the Western Reserve.
    This industrial town has handsome buildings lining its level downtown streets, and the greenery of a parkway adds to its inviting appearance. There are several hilly residential streets around the main part of town.

Agriculture - Truck, fruit and grain farming
Industry/Mfg. - Clay products, dairy
    products, matches, paint
Mayor - John D. Henson 335-1521
Chamber of Commerce - PO Box 324

•**WAITE HILL**, Village; Lake County; Pop. 529; Area Code 216; NE Ohio.

•**WAKEMAN**, Village; Huron County; Pop. 906; Area Code 216; Zip Code 44889; N Ohio; Named for one of the proprietors, *Jessup Wakeman.* Home of C.S.Clark Seed Company, one of the largest seed-corn producers in the world. A former Wakeman physician, *Edwin E. Beeman,* invented pepsin chewing gum.

•**WALBRIDGE**, Village; Wood County; Pop. 2,900; Area Code 419; Zip Code 43465; NW Ohio; 10 m. S of Toledo, just S of the 'Iaumee River in a residential area.

Mayor - Gary Revill 666-1830

•**WALDO**, Village; Marion County; Pop. 347; Area Code 614; Zip Code 43356; 10 m. S of city of Marion in a rural area. Named after *Milo D. Pettibone's* son Waldo who laid out the town in 1831.

•**WALTON HILLS**, Village; Cuyahoga County; Pop. 2,199; Area Code 216; N Ohio.

Mayor - Thomas G. Young 232-7800
Chamber of Commerce - 18205 Fern Lane

•**WAPAKONETA**, City; Seat of Auglaize County; Pop. 8,402; Area Code 419; Zip Code 45895; Elev. 898'; W Ohio; 15 m. S of Lima on the Auglaize River.

According to local history, Wapaghkonetta (the town's original name) was derived from the names of an Indian chief and his squaw, Wapaugh and Konetta. After the town was established in 1833 it grew steadily, attracting a large influx of German settlers to the region. Wapakoneta was known for many years for its outstanding woodwork. Nearby is a monument which marks the site of Fort Amanda, a stockade built by *Colonel Thomas Poague* to protect settlers from British troops during the war with England. The fort was named after Poague's wife.

Wapakoneta was the birthplace of *Neil Armstrong,* U.S. astronaut, first man to set foot on the moon.

Agriculture - Varied farming
Industry/Mfg. - Dairy products, plastics

233

Mayor - William V. Lietz 738-6111
Daily Newspaper - The News, 8 Willipie St.
Chamber of Commerce - 105-1/2 S. Blackhoof
        Street

•WARREN, City; Seat of Trumball County; Pop. 56,629; Area Code 216; Zip Code 444 + zone; Elev. 904'; 15 m. NW of Youngstown in NE Ohio; the second largest steel center in the Mahoning Valley.

In 1798 *Ephraim Quinby* and *Richard Storr*, stockholders in the Connecticut Land Company, came from Pennsylvania and selected their home sites in the area that they named for *Moses Warren*, a county surveyor. Two years later the little settlement became the seat of the Western Reserve, and in July of the same year it was made the seat of the newly formed Trumball County. Incorporated as a city in 1869. *J.Ward Packard* made the first Packard automobiles here in 1899 then moved to Detroit in 1903. It was also an important port along the old Ohio and Erie Canal.

Steel is the major product of this city, but electrical goods are also made in factories here.

Industry/Mfg. - Auto parts, automobiles,
        steel, barries, motors, steel, barrels,
        motors
Mayor - Arthur J. Richards 399-3681
Daily Newspaper - The Tribune Chronicle, 240 Franklin
St. S.E.
Chamber of Commerce - 280 N. Park Ave.,
        PO Box 1147

•WARREN COUNTY, SW Ohio; Area 408 sq. miles; Pop. 99,276; County seat Lebanon; Est., March 24, 1803; Named for county in Pennsylvania, Named for *Joseph Warren* ; Crossed by two branches of the Miami River.

•WARRENSVILLE HEIGHTS, City; Cuyahoga County; Pop. 16,565; Area Code 216; N Ohio.

Mayor - Raymond J. Grabow 662-5858
Chamber of Commerce - 4353 Northfield Rd.

•WARSAW, Village; Coshocton County; Pop. 765; Zip Code Area Code 614; Zip Code 43844; E Ohio; 10 m. NW of Coshocton city, on the Walhonding River.

•**WASHINGTON COUNTY**, SE Ohio; Area 641 sq. miles; Pop. 64,266; County seat Marietta; Est., July 27, 1788; Named for *George Washington*, first President of the U.S.; Bordered to S and E by Ohio River; Wayne National Forest covers much of E county; and Muskingum River feeds farmlands to the W; Coal mining is not as important today as it was in the late nineteenth century here.

•**WASHINGTON COURT HOUSE**, City; Seat of Fayette County; Pop. 12,648; Area Code 614; Zip Code 43160; Elev. 973'; 30 m. NW of Chillicothe in SW Ohio; Originally named Washington, the city adopted the larger name in 1810 after the first court of common pleas was held in the cabin of one of the town's resident's, *John Devault*. The city is often referred to by only its original name.

•**WASHINGTONVILLE**, Village; Columbiana and Mahoning Counties; Pop. 865; Area Code 216; Zip Code 44490; 20 m. SW of Youngstown in E Ohio; Rural -residential community.

•**WATERVILLE**, Village; Lucas County; Pop. 3,884; Area Code 419; Zip Code 43567; Elev. 654'; NW Ohio; Platted in 1818 by *John Pray*.

> *Mayor* - Rodger Herringshaw 878-3951

•**WAUSEON**, Village; Seat of Fulton County; Pop. 6,173; Area Code 419; Zip Code 4356; 30 m. W of Toledo in NW Ohio.

> *Agriculture* - Cattle truck and varied
> farming
> *Industry/Mfg.* - Electronics, food packing,
> auto parts, furniture
> *Mayor* - Richard G. Volk 335-9022
> *Chamber of Commerce* - Municipal Bldg.,
> 230 Clinton St.

•**WAVERLY CITY**, City; Seat of Pike County; Pop. 4,603; Area Code 614; Zip Code 45690; Elev. 604'; 15 m. S of Chillicothe in S Ohio; founded in 1829 by *James Emmitt* as Uniontown, the village was renamed Waverly the following year. It is named after the novelist, *Scott Waverly*. The construction of the Ohio and Erie canal here in the mid-nineteenth century made Waverly an important commerce center for several years. But like many other Ohio cities that relied on the canal for trade, Waverly began losing importance as the state's transportation system became more dependent on railroads and highways. Two miles outside of Waverly is the Lake White State Park, a beautiful wooded park surrounding a 323-acre lake.

Agriculture - Grain, cattle and varied
farming
Industry/Mfg. - Lumber, dairy products.
Resort area
Mayor - William T. Urwin 947-5162
Chamber of Commerce - Box 107

•WAYNE, Village; Wood County; Pop. 894; Area Code 419; Zip Code 43466; NW Ohio.

•WAYNE COUNTY, NE central Ohio; Area 561 sq. miles; Pop. 97,408; County seat Wooster; Est., August 15, 1796; Named for *General "Mad Anthony" Wayne*, Revolutionary War soldier and Indian fighter in Ohio territory; Bordered to W by Mohican River; Vegetagle and fruit farming take up most of the county, and oil derricks serve as a reminder of the drilling days which climaxed in the 1890s.

•WAYNE NATIONAL FOREST, S Ohio, in three general locations near or along the Ohio River; 1,464,000 acres in 14 counties; Hilly land covered mostly with hardwood forests.

Settlers came to this section of Ohio in 1788 and began clearing the land for home sites; they found the forest floor rich and productive, particularly along the Ohio River. As facilities for marketing timber increased in the period before the Civil War, Ohio rose to preeminence as a hardwood lumber state. Wide areas were cmpletely denuded of trees, and heavy rains plundered the fertile topsoil, carrying it in muddy torrents toward the Ohio River. Owners of land here finally admitted being "starved out" when they found their soil was untillable, and thousands of acres were abandoned. Soon afterwards, the Federal Government stepped in and began a reforestation program, which has restored some of the forest and helped prevent further erosion.

Trails, camping, and picnicing sites, fire control stations, and historical markers show the visitor around the various areas of the forest.

•**WAYNESBURG**, Village; Stark County; Pop. 1,160; Area Code 216; Zip Code 44688; NE central Ohio; 13 m. S of Canton in a residential area along the Sandy Creek.

•**WAYNESFIELD**, Village; Auglaize County; Pop. 826; Area Code 419; Zip Code 45896; W Ohio; 15 m. S of Lima in a region once traversed by *General Anthony Wayne* and his men on their anti-Indian expeditions.

•**WAYNESVILLE**, Village; Warrn County; Pop. 1,796; Area Code 513; Zip Code 45068; Elev. 750'; SW Ohio; Laid out in 1796 by *Samuel Highway* and *Dr. Evan Banes*, and named for *General Anthony Wayne.*

Early in the 19th century this vicinity was dominated by Quakers from Carolina and Pennsylvania, (1748-1830), whose founding of the Hicksite Church, which still exists, caused a schism in the ranks of Orthodox Quakers. In Waynesville is a Quaker boarding home, the only one of its kind in Ohio.

•**WELLINGTON**, Village; Lorain County; Pop. 4,146; Area Code 216; Zip Code 44090; Elev. 860'; 35 m. SW of Cleveland in N Ohio; In a dairy and grain region.

Here and in the immediate vicinity are a number of fine old houses of the "Firelands" type, characterized by ingenious fret around the eaves and porticoes, and occasional recessed second story porches.

Prior to the Civil War, Wellington, a seething abolitionist center, was the scene of several conflicts over concealed fugitive slaves.

Archibald M. Willard (1836-1918), the painter of the classic "Spirit of '76", lived here for a time. He is buried outside of town in the Greenwood Cemetery.

Agriculture - Grain, cattle and varied
farming
Industry/Mfg. - Dairy products, iron cast-
ings, rubber products
Mayor - Lethel Lum Edwards 647-4626
Chamber of Commerce - PO Box 117

•**WELLSTON**, City; Jackson County; Pop. 6,016; Area Code 614; Zip Code 45692; Elev. 700'; On hilly land near the Little Raccoon Creek in S Ohio; 40 m. NE of Portsmouth.

It was named for *Harvey Wells*, who constructed a blast

furnace in 1874 and platted a town around it. Wellston flourished for many years by exploiting the iron, coal, limestone, and clay deposits in the vicinity. Iron ore is no longer smelted, and the richest coal veins have been exhausted, but numerous small mines about the city still ship out their product.

Agriculture - Fruit, cattle and varied
farming
Industry/Mfg. - Clothing, food packing,
lumber, coal
Mayor - Harold G. Souders 384-2040

•WELLSVILLE, City; Columbiana County; Pop. 5,095; Area Code 216; Zip Code 43968; Elev. 708'; E Ohio.
Since its founding by *William Wells* in 1797, the city has been successively a stagecoach stop on the Cleveland-Ohio River route, a busy shipping mart during the steamboat era.

•WEST ALEXANDRIA, Village; Preble County; Pop. 1,313; Area Code 513; Zip Code 45381; SW Ohio; On Twin Creek, 30 m. W of Dayton in a rural area.

•WEST CARROLLTON, City; Montgomery County; Pop. 13,148; Area Code 513; Zip Code 454 + zone; Elev. 714'; 10 m. S of Dayton along the E side of the Great Miami River; Suburban.

Mayor - A.A.Hintermeister 859-5181

•WEST ELKTON, Village; Preble County; Pop. 277; Area Code 513; Zip Code 45070; W Ohio; 30 m. SW of Dayton in a farming area.

•WESTERVILLE, City; Delaware and Franklin Counties; Pop. 23,414; Area Code 614; Zip Code 43081; 10 m. NE of Columbus in a residential-educational setting.
This city was settled in 1813 by Virginia Cavalier families and Quakers from Pennsylvania. Evidently the Quaker influence prevailed, for Westerville is generally regarded as the most straight-laced town for its size in the state, and the "dry capital" of America. The Anti-Saloon League was established here permanently in 1909 when Westerville citizens presented a lot for the erection of a printing plant.

Otterbein College was founded here in 1847 by the United Brethren Church, and has been connected with the city's dry crusade. It is a coeducational arts college on a 40 acre campus.

Author and composer *Benjamin Hanby* lived in a pre-Civil War home which is still standing here.

Industry/Mfg. - Dairy products, machine shops
Higher Education - Otterbein College
Mayor - James A. Tressler 882-2317
Chamber of Commerce - 5 W. College Ave.

•WEST FARMINGTON, Village; Trumbull County; Pop. 563; Area Code 216; Zip Code 44491; NE Ohio, approx. 20 m. Nw of Warren in a rural area.

•WESTFIELD CENTER, Village; Medina County; Pop. 791; Area Code 216; Zip Code 44251; NE central Ohio; 25 m. W of Akron in a rural area.

•WEST LAFAYETTE, Village; Coshocton County; Pop. 2,225; Area Code 614; Zip Code 43845; Elev. 809'; lies in the middle of White Eyes Plains, a region named for the Delaware chief who was friendly to the white man. The plain extends for two miles east-to-west, where it abuts a range of high broken hills. The town's growth began modestly when *John Coles,* an Englishman, opened a store here in 1850; it gained impetus with the arrival of the Pennsylvania Railroad. An enameling plant, a metal-products company, and a novelty factory are the leading industries.

•WESTLAKE, City; Cuyahoga County; Pop. 19,483; Area Code 216; Zip Code 44145; NE Ohio; 13 m. W of Cleveland, just S of Lake Erie's shoreline in a residential-suburban area.

Agriculture - Grapes, grain and varied
    farming
Industry/Mfg. - Wine, building material,
    cosmetics, plastics
Mayor - Alexander R. Roman 781-3300

•WEST LEIPSIC, Village; Putnam County; Pop. 298; Area Code 419; NW Ohio.

•**WEST LIBERTY**, Village; Logan County; Pop. 1,653; Area Code 419; Zip Code 43357; Elev. 1,099'; W Ohio; 8 m. S of Bellefontaine; A rural trading center grouped about a milk plant, flour mill and grain elevators.

Two estates built in the late 1800s are in the area, known as Mac-O-Chee (1879) and Mac-O-Cheek (1864). Also nearby are the Ohio Caverns, with dramatic stalactites and stalagmites.

•**WEST MANCHESTER**, Village; Preble County; Pop. 448; Area Code 513; Zip Code 45382; SW Ohio; 12 m. S of Greenville in a rural area.

•**WEST MANSFIELD**, Village; Logan County; Pop. 716; Area Code 419; Zip Code 43358; 12 m. E of Bellefontaine in W Ohio; Rural.

•**WEST MILLGROVE**, Village; Wood County; Pop. 205; Area Code 513; Zip Code 45383; NW Ohio; On the E Branch of the Portage River, 40 m. S of Toledo.

•**WEST MILTON**, Village; Miami County; Pop. 4,119; Area Code 513; Zip Code 45383; W Ohio; On the Stillwater River, 16 m. N of Dayton.

Agriculture - Tobacco, grain and varied farming
Industry/Mfg. - Cement products, dairy products, hatcheries
Mayor - Don Thompson 698-4191
Chamber of Commerce - PO Box 3

•**WESTON**, Village; Wood County; Pop. 1,708; Area Code 419; Zip Code 43569; NW Ohio; 8 m. W of Bowling Green; Residential area.

•**WEST RUSHVILLE**, Village; Fairfield County; Pop. 159; Area Code 614; Zip Code 43163; S Ohio; 10 m. NE of Lancaster, adjacent to the village of Rushville.

•**WEST SALEM**, Village; Wayne County; Pop. 1,357; Area Code 216; Zip Code 44287; Elev. 1,092; NE central Ohio; Laid out in 1834 by the *Rickel brothers*, who trekked here over a road blazed from Wooster by the fighting *Poes*, famous frontier scouts and Indian fighters.

•WEST UNION, Village; Seat of Adams County; Pop. 2,791; Area Code 614; Zip Code 45693; 55 m. SE of Cincinnati, 10 m. N of Kentucky state line in S Ohio.

•WEST UNITY, Village; Williams County; Pop. 1,639; Area Code 419; Zip Code 43570; NW Ohio; 55 m. W of Toledo in the stockraising region S of Michigan.

•WHARTON, Village; Wyandot County; Pop. 432; Area Code 419; Zip Code 43369; NW central Ohio; 20 m. SE of Findlay in a rural area.

•WHITEHALL, City; Franklin County; Pop. 21,299; Area Code 614; Zip Code 43213; Central Ohio; 6 m. E of Columbus, overlooking the city on Big Walnut Creek; Residential suburb.

Mayor - John A. Bishop 237-8611

•WHITEHOUSE, Village; Lucas County; Pop. 2,137; Area Code 419; Zip Code 43571; NW Ohio; 20 m. SW of Toledo in a rural-residential section outside of the city area.

•WICKLIFFE, City; Lake County; Pop. 16,790; Area Code 216; Zip Code 44092; 15 m. NE of Cleveland, just S of the Lake Erie shoreline; Residential.

Higher Education - Rabbinical College,
Borromeo College
Mayor - Mel Buchheit 944-4400

•WILBERFORCE, Village and University; Greene County; Pop. 800; Area Code 513; Zip Code 45314; Elev. 1,020'; SW Ohio; NE of Xenia; It is a Negro college community named for *William Wilberforce*, an English reformer who fought the slave trade. It has developed along with Wilberforce University and has become a cultural center for Black people.

•WILKESVILLE, Village; Vinton County; Pop. 189; Area Code 614; Zip Code 45695; 20 m. N of Gallipolis in a hilly area in S Ohio.

241

•**WILLARD**, Cit; Huron County; Pop. 5,674; Area Code 513; Zip Code 44890; N central Ohio; 20 m. N of Mansfield in a farming region.

Agriculture - Fruit, grain and varied
    farming
Industry/Mfg. - Publishing, dairy products,
    steel
Mayor - Kenneth Sommers 933-2581
Chamber of Commerce - 119 Myrtle Ave.,
    PO Box 73

•**WILLIAMSBURG**, Village; Clermont County; Pop. 1,952; Area Code 513; Zip Code 45176; SW Ohio; On the E Fork of the Miami River, 25 m. E of Cincinnati. Named for the town in Virginia.

•**WILLIAMSPORT**, Village; Pickaway County; Pop. 792; Area Code 614; Zip Code 43164; Elev. 771'; S central Ohio; On Deer Creek, a village of retired farmers.

•**WILLIAMS COUNTY**, NW Corner Ohio; Area 421 sq. miles; Pop. 36,369; County seat Bryan; Est., February 12, 1820,; Named for *David Williams*, Revolutionary War soldier who helped capture the traitor *John Andre* ; St. Joseph and Tiffin Rivers flow through this region, which is mainly agricultural.

•**WILLOUGHBY**, City; Lake County; Pop. 19,329; Area Code 216; Zip Code 44094; Elev. 649'; 20 m. NE of Cleveland in NE Ohio.
    Originally called Chagrin, this city was named for an instructor in the Willoughby Medical College. The school grew rapidly after its establishment in 1834.

Agriculture - Varied Farming
Industry/Mfg. - Machine shop, food packing
    tools and dies, steel works
Mayor - Eric R. Knudson 951-2800
Daily Newspaper - The News-Herald, 38879
    Mentor Ave.
Chamber of Commerce - 38131 Euclid Ave.
Community Event(s) : Outdoor Art Festival;
    Annual, July

•**WILLOUGHBY HILLS**, City; Lake County; Pop. 8,612; Area Code 216; is a residential suburb of Willoughby for the most part.

Mayor - Melvin G. Schaefer 585-3700

•**WILLOWICK**, City; Lake County; Pop. 17,834; Area Code 216; Zip Code 44094; 10 m. NE of Cleveland, in a suburban area near Willoughby on Lake Erie in NE Ohio; Residential.

Mayor - Raymond W. Kaluba 585-3700

•**WILLSHIRE**, Village; Van Wert County; Pop. 564; Area Code 419; Zip Code 45898; Elev. 798'; NW Ohio; On St. Marys River, just E of Indiana state line.

The oldest settlement in Van Wert County, Willshire is one of those country villages where farmers sit on wooden benches discussing the weather, bragging about the number of shocks of corn they can cut in a day, and wondering how the bass are biting on the St. Marys River. The first county courthouse is in town, built in 1826.

Agriculture - Varied farming
Industry/Mfg. - Dairy products

•**WILMINGTON**, City; Seat of Clinton County; Pop. 10,431; Area Code 513; Zip Code 45177; Elev. 1,033'; 30 m. SE of Dayton; Founded in 1810. Named after Wilmington, N.C. and originally known as Clinton.

In the center of a prosperous agricultural area, is proud of its big white houses and wide streets. A large plant that manufactures steel drill bits, and one of the oldest bridge companies in the world, founded in 1872, are here.

Higher Education - Wilmington College
Mayor - Robert W. Moyer 382-3833
Daily Newspaper - The News-Journal, 47 S.
    South Street
Chamber of Commerce - 125 S. South

•**WILMONT**, Village; Stark County; Pop. 329; Area Code 216; Zip Code 44689; In 1836 known as Milton. Named after *Congressman David Wilmot*. A trading center in the midst of the Amish country. It was platted in 1836 and had a number of small factoris during the canal days.

•**WILSON**, Village; Belmont and Monroe Counties; Pop. 136; Area Code 614; E Ohio.

243

•WINCHESTER, Village; Adams County; Pop. 1,080; Area Code 614; Zip Code 45697; S Ohio; 45 m. E of Cincinnati in a farming area.

•WINDHAM, Village; Portage County; Pop. 3,721; Area Code 216; Zip Code 44288; NE Ohio; 12 m. W of Warren in a farm trading area.

Mayor - John Stamm 326-2211

•WINESBURG, Village; Holmes County; Pop. (Rural); Area Code 216; Zip Code 44690; Elev. 1,311'; NE Ohio.

This town is as neat as a pin, a hamlet of frame houses occupied by people of Swiss and German extraction. It was laid out in 1832 and called Weinsburg for a town in Germany; later, the Post Office Department altered the spelling.

•WINTERSVILLE, Village; Jefferson County; Pop. 4,724; Area Code 614; Zip Code 43952; E Ohio; 5 m. E of Steubenville in a steel milling and residential part of the greater city.

Mayor - Frank P. Layman 264-5533
Chamber of Commerce - PO Box 2098

•WOODLAWN, Village; Hamilton County; Pop. 2,715; Area Code 513; SW corner of Ohio.

Mayor - James D. Keels 771-6130

•WOODMERE, Village; Cuyahoga County; Pop. 772; Area Code 216; N Ohio.

•WOODSFIELD, Village; Seat of Monroe County; Pop. 3,145; Area Code 614; Zip Code 43793; 30 m. NE of Marietta in SE Ohio; Archibald Woods founded the town in 1815.

Agriculture - Grain and varied farming
Industry/Mfg. - Clothing, dairy products,
oil, coal, aluminum
Mayor - LGeorge Zonker 472-0418
Chamber of Commerce - PO Box 311

•**WOODSTOCK**, Village; Champaign County; Pop. 292; Area Code 513; Zip Code 43084; W central Ohio; 45 m. NW of Columbus in a grain and vegetable farming region.

•**WOODVILLE**, Village; Sandusky County; Pop. 2,050; Area Code 419; Zip Code 43469; N Ohio; 25 m. SE of Toledo in an area which was once heavily wooded, along the Portage River. Named for the man who laid the town out in 1838, *Amos Wood*.

•**WOOD COUNTY**, NW Ohio; Area 619 sq. miles; Pop. 107,372; County seat Bowling Green; Est., February 12, 1820; Named for *Eleazer D. Wood* (1783-1814), early pioneer in Ohio, and builder of Ft. Meigs, Ohio in 1813; Maumee River cuts a deep and wide gouge in this county, which has its northernmost limits in the Toledo metropolitan area; Rich corn and wheat-raising belt to S.

Crude oil bubbling in this area was used as a medicine by the Indians, and early settlers bottled and sold it as a cure-all. Large scale development of the region followed a strike at Lima in 1885. Although the peak years have passed, oil is still pumped and the pungent odor of the crude product hangs heavily over the countryside.

•**WOOSTER**, City; Seat of Wayne County; Pop. 19,289; Area Code 216; Zip Code 44691; Elev. 910'; NE central Ohio.

The *Larwills* came in 1807 to build the first home. A land office and an army headquarters established here during the War of 1812 brought an influx of speculators and landseekers, some of whom stayed on in the town that was named for the Revolutionary War general, *David Wooster*. Incorporation took place in 1817.

College of Wooster, a coeducational liberal arts institution chartered in 1866 by Presbyterians.

Agriculture - Varied farming
Industry/Mfg. - Food packing, rubber goods,
    plastics, boxes, oil, gas
Higher Education - College of Wooster,
    Ohio State University
Mayor - Robert M. Anderson 436-3100
Daily Newspaper - The Record, 212 E. Liberty
Chamber of Commerce - Public Square, North,
    PO Box 12

•**WORTHINGTON**, City; Franklin County; Pop. 15,016; Area

Code 614; Zip Code 43085; Elev. 908'; Central Ohio; 10 m. N of Columbus; On a slope overlooking the wide Olentangy bottoms.

Led by *Colonel James Kilbourne,* who named the place Worthington after a parish in Connecticut, 100 settlers arrived in 1803; the first cabin erected was used as a school and church — the first Episcopal church organized in Ohio.

Higher Education - Pontifical College
Josephine
Mayor - J.J.Lorimer 436-3100
Chamber of Commerce - 666 High Street

•WREN, Village; Van Wert County; Pop. 282; Area Code 419; Zip Code 45899; 15 m. SW of Van Wert city, near the Indiana state line in NW Ohio.

•WYANDOT COUNTY, NW central Ohio; Area 406 sq. miles; Pop. 22,651; County seat Upper Sandusky; Est., February 3, 1845; Named for the Indian tribe which lived in this plains region; Site of several Indian - white man battles, since the Wyandot had lived all along the Sandusky River valley since ancient times.

Early pioneers were amazed at the seemingly endless stretch of wild land here when they saw it in 1782. *Daniel Boone* came here regularly to hunt turkeys and pigeons. During his last trip (1776) he lost his powder horn; it was fund later and is now exhibited at the Wyandot National Museum in Upper Sandusky.

•WYOMING, City; Hamilton County; Pop. 8,282; Area Code 513; Zip Code (with Cincinnati); SW Ohio; 10 m. N of Cincinnati in a residential area; Named for the county in Pennsylvania.

Mayor - Lee c. Weber 821-7500

•XENIA, Seat of Greene County; Pop. 24,653; Area Code 513; Zip Code 45385; Elev. 925'; 15 m. SE of Dayton and 3 m. E of the Little Miami River in SW Ohio.

Although it has been a major producer of twine and rope for many years, Xenia now hosts numerous industries which bring money to the city. These include the manufacturing of automobile parts, paper products and furniture. In the late 1700's, the area around the Little Miami River was the scene of numerous battles between the native Indians (mainly Miami Indians) and the westward moving whites. *Judge John Cleves Symmes* of New Jersey purchased 30,000 acres of land around Xenia and the Miami River in 1792, opening the door for settlers to the region. Among the most numerous settlers came a large influx of German imigrants. In 1869, the Ohio Soldiers' and Sailors' Home was built here to care for the orphans of civil war veterans. The Greene County Historical Museum in downtown Xenia traces the history of the area. About three miles to the north, is Wilberforce village.

> *Agriculture* - Varied farming
> *Industry/Mfg.* - Auto parts, rope, furniture, motors
> *Mayor* - Walter L. Marshall 372-7611
> *Daily Newspaper* - The Gazette, 37 S. Detroit Street
> *Chamber of Commerce* - 50 S. Detroit St.

•**YANKEE LAKE**, Village; Trumbull County; Pop. 99; Area Code 216; Zip Code (Rural); NE Ohio; Near a small lake by the same name.

•**YELLOW SPRINGS**, Village; Greene County; Pop. 4,077; Area Code 513; Zip Code 45387; Elev. 974'; SW Ohio; 9 m. S of Springfield in a great metal and rubber industrial area along the Miami River.

Antioch College has focused worldwide attention on this quiet, heavily shaded town. It was founded in 1804, and took its name from the yellow discharges of the neighboring iron springs whose health-giving waters attracted visitors here for several decades.

Antioch College was founded in 1853, and today sits on a large 1,000 acre-plus campus. Antioch's first president was *Horace Mann*, who came here from Massachusetts to create a college that would develop the complete personality and not merely foster learning. However, amid opposition to his plans, he died here in 1859. Today, the school is known for its practical emphasis on education, and most students complete field studies along with their majors.

> *Agriculture* - Grain, poultry and varied farming

Industry/Mfg. - Rubber goods, aluminum
products
Higher Education - Antioch College
Mayor - Farrell Ballenger 767-7202

•YORKSHIRE, Village; Darke County; Pop. 146; Area Code 513; Zip Code 45388; W Ohio; 20 m. NE of Greenville.

•YORKVILLE, Village; Belmont and Jefferson Counties; Pop. 1,447; Area Code 614; Zip Code 43971; Elev. 669'; E Ohio; Named for its early settlers, who came from York, Pennsylvania; Hot mills of the Wheeling Steel Corporation.

•YOUNGSTOWN, City; Seat of Mahoning County; Pop. 115,436; Area Code 216; Zip Code 445 + zone; On Mahoning river 45 m. E of Akron in NE Ohio.

Little is recorded of the Youngstown area prior to the arrival in 1797 of *John Young* of Whitestown, New York, and his party of settlers. He had purchased the land around the junction of Mill Creek and the Mahoning River from the Connecticut Land Company for $16,085.16. Two days after he had encamped, Young was visited by *Colonel James Hillman* who was trading in the Mahoning Valley with the Indians. Young traded his last deerskin, a favorite medium of exchange, for a quart of whisky, and celebrated the founding of his village. Although it was Young's town, the infant sttlement owed its early security to Colonel Hillman's success in appeasing resentful Indians of the vicinity.

Within a year, Youngstown contained 10 families. In 1801 a physician cast his lot with the village, and it did not seem incongruous to his patients that he eked out his living by doubling as an undertaker. Almost immediately, as usual with the pioneers, a school and a church were established. At the falls of Mill Creek the first gristmill in the Western Reserve was erected.

Youngstown's interest in iron production began early, when *James and Daniel Heaton* set up a crude smelter on Yellow Creek (the present city of Struthes) in 1802. Here they utilized the native bog ores and limestones, and found an ample wood supply for charcoal in the virgin forests. This furnace, the remains of which can be seen in Yellow Creek Park, was succeeded by a larger one, the Hopewell Furnace, erected on Yellow Creek near by.

Because of its proximity to the same native ores and coal

248

beds that created iron furnaces around Pittsburgh. Youngstown from its early years assumed an economy similar to that of western Pennsylvania rather than that of Ohio proper. In 1826 the first coal mine was opened in the Mahoning Valley, and soon the operators of two charcoal-burning furnaces in Youngstown discovered that Mahoning coal could be used in the reduction of iron ore. With the opening of the Pennsylvania-Ohio Canal in 1839, trade in coal was extended to farther markets, a develoment that was accelerated by the laying of the first railroad through the valley in 1853 and the increase in iron productin during the Civil War. Lacking the early water transportation to Lake Erie which boomed the commercial activity of towns along the route of the Ohio and Erie Canal, Youngstown's growth was predicated on the general progress of the iron industry in the western Pennsylvania district, from which the Mahoning Valley stemmed like a fiery arm.

Following the Civil War, the city instlled a water system and a horsecar line. The pre-Civil War village of 2,759 had tripled its population in 10 years. The time had come, its citizens concluded, to assert its superiority over the centrally situated Canfield, and Youngstown made application for removal of the county seat from that Village to Youngstown. This was done in 1876, but only after a legal fight that was concluded in the United States Supreme Court.

The town continued to grow as the metropolis of the Mahoning Valley, but it was not until Youngstown became the home of the first steel plant in the valley, the Union Iron & Steel Company, in 1892, that the dominance of steel began. Soon the banks of the river were lined with Bessemer converters, open-hearth furnaces, strip and rolling mills, pipe plants, and manufactories of steel accessories and products. At the beginning of the twentieth century, the city had grown to 44,885.

Especially susceptible to recurrent booms and panics, Youngstown has had its share of luxury and stringency and of serious labor troubles. The World War years and the boom times that followed were a silk-shirt age for the steelworkers. A scarcity of labor brought recruits from the impoverished Negro population of the South. Then the depression of the 1930's struck Youngstown a body blow, and the merger practice in industry precipitated one of the most sensatinal legal struggles in the steel industry's history.

BUTLER ART MUSEUM - Italian Renaissance
style, designed by *McKim, Meade and
White* (1919)

Industry/Mfg. - Varied manufacturing, trade
    and services
Higher Education - Youngstown State
    Universtiy
Mayor - J. Philli Richley 746-1892
Daily Newspaper - The Vindicator, Vindicator
    Square
Chamber of Commerce - 200 Wick Bldg.
Community Event(s) : Ohio Ceramic and
    Sculpture Show; Annual, January-February

•ZALESKI, Village; Vinton County; Pop. 347; Area Code 614; Zip
Code 45698; 20 m. W of Athens near the outskirts of the Wayne National Forest in S central Ohio. Named after *Peter Zaleski* who
laid out this town in 1856 and was a Parisian banker who founded
several mines in this area of the county.
    The Zaleski State Forest surrounds ths village, which
serves as a trading post for a large recreational area. Much of the
forest here has been replanted after a lumber boom cleared the
area in the last century. Nearby is a 120-acre artificial lake
created by a damming of Raccoon Creek.

•ZANESFIELD, Village; Logan County; Pop. 269; Area Code
419; Zip Code 43360; 6 m. E of bellefontaine in the midst of rolling
hills in W central Oio.
    Zanesfield was settled in 1819 on the site of a blockhouse
built by the English during the French and Indian War. The land
belonged to *Issac Zane*, about whom center many of the lusty
events of early Ohio history. The Zane-Kenton Monument was
erected here in 1914 in the memory of the two frontiersmen. The
Sloan Library was given to Zanesfield by *Dr. Earl Sloan*, native,
who made a fortune from the manufacture of Sloan's Liniment in
the nineteenth century.
    Near the village are several remnants of Shawnee Indian
Villages, as are the Zane Caverns, a spectacular underground
formation of broad chambers, lofty corridors and solid rock walls
of amber color.

•ZANESVILLE, City; Seat of Muskingum County; Pop. 28,655;
Area Code 614; Zip Code 43701; On Muskingum river 50 m. E of
Columbus in SE central Ohio; Was settled in 1819 on the site of a

blockhouse built by the English during the French and Indian War.

The land once belonged to *Issac Zane*, about whom center many of the lusty events in early Ohio History.

In 1797 when *Ebenezer Zane* was surveying Zane's Trace he staked out a mile-square tract of land at the confluence of the two rivers, in accordance with the terms of his contract with the Government. Not as shrewd as he might have been, he soon sold the future site of Zanesville for $100 to his brother, *Jonathan Zane*, and his son-in-law, *John McIntire*. The latter, a leader in public and private enterprise in the early nineteenth century, donated the first free public school, the library, and a children's home to his adopted city.

Three little settlements, Zanesville (first called Westbourne), West Zanesville, and Natchez were established here by 1800. The same year carpenters, stonemasons, shoemakers, and weavers began to do business. *John and Increase Mathews* opened the first store at about this time, offering green tea at $1.21 a pound, stockings at $1.66 a pair, muslin at $1.93 a yard, and gingham at $1.58 a yard.

But the town grew slowly. *Fortescue Cuming's* tour to the West in 1807-8 brought him to Zanesville, which, he observed, "does not seem to thrive so much as Springfield." His observation may have been a little prejudiced, however, by his experience in the village, for he found the corpse of the innkeeper's sister in the tavern, and went out to stop the stage for "Harvey's very good inn, where we found an excellent supper, clean beds, a consequencial host and hostess, and the highest charges I had yet paid in Ohio."

Clay suitable for pottery-making was early discovered in the vicinity. By 1808 plain dishes, stoneware, and bricks were bearing the Zanesville imprint. As only a small outlay of capital was required to start a pottery, many farmers turned their efforts to this type of work during the winter months. In the spring of the year they would hire a young man to float the wares by barge down the Muskingum, the Ohio, and the Mississippi Rivers, selling it along the way at extremely high prices. The hazards of the industry were great, however, many a small busines man was completely wiped out when a kiln failed or a barge was wrecked.

One of Ohio's first glass plants was started in Zanesville in 1815, and for many years the town was the center for this industry in the State. Local sands were used exclusively. Zanesville goblets and water pitchers of the early nieteenth century are highly prized by collectors today.

The Ohio Legislature designated Zanesville the State capital on February 19, 1810. The day following this action, however, the legislature adopted a resolution providing for the location of a permanent capital "not more than forty miles from what shall be deemed to be the common center of the state." Unfortunately Zanesville was outside this area, and the day of its political importance passed almost before it had dawned. Several citizens the year before had raised sufficient funds by popular subscription for the erection of a building, later known as Old 1809. An earthquake during the first session of the legislature caused much confusino, and senators and representaives scrambled from Old 1809 with little semblance of dignity or order. The building served as the capitol from December 1810 until May 1812, after which it became the Muskingum County Courthouse. In the latter year Zanesville had a population of 1,200 and ranked third in size among the settlements in Ohio.

The arrival of the steamboat Rufus Putnam from Marietta in 1824 marked the beginning of a new era in transportation. Shipbuilding became a prominent industry, over 100 boats being launched from the Zanesville docks in the next quarter-century. The dredging and damming of the Muskingum River in 1841 was but another step in water transportation, which had been given great impetus with the completion of the Ohio and Erie Canal to the head of navigation on the Muskingum at Dresden in the late 1820's. At about the same time the National Road was improved from Wheeling to Zanesville.

These new agencies were not wholly beneficial, however. The local markets became glutted with manufactured articles and farm produce. A veritable panic existed in 1840. Corn was selling at 25 cents a bushel, oats at 12 cents a bushel, flour at $3 a barrel, eggs at 4 cents a dozen, chickens at from 50 cents to 75 cents a dozen. In the same year, however, a Government report indicated that approximately one fourth of the potteries in Ohio were located in or near Zanesville. And in that yer potters and clay workers from Staffordshire, England, settled in the vicinity and began the production of Rockingham ware.

Residents were thrown into panic on July 23, 1863, with news that Morgan's raiders were approaching the city from the southwest. Militia companies were hastily organized, and little-used weapons were assembled. After hours of anxious waiting the alarmed citizens learned that Morgan had crossed the Muskingum River a score of miles to the south, and that the threat had passed.

The closing decades of the nineteenth century witnessed many changes in the city's industrial life. Floor tile bearing the

Zanesville imprint was placed on the market. By the 1890's the demand for such products had become sufficiently large to make feasible the construction of the immense plant of the American Encaustic Tiling Company (1891), which was dedicated by *Governor William McKinley*. Before its financial collapse in recent years, "the A.E.," as it was familiarly known, was the largest manufacturer of floor and wall tile in the United States. These years also witnessed the founding of several other clay products industries, including the S.A.Weller Pottery in 1888, the Roseville Pottery in 1892, and the Mosaic Tile Company in 1894. Several years earlier the now defunct Burton-Townsend Brick Company, founded in 1887, had begun to utilize local clays. For a number of yers around 1900, Zanesville was one of the leading producers of farm wagons in the United States.

The 1913 flood, general throughout Ohio, inundated many parts of the city, inflicting property damage of approximately $3,000,000. The prosperous World War years hastened recovery from this severe blow. Large numbers of foreign immigrants settled during this period in the Putnam section where they were employed at the Mark Manufacturing Plant, producing tubing and pipe. When the plant was razed in the early 1920's, many of these residents moved away, and those who remained were almost completely assimilated.

POINTS OF INTEREST

ZANE GREY BIRTHPLACE - *Ebenezer Zane.* namesake f the city was great-great-grandfather of the novelist.

Industry/Mfg. - Quarrying, clay products, coal, oil, electronics
Higher Education - Ohio University
Mayor - George Walt Frueh 452-5441
Daily Newspaper - The Times Recorder, 34 South Fourth Street
Chamber of Commerce - 47 N. 4th Street
Community Event(s) : Zane's Trace Commemoration; Annual. June

•**ZOAR**, Village; Tuscarawas County; Pop. 264; Area Code 614; Zip Code 44697; 15 m. S of Canton along the Tuscarawas River in E central Ohio.

To this place in 1817 came a group of Separatists from southern Germany to enjoy religious freedom on the 5,600 acres they purchased. The problems of individualism the group led to the formation of a communal corporation, chartered in 1832 as the Separatist society of Zoar. (The town was named for the biblical city to which Lot fled after leaving Sodom). The Society folded in 1898 after many prosperous years.

BIOGRAPHY INDEX

255

256

258

259

261